DYNAMITE®

ISBN13: 978-1-5241-0422-9
First Printing   10 9 8 7 6 5 4 3 2 1

Nick Barrucci, CEO / Publisher
Juan Collado, President / COO
Brandon Dante Primavera, V.P. of IT and Operations
Rich Young, Director of Business Development

Joe Rybandt, Executive Editor
Matt Idelson, Senior Editor
Anthony Marques, Associate Editor
Kevin Ketner, Associate Editor

Geoff Harkins, Creative Director
Cathleen Heard, Senior Graphic Designer
Alexis Persson, Graphic Designer
Rachel Kilbury, Digital Multimedia Associate
Katie Hidalgo, Graphic Designer

Alan Payne, V.P. of Sales and Marketing
Pat O'Connell, Sales Manager

Amy Jackson, Administrative Associate

Online at **www.DYNAMITE.com** | On Facebook **/Dynamitecomics** | On Twitter **@dynamitecomics**

Delia, a young girl with blossoming and as yet untamed supernatural powers, accidentally unleashes her powers in a school. A danger to herself and others, she draws the attention of Phoebe, Piper, and Paige - three witches with experience managing innate abilities! With their help, Delia begins to make a new life for herself... but magic has a way of making its presence known, and it's only a matter of time before this incredibly powerful novice draws the unwanted attention of sinister forces!

BASED ON THE TELEVISION SERIES CREATED BY
CONSTANCE M. BURGE

◆

WRITTEN BY
KATY REX

ILLUSTRATED BY
JONATHAN LAU

ILLUSTRATIONS TONED BY
PIPPA MATHER

LETTERED BY
SIMON BOWLAND

◆

COVER ILLUSTRATED BY
JONATHAN LAU

COVER COLORED BY
PIPPA MATHER

◆

GRAPHIC NOVEL DESIGNED BY
ALEXIS PERSSON

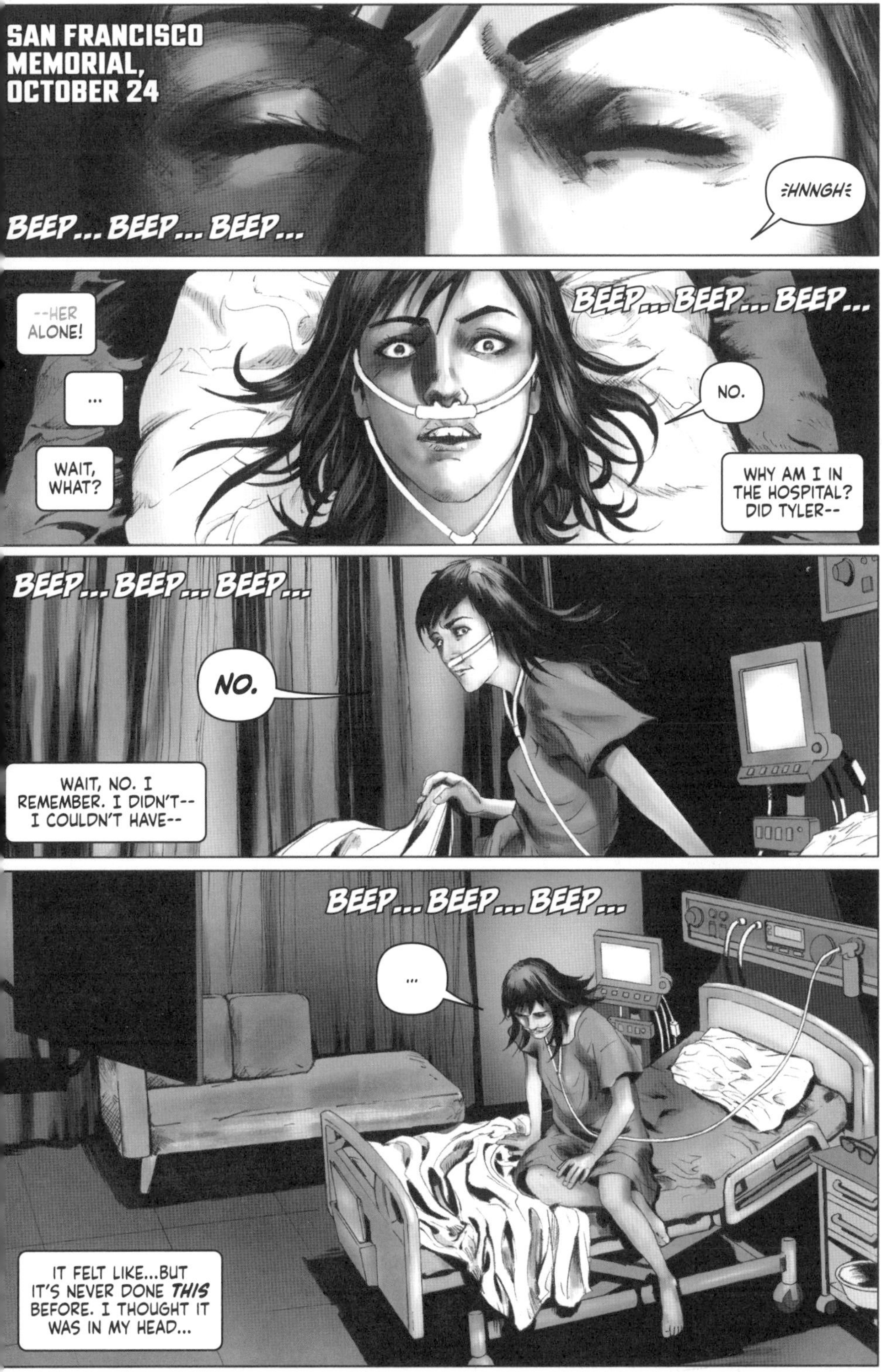
SAN FRANCISCO MEMORIAL, OCTOBER 24
BEEP... BEEP... BEEP...
HNNGH
--HER ALONE!
...
WAIT, WHAT?
BEEP... BEEP... BEEP...
NO.
WHY AM I IN THE HOSPITAL? DID TYLER--
BEEP... BEEP... BEEP...
NO.
WAIT, NO. I REMEMBER. I DIDN'T-- I COULDN'T HAVE--
BEEP... BEEP... BEEP...
...
IT FELT LIKE...BUT IT'S NEVER DONE *THIS* BEFORE. I THOUGHT IT WAS IN MY HEAD...

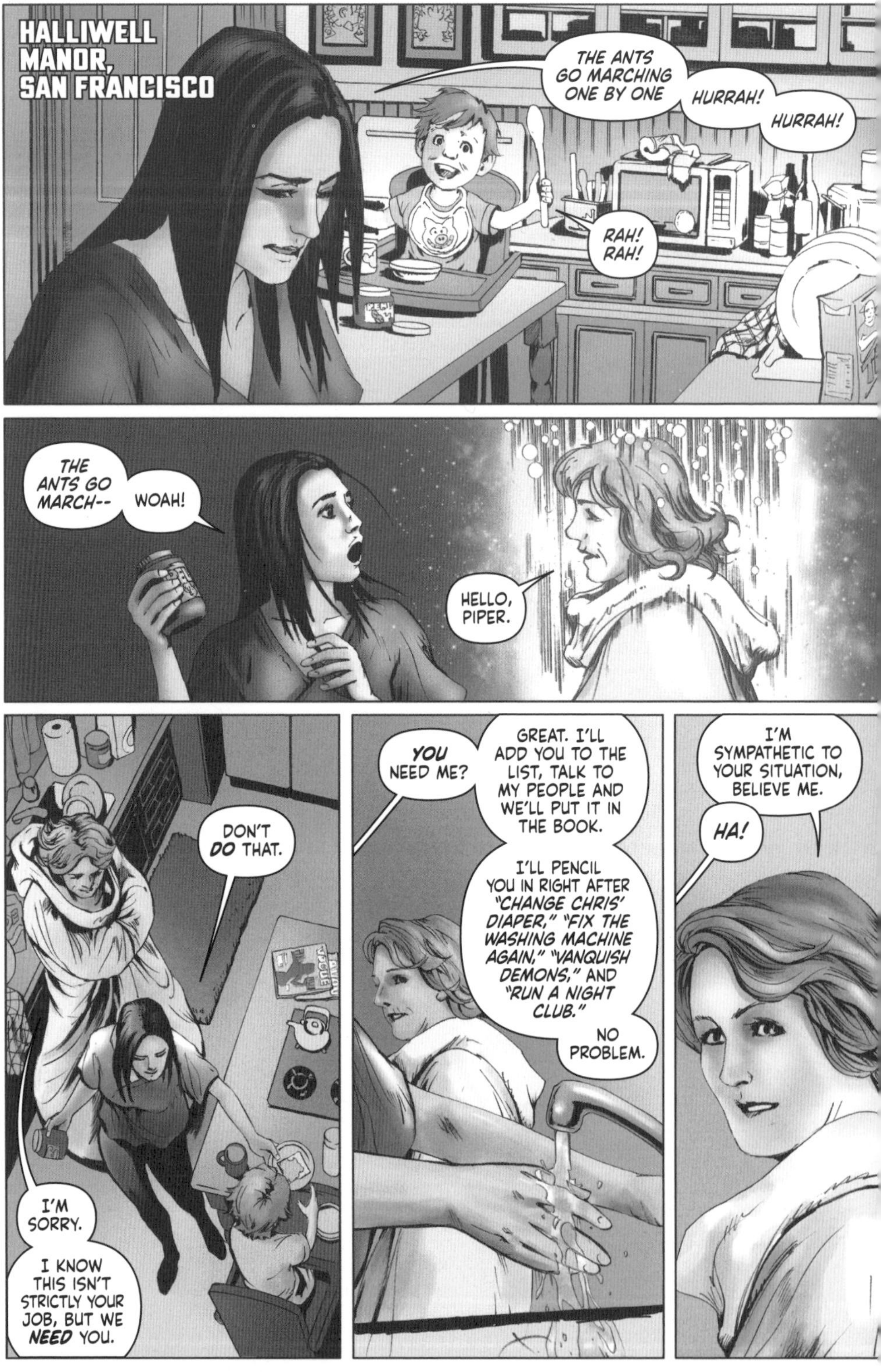
HALLIWELL MANOR, SAN FRANCISCO
THE ANTS GO MARCHING ONE BY ONE
HURRAH!
HURRAH!
RAH! RAH!
THE ANTS GO MARCH--
WOAH!
HELLO, PIPER.
DON'T DO THAT.
I'M SORRY.
I KNOW THIS ISN'T STRICTLY YOUR JOB, BUT WE NEED YOU.
YOU NEED ME?
GREAT. I'LL ADD YOU TO THE LIST, TALK TO MY PEOPLE AND WE'LL PUT IT IN THE BOOK.
I'LL PENCIL YOU IN RIGHT AFTER "CHANGE CHRIS' DIAPER," "FIX THE WASHING MACHINE AGAIN," "VANQUISH DEMONS," AND "RUN A NIGHT CLUB."
NO PROBLEM.
I'M SYMPATHETIC TO YOUR SITUATION, BELIEVE ME.
HA!

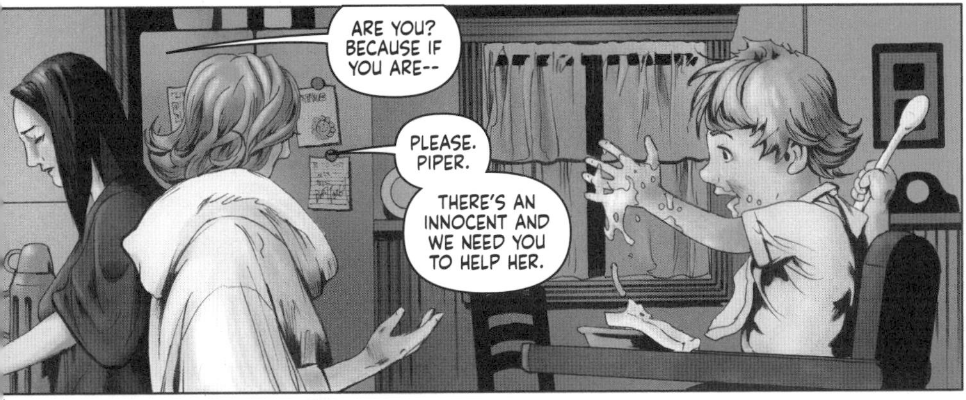
ARE YOU? BECAUSE IF YOU ARE--
PLEASE. PIPER.
THERE'S AN INNOCENT AND WE NEED YOU TO HELP HER.

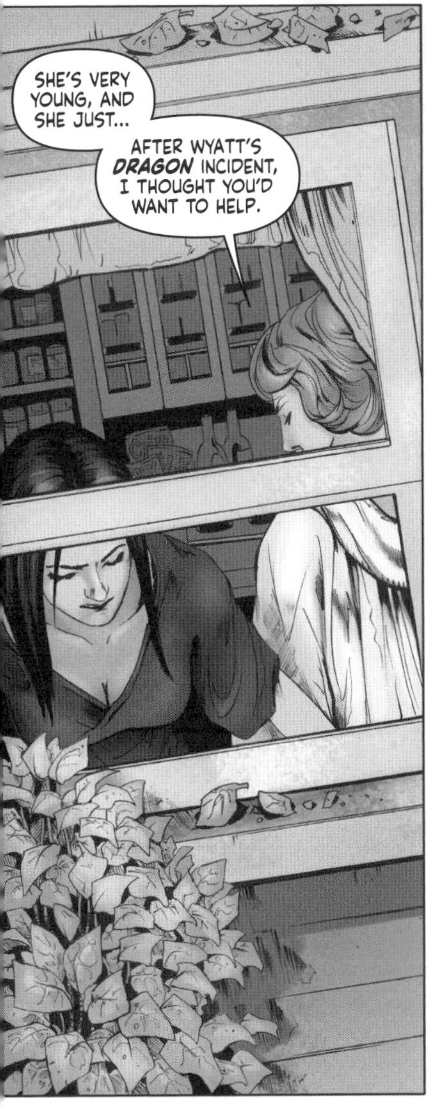
SHE'S VERY YOUNG, AND SHE JUST...
AFTER WYATT'S ***DRAGON*** INCIDENT, I THOUGHT YOU'D WANT TO HELP.

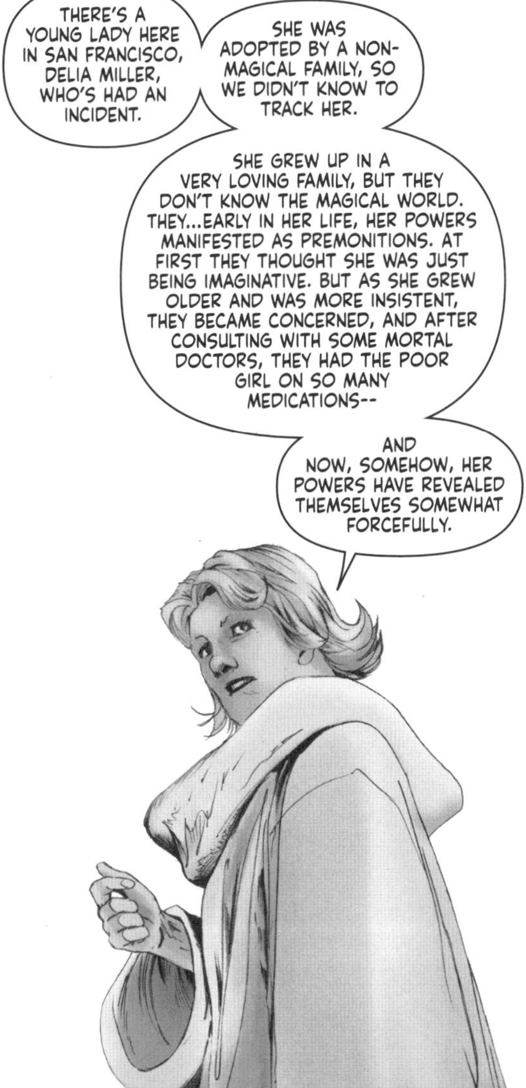
THERE'S A YOUNG LADY HERE IN SAN FRANCISCO, DELIA MILLER, WHO'S HAD AN INCIDENT.
SHE WAS ADOPTED BY A NON-MAGICAL FAMILY, SO WE DIDN'T KNOW TO TRACK HER.
SHE GREW UP IN A VERY LOVING FAMILY, BUT THEY DON'T KNOW THE MAGICAL WORLD. THEY...EARLY IN HER LIFE, HER POWERS MANIFESTED AS PREMONITIONS. AT FIRST THEY THOUGHT SHE WAS JUST BEING IMAGINATIVE. BUT AS SHE GREW OLDER AND WAS MORE INSISTENT, THEY BECAME CONCERNED, AND AFTER CONSULTING WITH SOME MORTAL DOCTORS, THEY HAD THE POOR GIRL ON SO MANY MEDICATIONS--
AND NOW, SOMEHOW, HER POWERS HAVE REVEALED THEMSELVES SOMEWHAT FORCEFULLY.

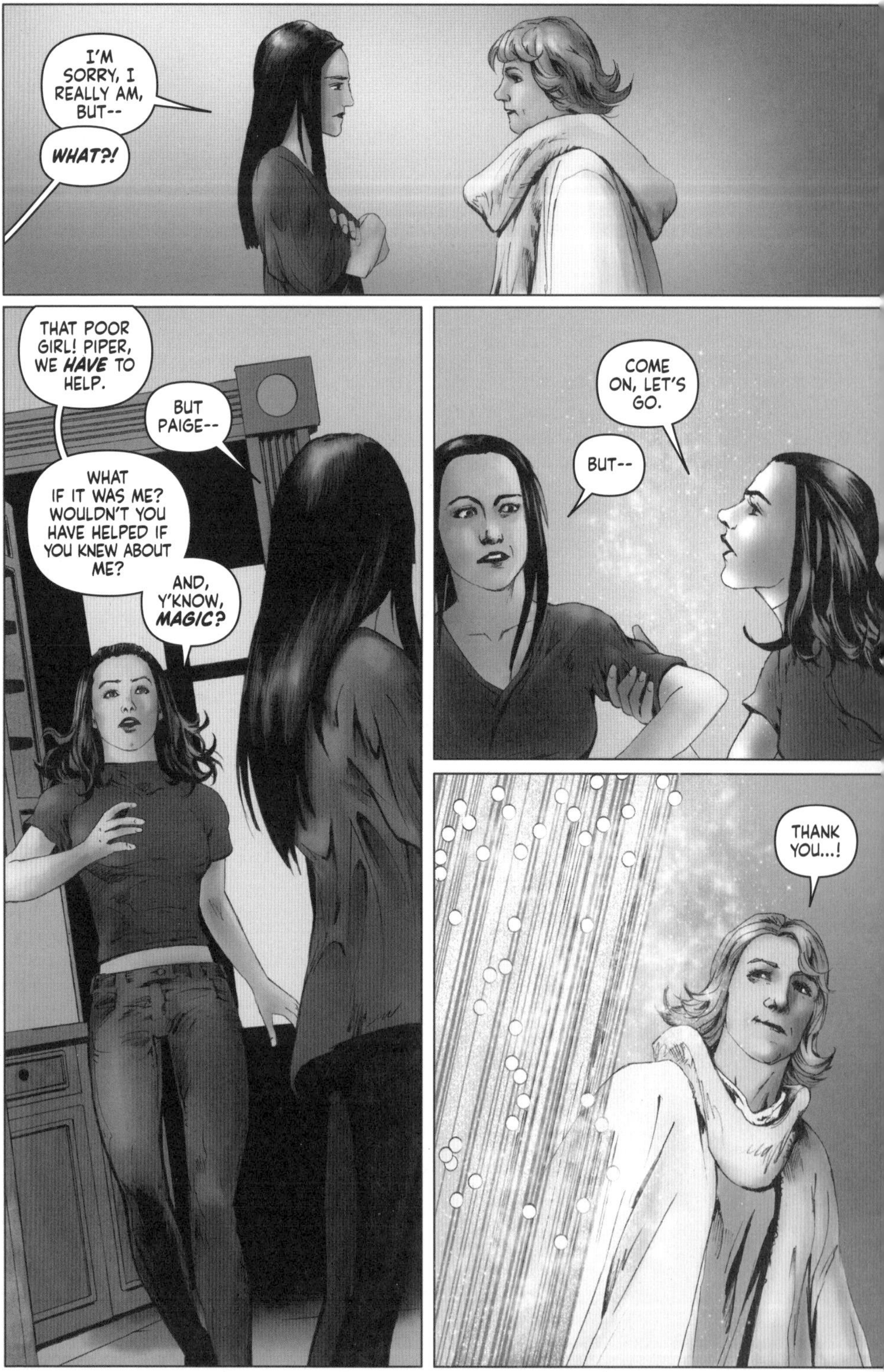
I'M SORRY, I REALLY AM, BUT--
WHAT?!
THAT POOR GIRL! PIPER, WE HAVE TO HELP.
BUT PAIGE--
WHAT IF IT WAS ME? WOULDN'T YOU HAVE HELPED IF YOU KNEW ABOUT ME?
AND, Y'KNOW, MAGIC?
COME ON, LET'S GO.
BUT--
THANK YOU...!

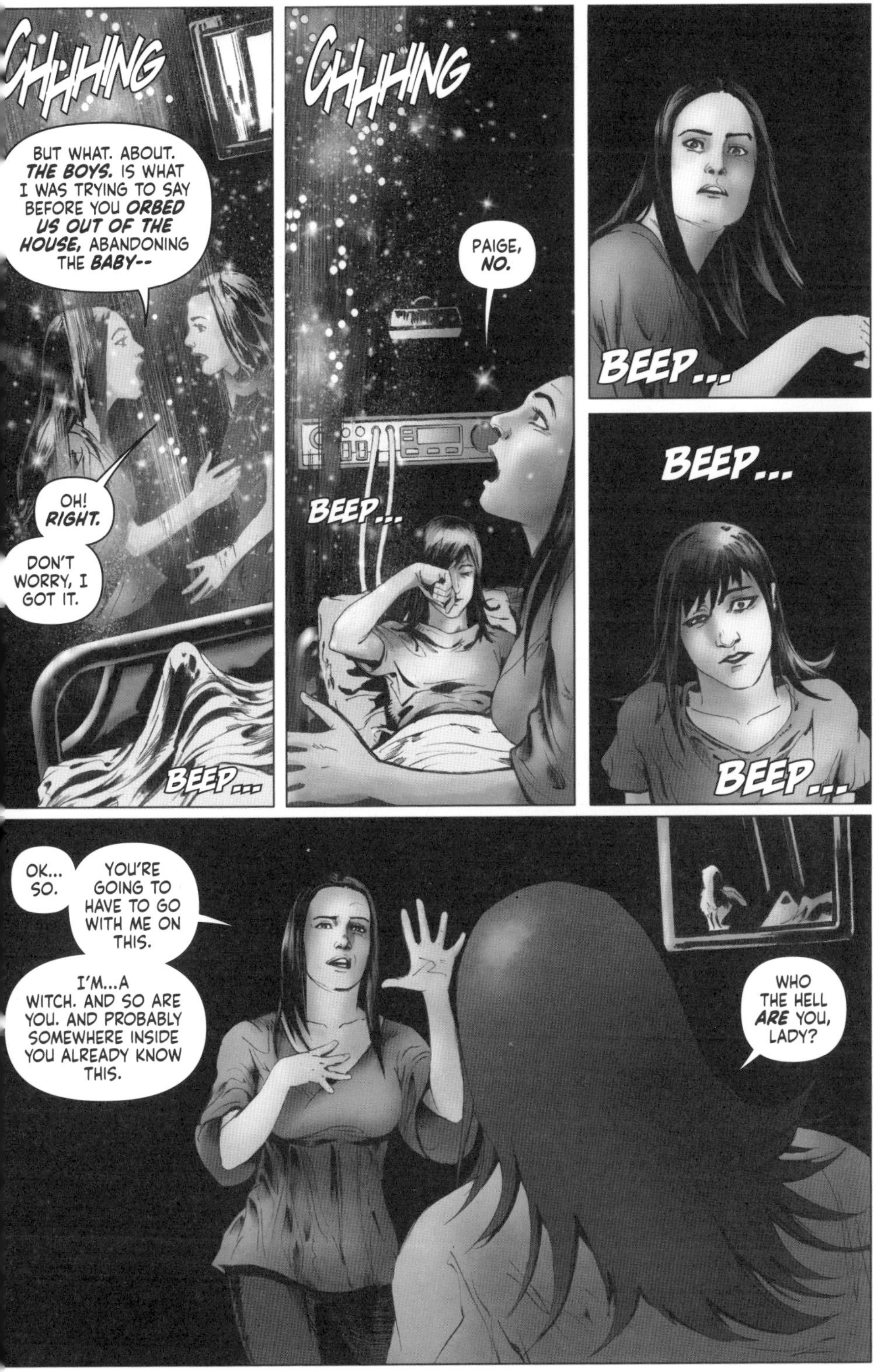
CHHHING
BUT WHAT. ABOUT. THE BOYS. IS WHAT I WAS TRYING TO SAY BEFORE YOU ORBED US OUT OF THE HOUSE, ABANDONING THE BABY--
OH! RIGHT.
DON'T WORRY, I GOT IT.
BEEP...
CHHHING
PAIGE, NO.
BEEP...
BEEP...
BEEP...
BEEP...
OK... SO.
YOU'RE GOING TO HAVE TO GO WITH ME ON THIS.
I'M...A WITCH. AND SO ARE YOU. AND PROBABLY SOMEWHERE INSIDE YOU ALREADY KNOW THIS.
WHO THE HELL ARE YOU, LADY?

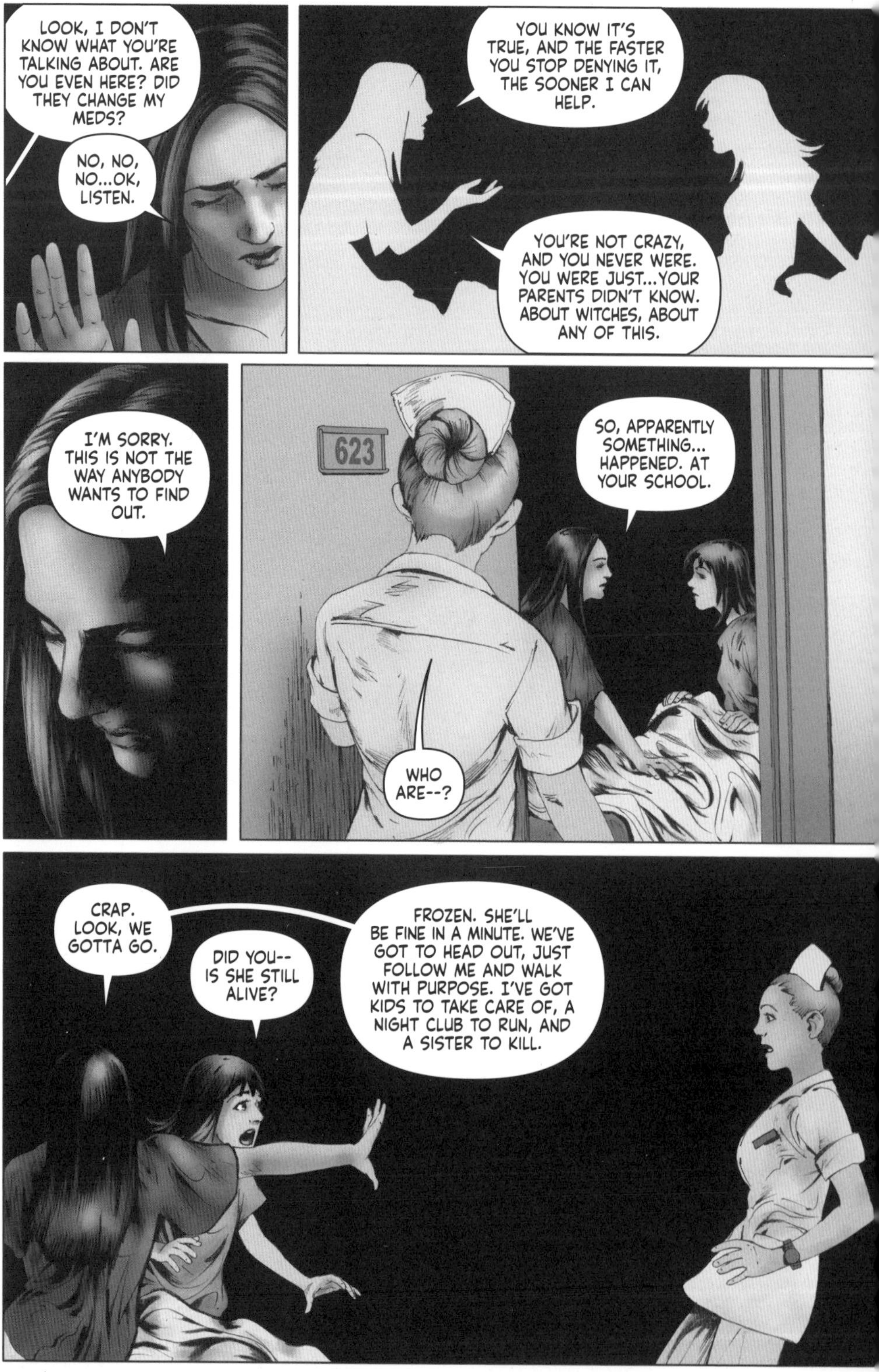
LOOK, I DON'T KNOW WHAT YOU'RE TALKING ABOUT. ARE YOU EVEN HERE? DID THEY CHANGE MY MEDS?
NO, NO, NO...OK, LISTEN.
YOU KNOW IT'S TRUE, AND THE FASTER YOU STOP DENYING IT, THE SOONER I CAN HELP.
YOU'RE NOT CRAZY, AND YOU NEVER WERE. YOU WERE JUST...YOUR PARENTS DIDN'T KNOW. ABOUT WITCHES, ABOUT ANY OF THIS.
I'M SORRY. THIS IS NOT THE WAY ANYBODY WANTS TO FIND OUT.
623
SO, APPARENTLY SOMETHING... HAPPENED. AT YOUR SCHOOL.
WHO ARE--?
CRAP. LOOK, WE GOTTA GO.
DID YOU-- IS SHE STILL ALIVE?
FROZEN. SHE'LL BE FINE IN A MINUTE. WE'VE GOT TO HEAD OUT, JUST FOLLOW ME AND WALK WITH PURPOSE. I'VE GOT KIDS TO TAKE CARE OF, A NIGHT CLUB TO RUN, AND A SISTER TO KILL.

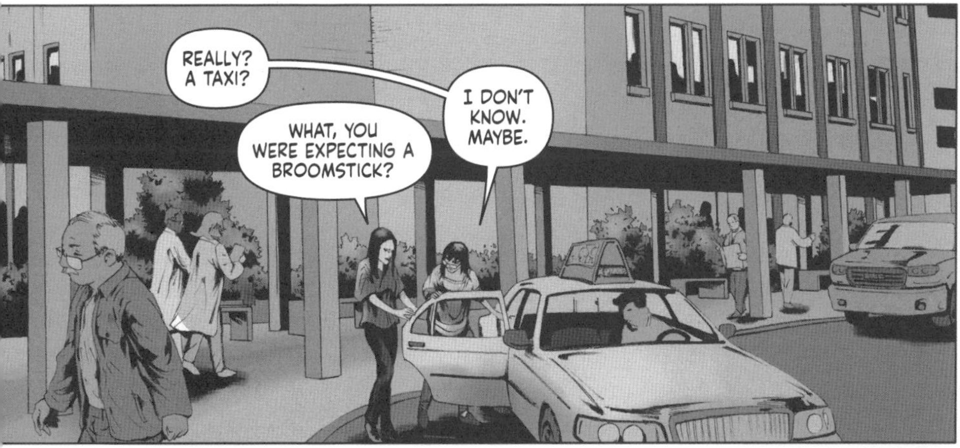
REALLY? A TAXI?
WHAT, YOU WERE EXPECTING A BROOMSTICK?
I DON'T KNOW. MAYBE.
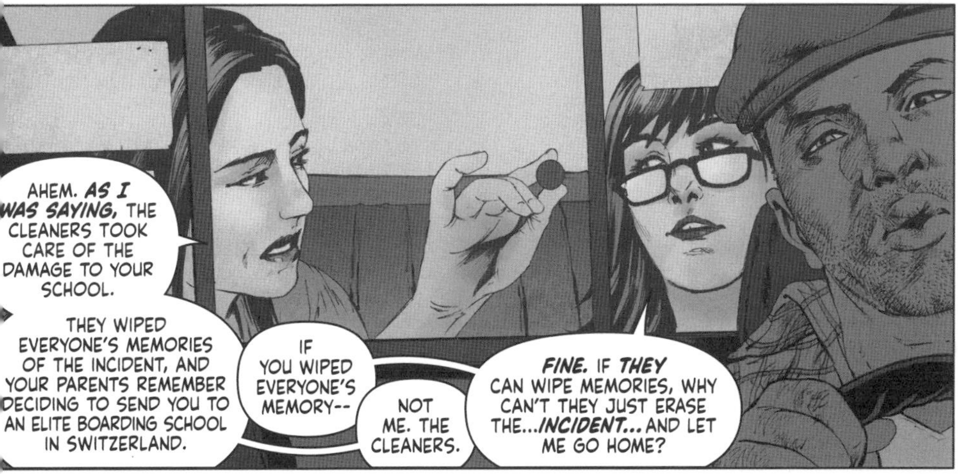
AHEM. ***AS I WAS SAYING,*** THE CLEANERS TOOK CARE OF THE DAMAGE TO YOUR SCHOOL.
THEY WIPED EVERYONE'S MEMORIES OF THE INCIDENT, AND YOUR PARENTS REMEMBER DECIDING TO SEND YOU TO AN ELITE BOARDING SCHOOL IN SWITZERLAND.
IF YOU WIPED EVERYONE'S MEMORY--
NOT ME. THE CLEANERS.
FINE. IF ***THEY*** CAN WIPE MEMORIES, WHY CAN'T THEY JUST ERASE THE...***INCIDENT...*** AND LET ME GO HOME?
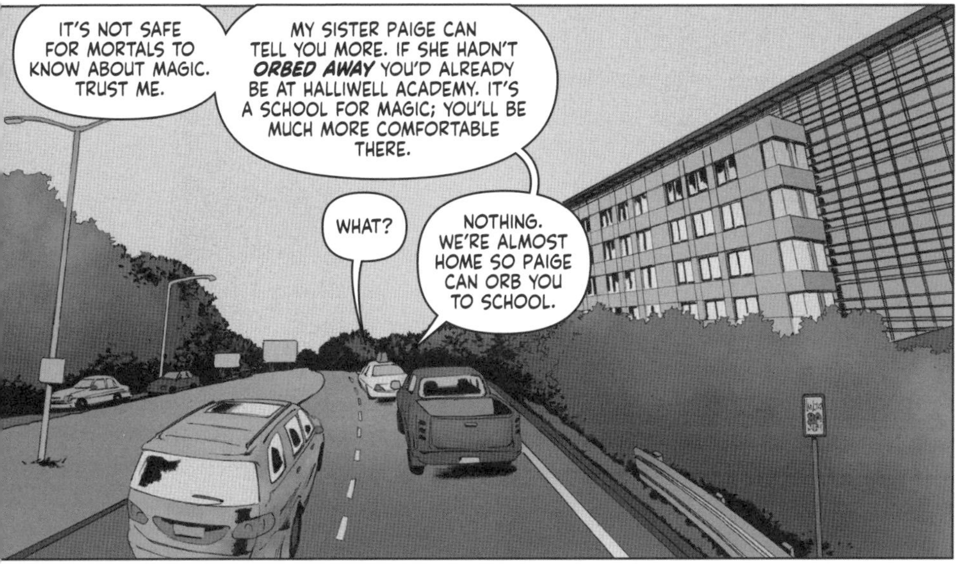
IT'S NOT SAFE FOR MORTALS TO KNOW ABOUT MAGIC. TRUST ME.
MY SISTER PAIGE CAN TELL YOU MORE. IF SHE HADN'T ***ORBED AWAY*** YOU'D ALREADY BE AT HALLIWELL ACADEMY. IT'S A SCHOOL FOR MAGIC; YOU'LL BE MUCH MORE COMFORTABLE THERE.
WHAT?
NOTHING. WE'RE ALMOST HOME SO PAIGE CAN ORB YOU TO SCHOOL.

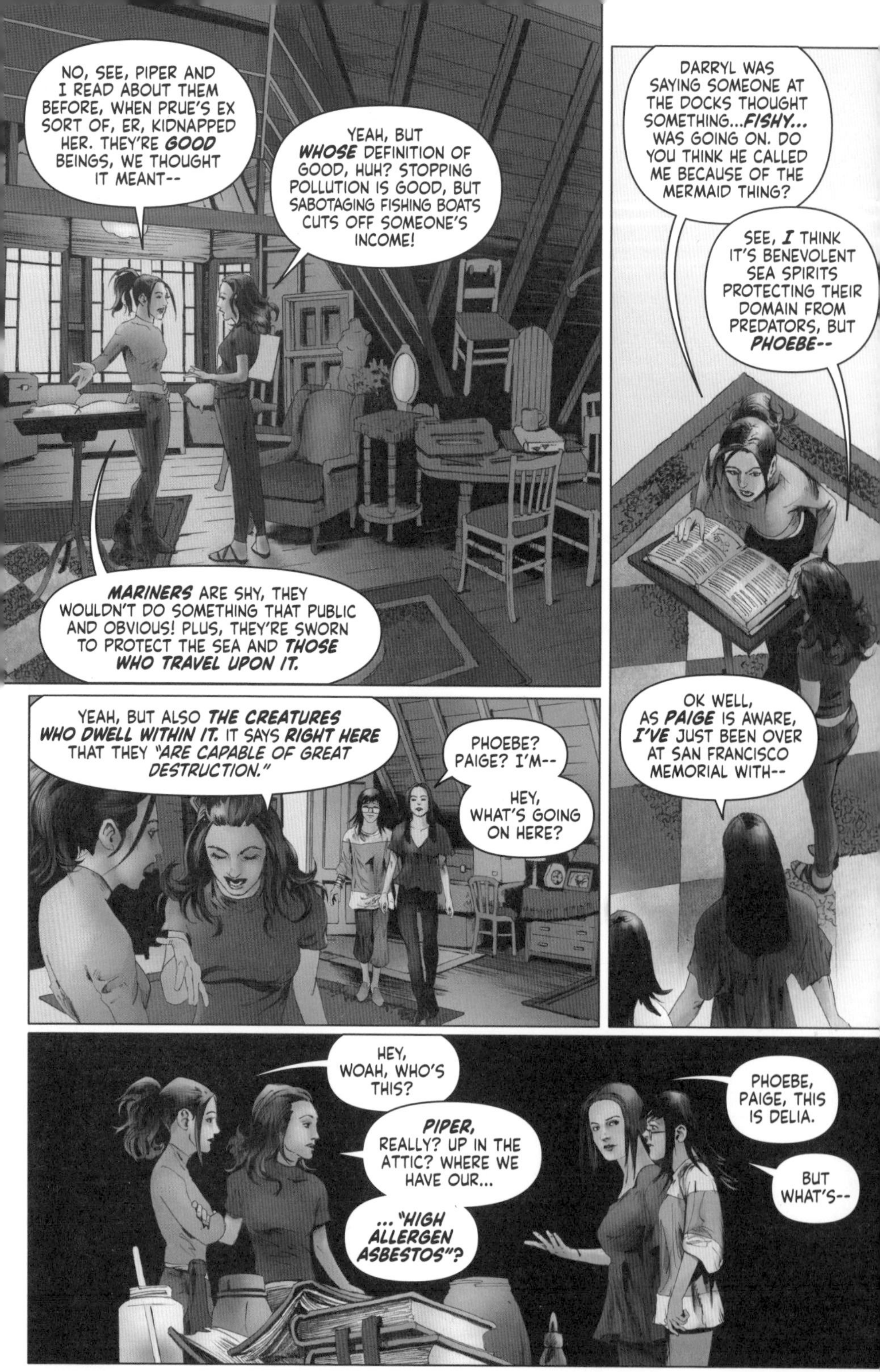
NO, SEE, PIPER AND I READ ABOUT THEM BEFORE, WHEN PRUE'S EX SORT OF, ER, KIDNAPPED HER. THEY'RE GOOD BEINGS, WE THOUGHT IT MEANT--
YEAH, BUT WHOSE DEFINITION OF GOOD, HUH? STOPPING POLLUTION IS GOOD, BUT SABOTAGING FISHING BOATS CUTS OFF SOMEONE'S INCOME!
MARINERS ARE SHY, THEY WOULDN'T DO SOMETHING THAT PUBLIC AND OBVIOUS! PLUS, THEY'RE SWORN TO PROTECT THE SEA AND THOSE WHO TRAVEL UPON IT.
DARRYL WAS SAYING SOMEONE AT THE DOCKS THOUGHT SOMETHING...FISHY... WAS GOING ON. DO YOU THINK HE CALLED ME BECAUSE OF THE MERMAID THING?
SEE, I THINK IT'S BENEVOLENT SEA SPIRITS PROTECTING THEIR DOMAIN FROM PREDATORS, BUT PHOEBE--
YEAH, BUT ALSO THE CREATURES WHO DWELL WITHIN IT. IT SAYS RIGHT HERE THAT THEY "ARE CAPABLE OF GREAT DESTRUCTION."
PHOEBE? PAIGE? I'M--
HEY, WHAT'S GOING ON HERE?
OK WELL, AS PAIGE IS AWARE, I'VE JUST BEEN OVER AT SAN FRANCISCO MEMORIAL WITH--
HEY, WOAH, WHO'S THIS?
PIPER, REALLY? UP IN THE ATTIC? WHERE WE HAVE OUR...
..."HIGH ALLERGEN ASBESTOS"?
PHOEBE, PAIGE, THIS IS DELIA.
BUT WHAT'S--

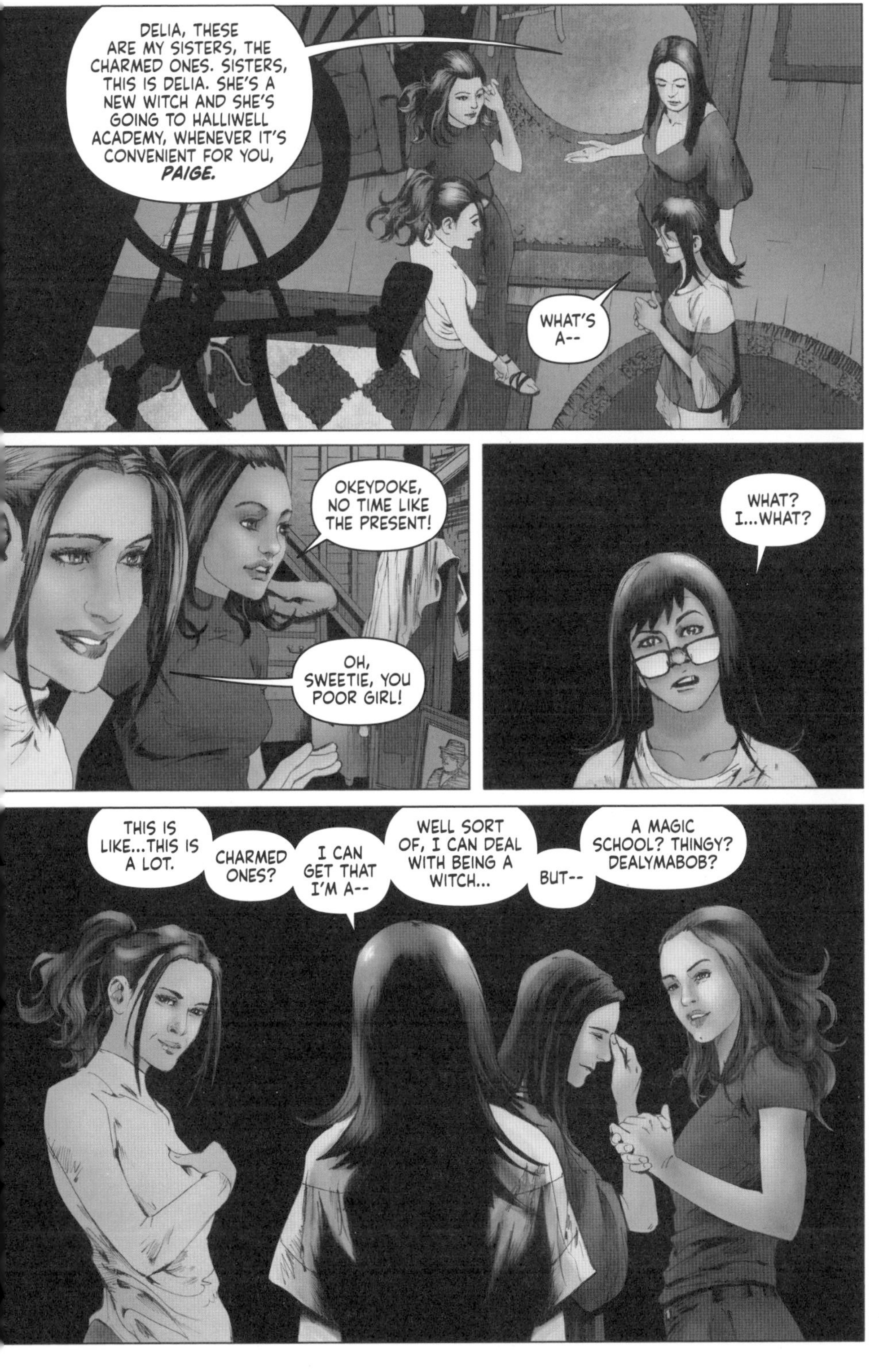
DELIA, THESE ARE MY SISTERS, THE CHARMED ONES. SISTERS, THIS IS DELIA. SHE'S A NEW WITCH AND SHE'S GOING TO HALLIWELL ACADEMY, WHENEVER IT'S CONVENIENT FOR YOU, *PAIGE.*
WHAT'S A--
OKEYDOKE, NO TIME LIKE THE PRESENT!
OH, SWEETIE, YOU POOR GIRL!
WHAT? I...WHAT?
THIS IS LIKE...THIS IS A LOT.
CHARMED ONES?
I CAN GET THAT I'M A--
WELL SORT OF, I CAN DEAL WITH BEING A WITCH...
BUT--
A MAGIC SCHOOL? THINGY? DEALYMABOB?

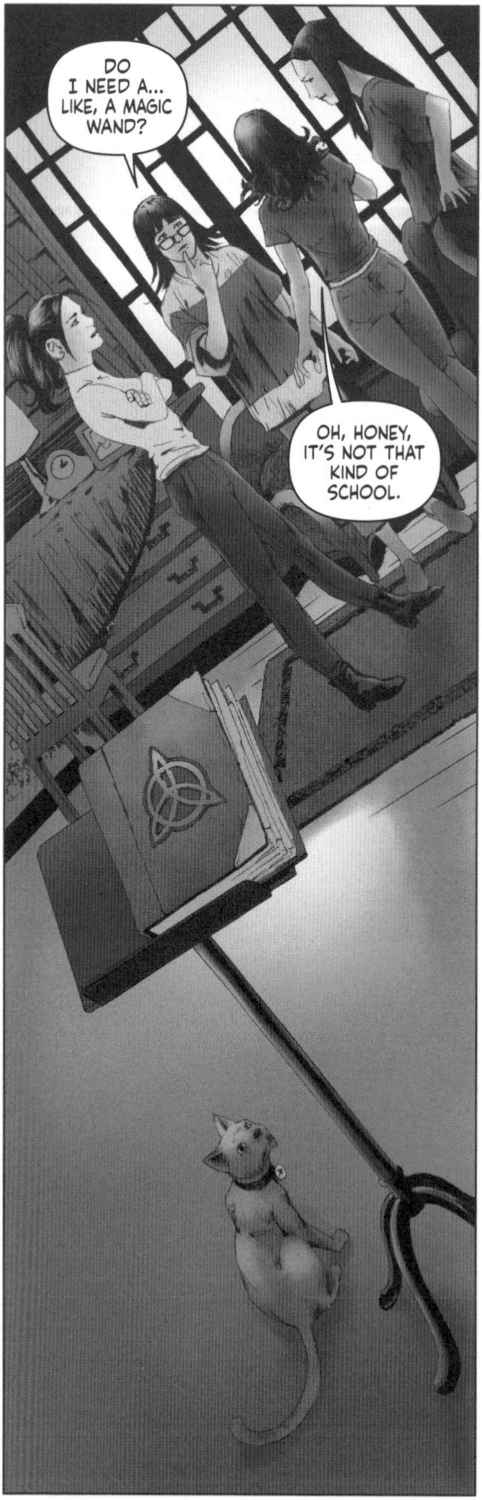
DO I NEED A... LIKE, A MAGIC WAND?
OH, HONEY, IT'S NOT THAT KIND OF SCHOOL.

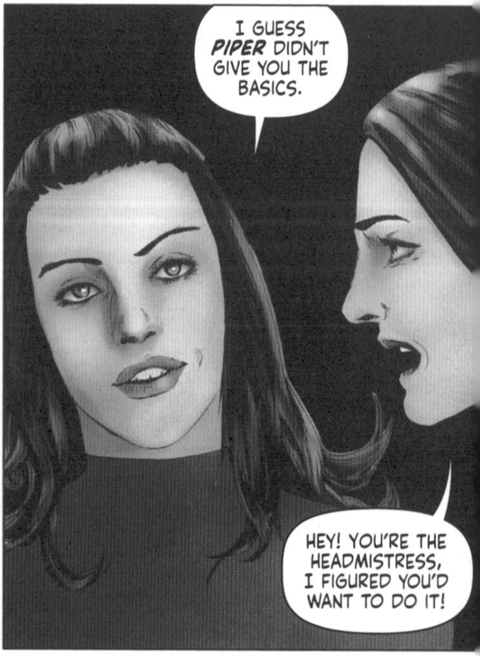
I GUESS PIPER DIDN'T GIVE YOU THE BASICS.
HEY! YOU'RE THE HEADMISTRESS, I FIGURED YOU'D WANT TO DO IT!

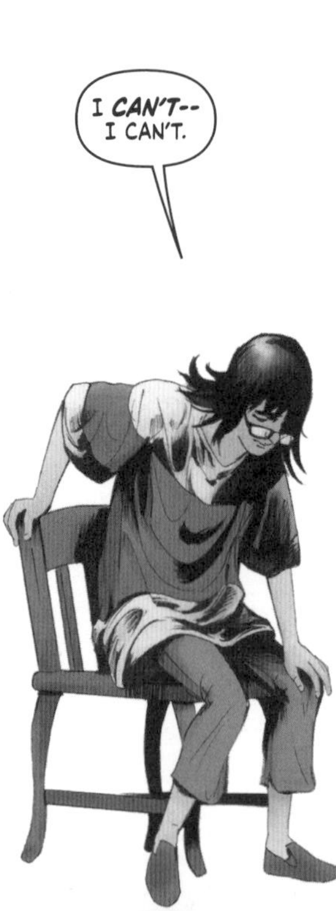
I CAN'T-- I CAN'T.

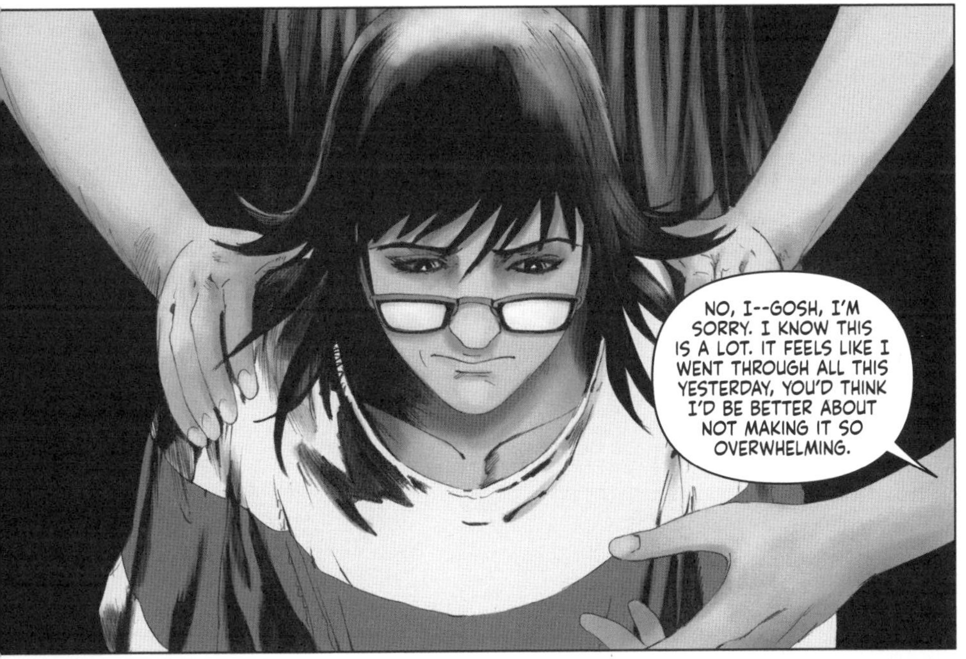
NO, I--GOSH, I'M SORRY. I KNOW THIS IS A LOT. IT FEELS LIKE I WENT THROUGH ALL THIS YESTERDAY, YOU'D THINK I'D BE BETTER ABOUT NOT MAKING IT SO OVERWHELMING.

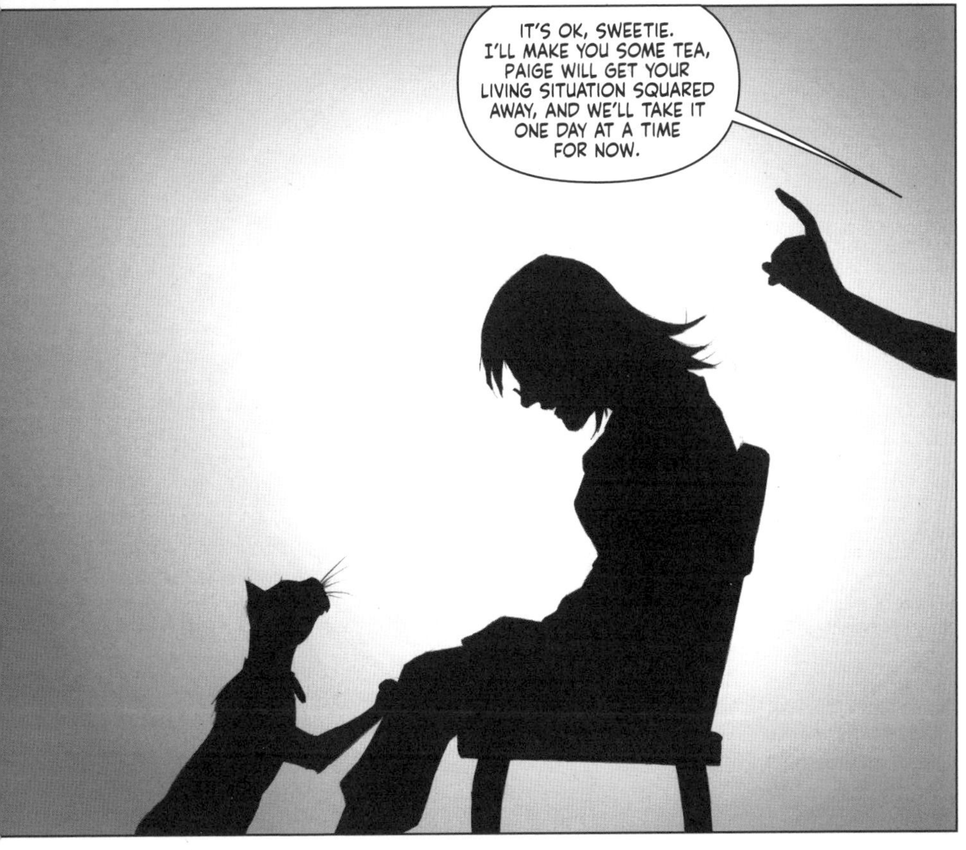
IT'S OK, SWEETIE. I'LL MAKE YOU SOME TEA, PAIGE WILL GET YOUR LIVING SITUATION SQUARED AWAY, AND WE'LL TAKE IT ONE DAY AT A TIME FOR NOW.

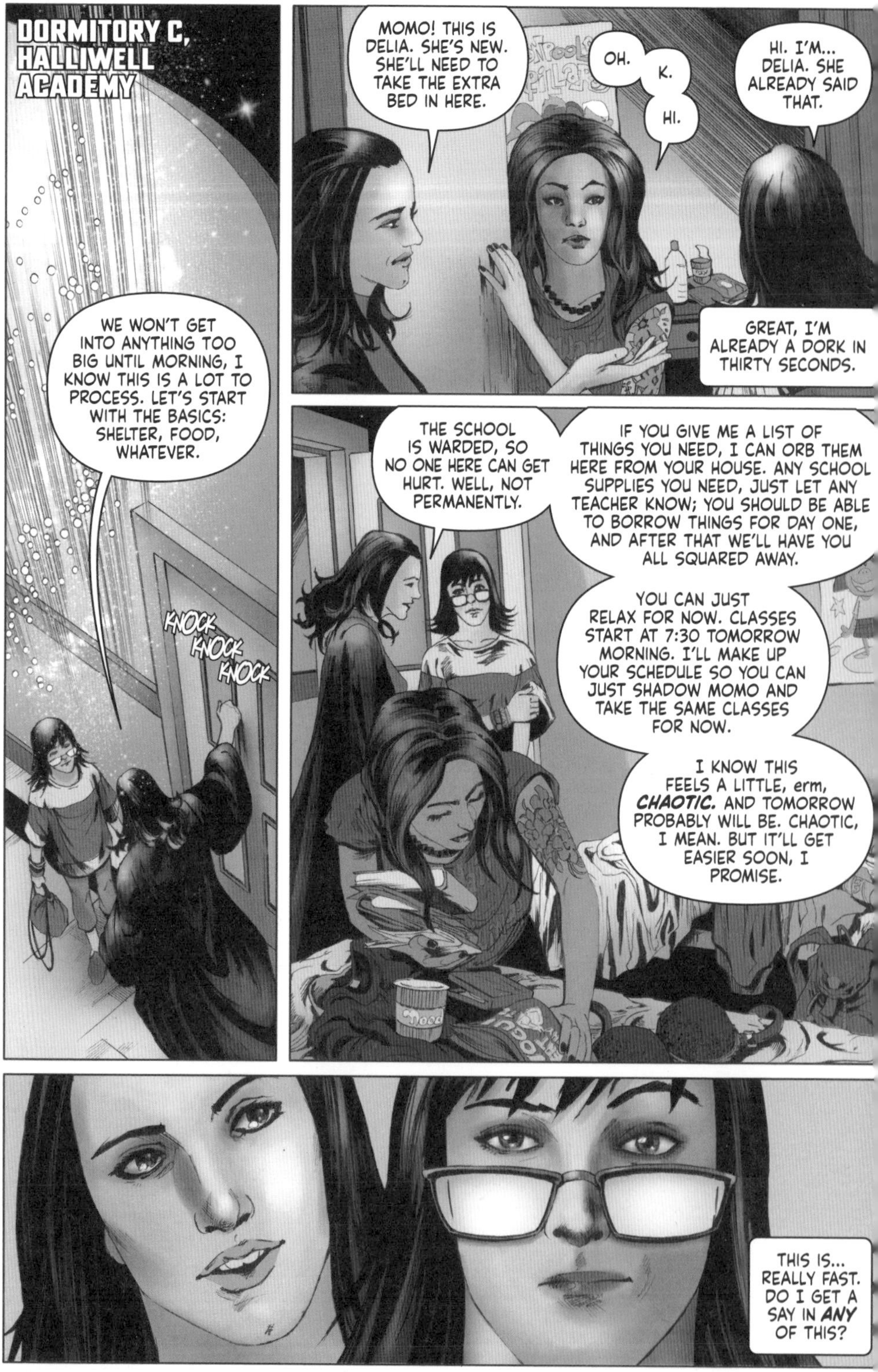
DORMITORY C, HALLIWELL ACADEMY
WE WON'T GET INTO ANYTHING TOO BIG UNTIL MORNING, I KNOW THIS IS A LOT TO PROCESS. LET'S START WITH THE BASICS: SHELTER, FOOD, WHATEVER.
KNOCK KNOCK KNOCK
MOMO! THIS IS DELIA. SHE'S NEW. SHE'LL NEED TO TAKE THE EXTRA BED IN HERE.
OH.
K.
HI.
HI. I'M... DELIA. SHE ALREADY SAID THAT.
GREAT, I'M ALREADY A DORK IN THIRTY SECONDS.
THE SCHOOL IS WARDED, SO NO ONE HERE CAN GET HURT. WELL, NOT PERMANENTLY.
IF YOU GIVE ME A LIST OF THINGS YOU NEED, I CAN ORB THEM HERE FROM YOUR HOUSE. ANY SCHOOL SUPPLIES YOU NEED, JUST LET ANY TEACHER KNOW; YOU SHOULD BE ABLE TO BORROW THINGS FOR DAY ONE, AND AFTER THAT WE'LL HAVE YOU ALL SQUARED AWAY.
YOU CAN JUST RELAX FOR NOW. CLASSES START AT 7:30 TOMORROW MORNING. I'LL MAKE UP YOUR SCHEDULE SO YOU CAN JUST SHADOW MOMO AND TAKE THE SAME CLASSES FOR NOW.
I KNOW THIS FEELS A LITTLE, erm, ***CHAOTIC.*** AND TOMORROW PROBABLY WILL BE. CHAOTIC, I MEAN. BUT IT'LL GET EASIER SOON, I PROMISE.
THIS IS... REALLY FAST. DO I GET A SAY IN ***ANY*** OF THIS?

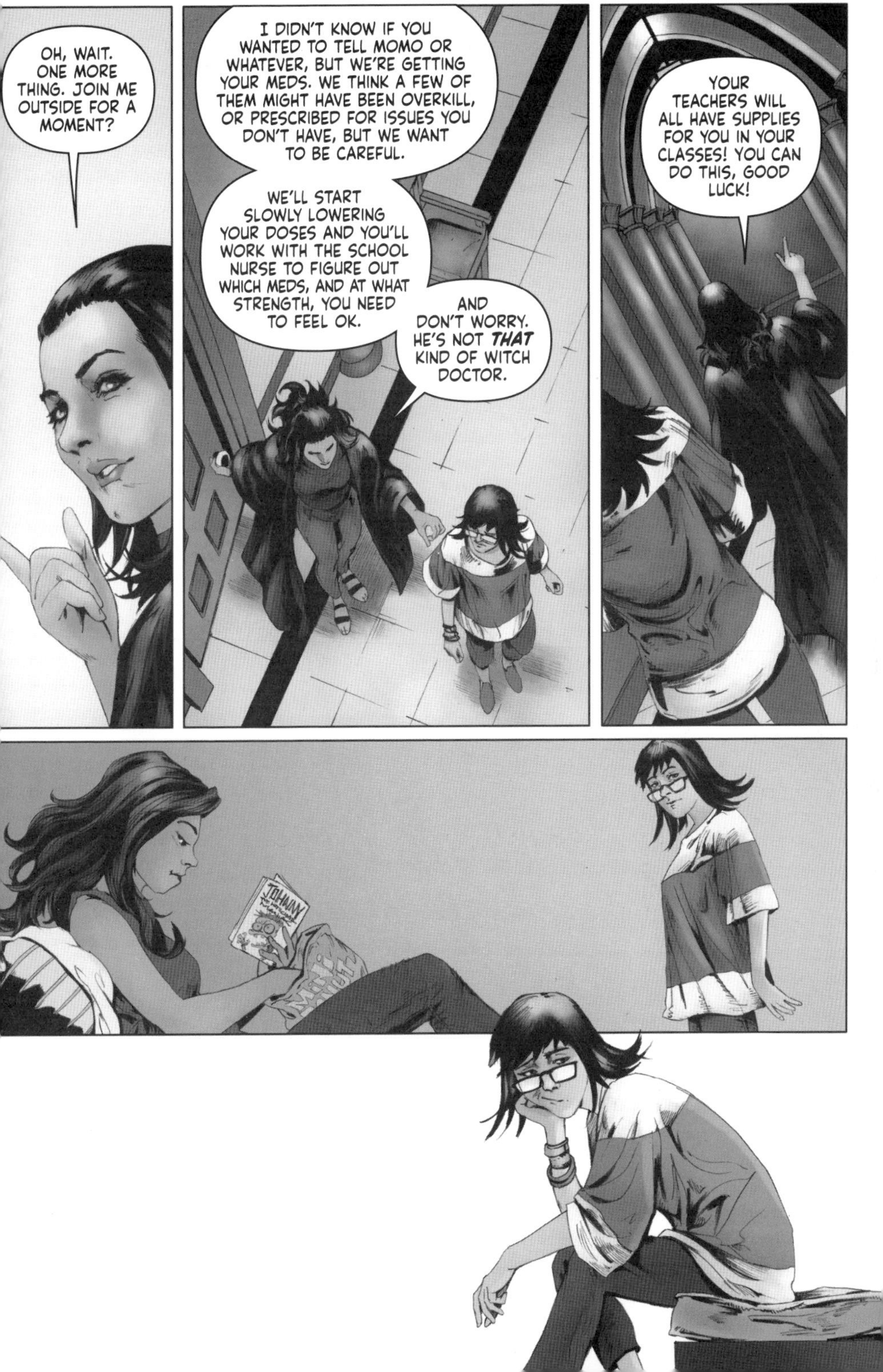
OH, WAIT. ONE MORE THING. JOIN ME OUTSIDE FOR A MOMENT?
I DIDN'T KNOW IF YOU WANTED TO TELL MOMO OR WHATEVER, BUT WE'RE GETTING YOUR MEDS. WE THINK A FEW OF THEM MIGHT HAVE BEEN OVERKILL, OR PRESCRIBED FOR ISSUES YOU DON'T HAVE, BUT WE WANT TO BE CAREFUL.
WE'LL START SLOWLY LOWERING YOUR DOSES AND YOU'LL WORK WITH THE SCHOOL NURSE TO FIGURE OUT WHICH MEDS, AND AT WHAT STRENGTH, YOU NEED TO FEEL OK.
AND DON'T WORRY. HE'S NOT ***THAT*** KIND OF WITCH DOCTOR.
YOUR TEACHERS WILL ALL HAVE SUPPLIES FOR YOU IN YOUR CLASSES! YOU CAN DO THIS, GOOD LUCK!

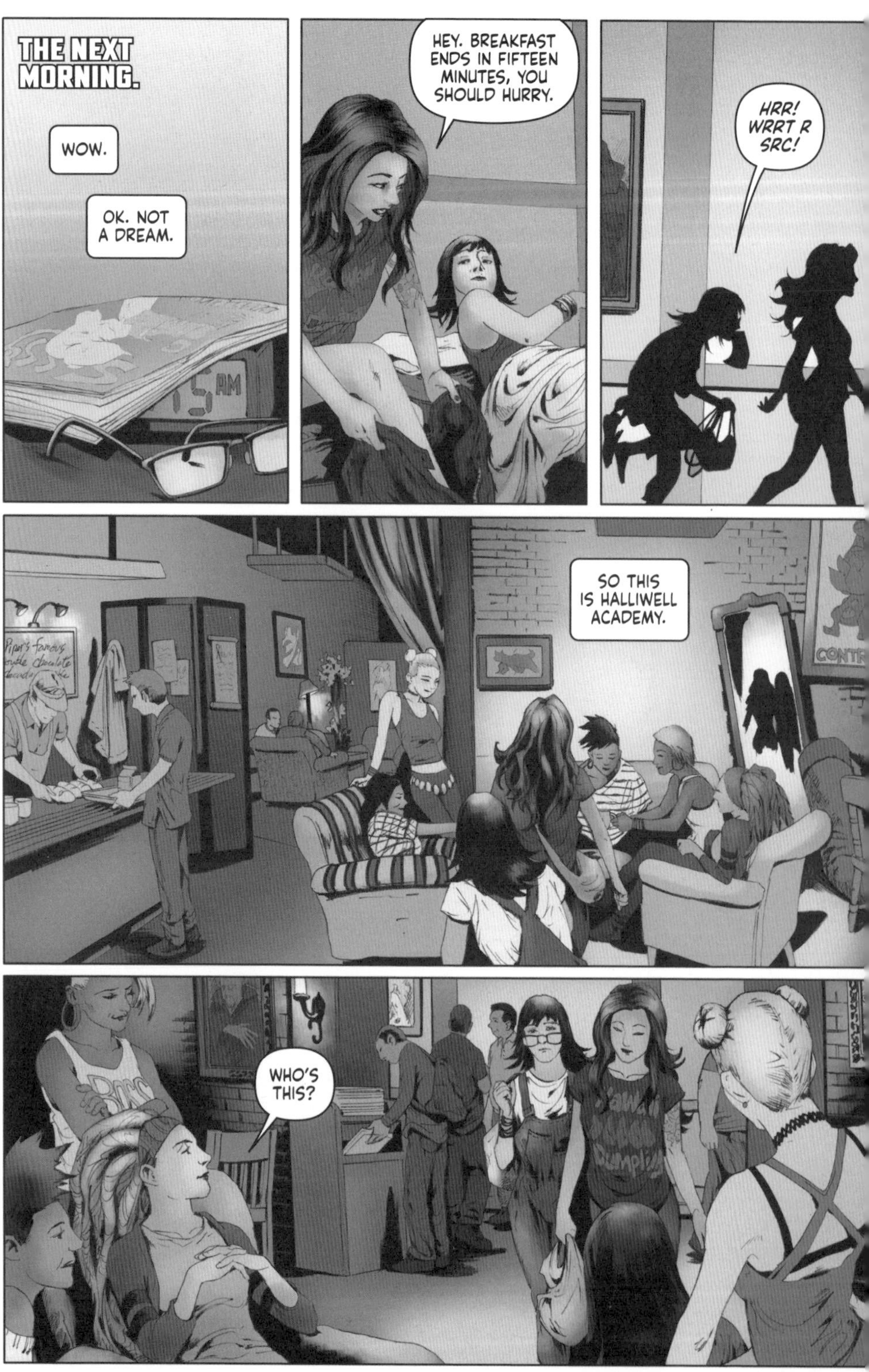
THE NEXT MORNING.
WOW.
OK. NOT A DREAM.
HEY. BREAKFAST ENDS IN FIFTEEN MINUTES, YOU SHOULD HURRY.
HRR! WRRT R SRC!
SO THIS IS HALLIWELL ACADEMY.
WHO'S THIS?

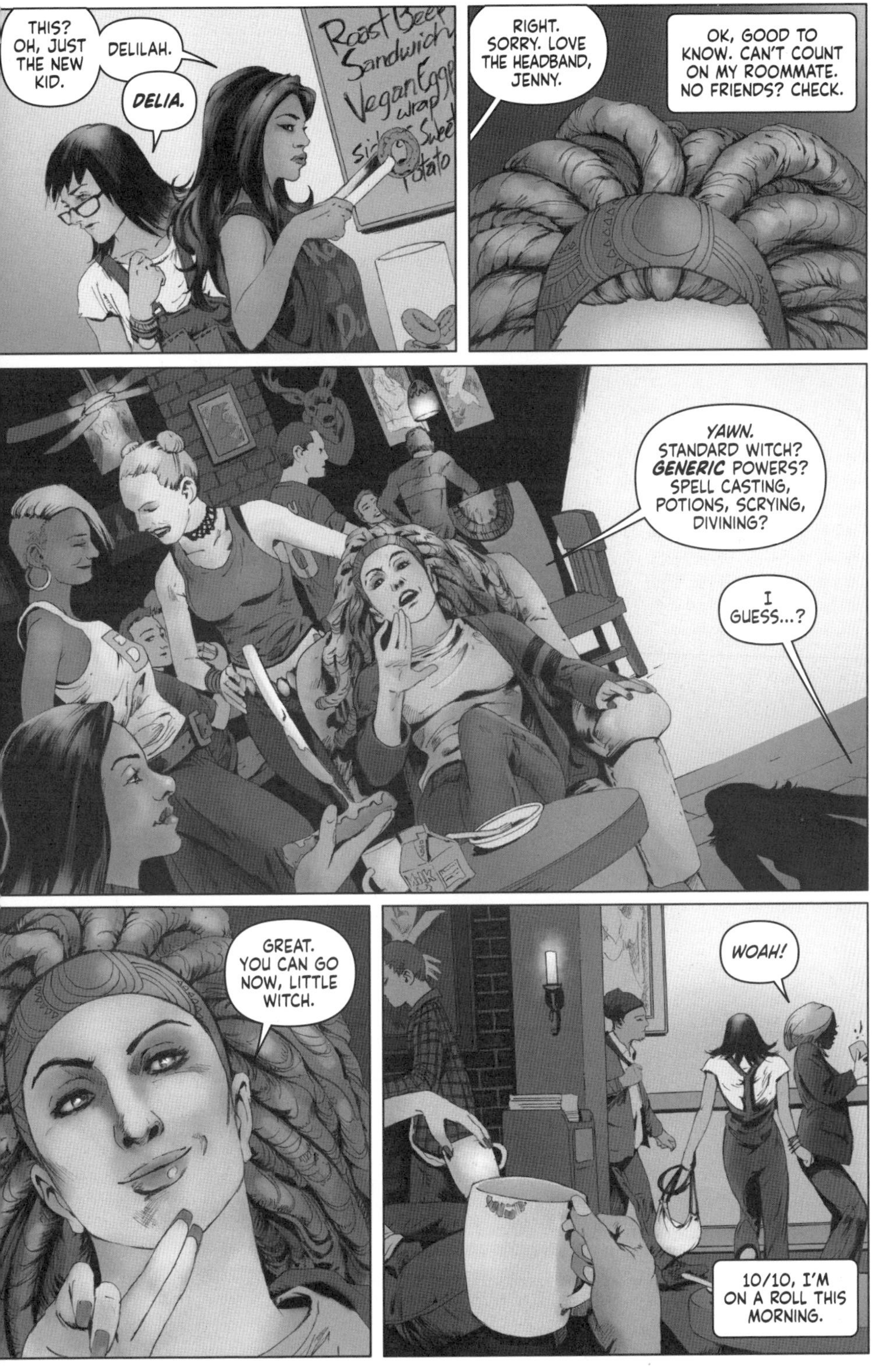
THIS? OH, JUST THE NEW KID.
DELILAH.
DELIA.
RIGHT. SORRY. LOVE THE HEADBAND, JENNY.
OK, GOOD TO KNOW. CAN'T COUNT ON MY ROOMMATE. NO FRIENDS? CHECK.
YAWN. STANDARD WITCH? ***GENERIC*** POWERS? SPELL CASTING, POTIONS, SCRYING, DIVINING?
I GUESS...?
GREAT. YOU CAN GO NOW, LITTLE WITCH.
WOAH!
10/10, I'M ON A ROLL THIS MORNING.

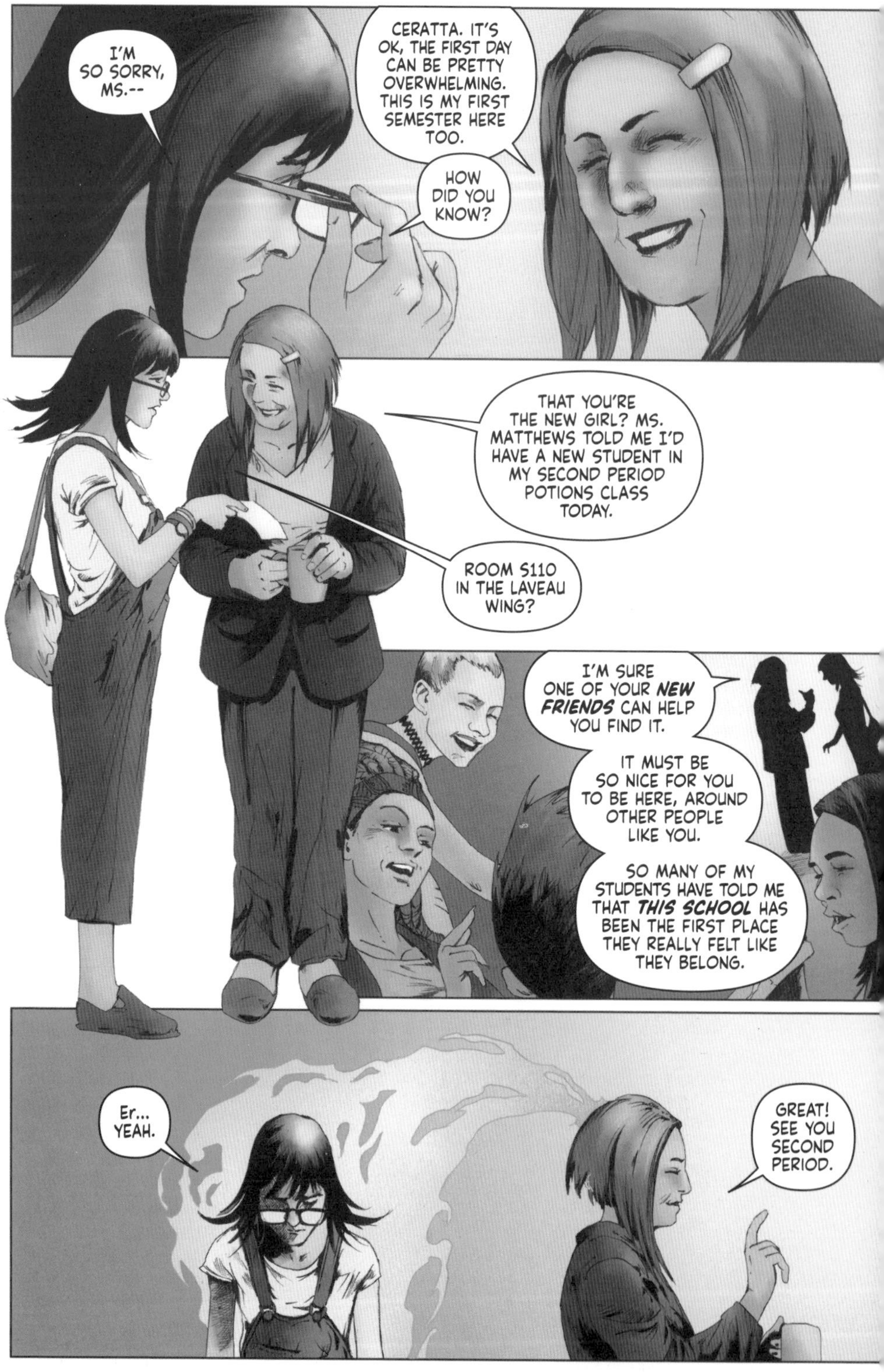
I'M SO SORRY, MS.--
CERATTA. IT'S OK, THE FIRST DAY CAN BE PRETTY OVERWHELMING. THIS IS MY FIRST SEMESTER HERE TOO.
HOW DID YOU KNOW?
THAT YOU'RE THE NEW GIRL? MS. MATTHEWS TOLD ME I'D HAVE A NEW STUDENT IN MY SECOND PERIOD POTIONS CLASS TODAY.
ROOM S110 IN THE LAVEAU WING?
I'M SURE ONE OF YOUR NEW FRIENDS CAN HELP YOU FIND IT.
IT MUST BE SO NICE FOR YOU TO BE HERE, AROUND OTHER PEOPLE LIKE YOU.
SO MANY OF MY STUDENTS HAVE TOLD ME THAT THIS SCHOOL HAS BEEN THE FIRST PLACE THEY REALLY FELT LIKE THEY BELONG.
Er... YEAH.
GREAT! SEE YOU SECOND PERIOD.

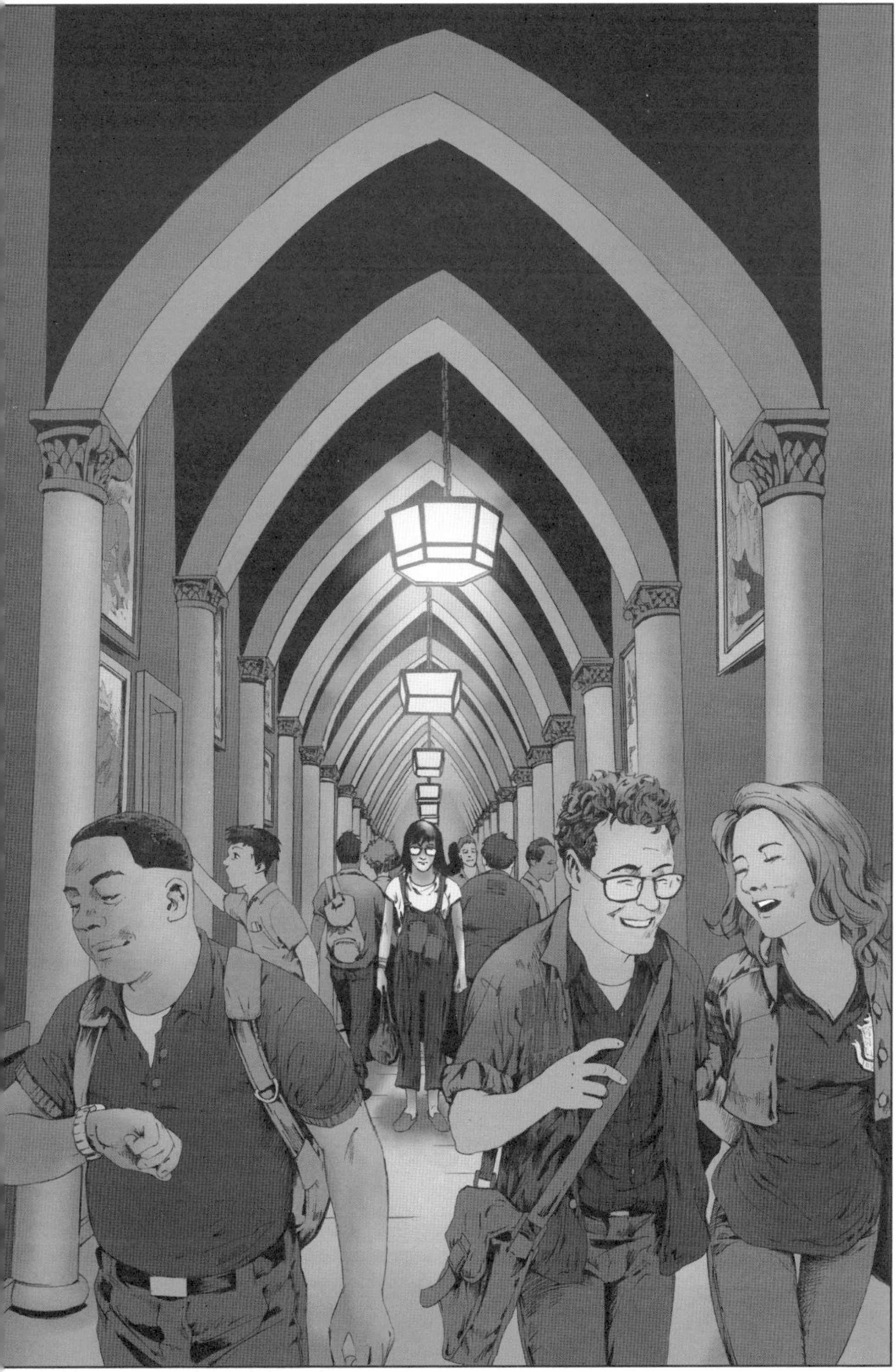

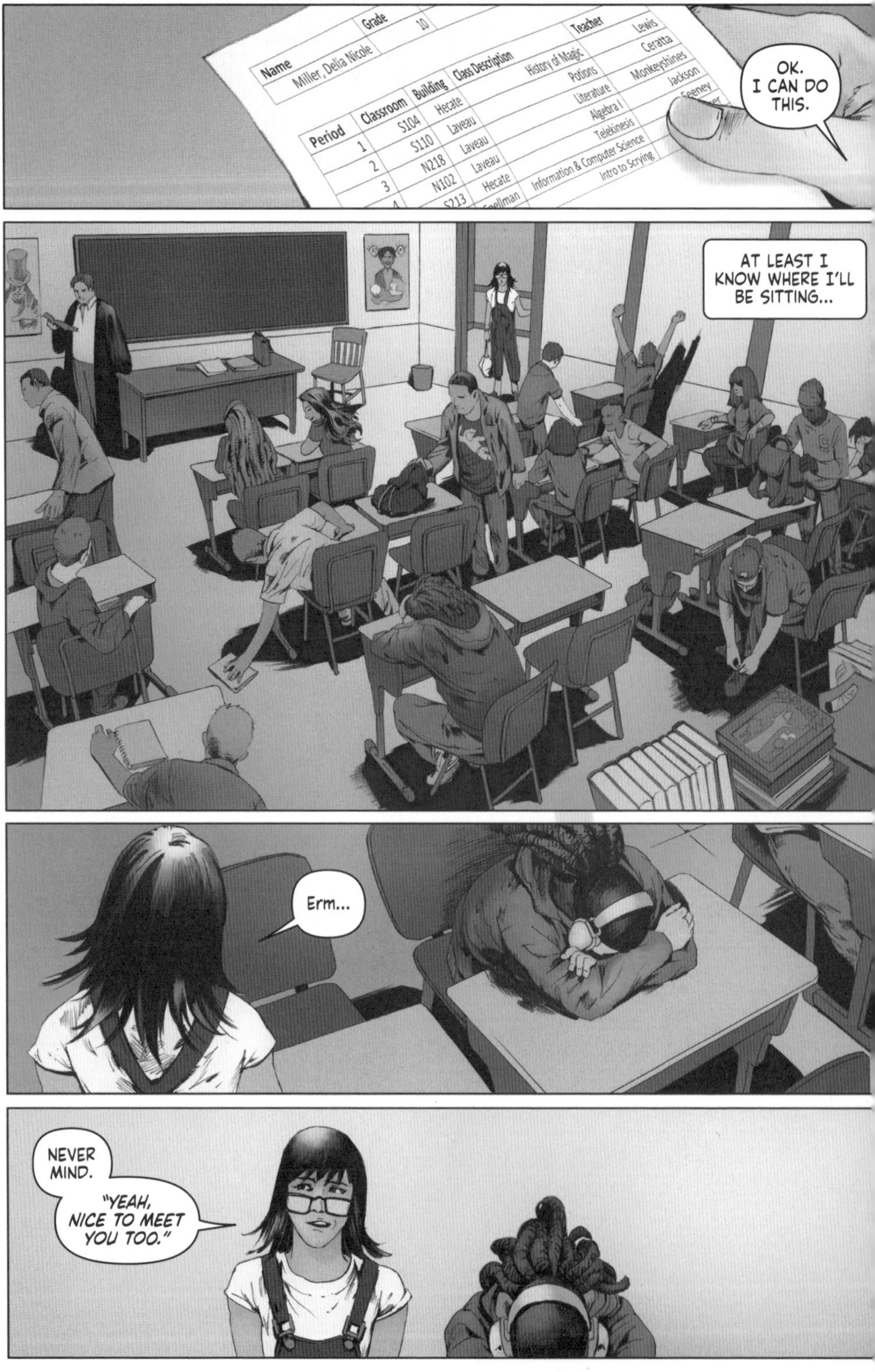
Name
Grade
Miller, Delia Nicole
10
Period
Classroom
Building
Class Description
Teacher
1
S104
Hecate
History of Magic
Lewis
2
S110
Laveau
Potions
Ceratta
3
N218
Laveau
Literature
Monkeyshines
N102
Laveau
Algebra I
Jackson
S213
Hecate
Telekinesis
Information & Computer Science
Intro to Scrying
OK. I CAN DO THIS.
AT LEAST I KNOW WHERE I'LL BE SITTING...
Erm...
NEVER MIND.
"YEAH, NICE TO MEET YOU TOO."

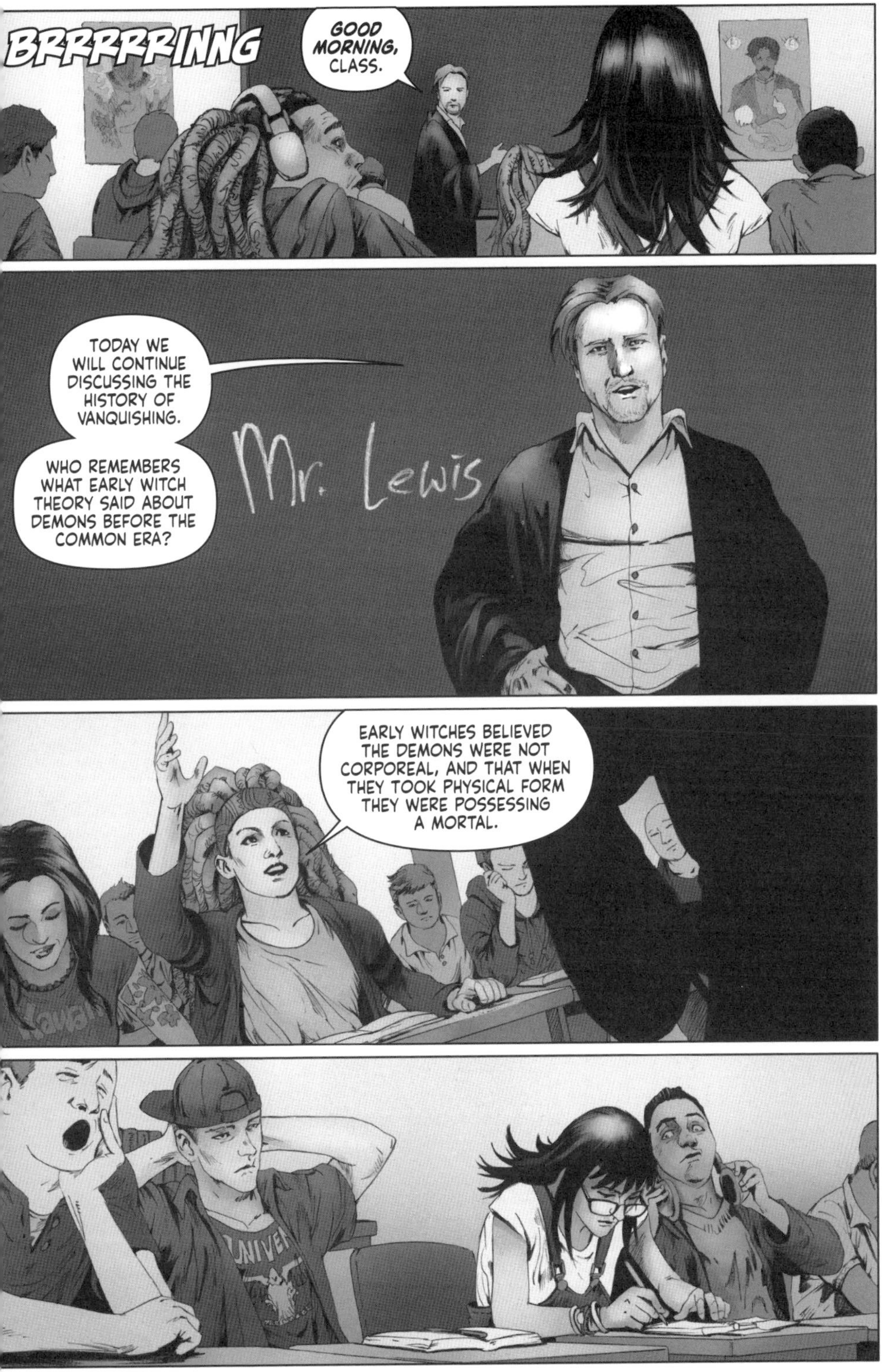
BRRRRRINNG
GOOD MORNING, CLASS.
TODAY WE WILL CONTINUE DISCUSSING THE HISTORY OF VANQUISHING.
WHO REMEMBERS WHAT EARLY WITCH THEORY SAID ABOUT DEMONS BEFORE THE COMMON ERA?
Mr. Lewis
EARLY WITCHES BELIEVED THE DEMONS WERE NOT CORPOREAL, AND THAT WHEN THEY TOOK PHYSICAL FORM THEY WERE POSSESSING A MORTAL.

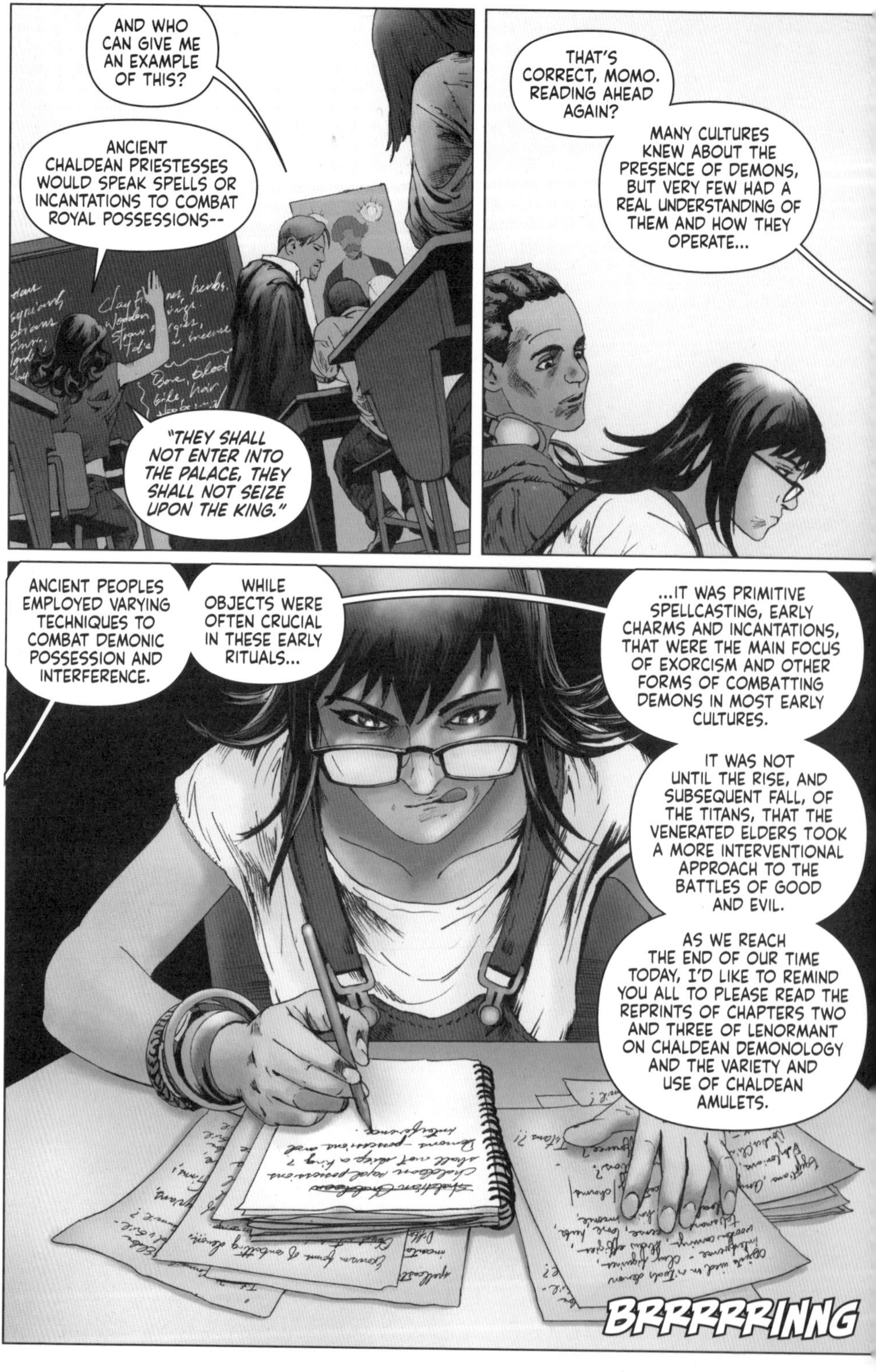
AND WHO CAN GIVE ME AN EXAMPLE OF THIS?
ANCIENT CHALDEAN PRIESTESSES WOULD SPEAK SPELLS OR INCANTATIONS TO COMBAT ROYAL POSSESSIONS--
"THEY SHALL NOT ENTER INTO THE PALACE, THEY SHALL NOT SEIZE UPON THE KING."
THAT'S CORRECT, MOMO. READING AHEAD AGAIN?
MANY CULTURES KNEW ABOUT THE PRESENCE OF DEMONS, BUT VERY FEW HAD A REAL UNDERSTANDING OF THEM AND HOW THEY OPERATE...
ANCIENT PEOPLES EMPLOYED VARYING TECHNIQUES TO COMBAT DEMONIC POSSESSION AND INTERFERENCE.
WHILE OBJECTS WERE OFTEN CRUCIAL IN THESE EARLY RITUALS...
...IT WAS PRIMITIVE SPELLCASTING, EARLY CHARMS AND INCANTATIONS, THAT WERE THE MAIN FOCUS OF EXORCISM AND OTHER FORMS OF COMBATTING DEMONS IN MOST EARLY CULTURES.
IT WAS NOT UNTIL THE RISE, AND SUBSEQUENT FALL, OF THE TITANS, THAT THE VENERATED ELDERS TOOK A MORE INTERVENTIONAL APPROACH TO THE BATTLES OF GOOD AND EVIL.
AS WE REACH THE END OF OUR TIME TODAY, I'D LIKE TO REMIND YOU ALL TO PLEASE READ THE REPRINTS OF CHAPTERS TWO AND THREE OF LENORMANT ON CHALDEAN DEMONOLOGY AND THE VARIETY AND USE OF CHALDEAN AMULETS.
BRRRRRINNG

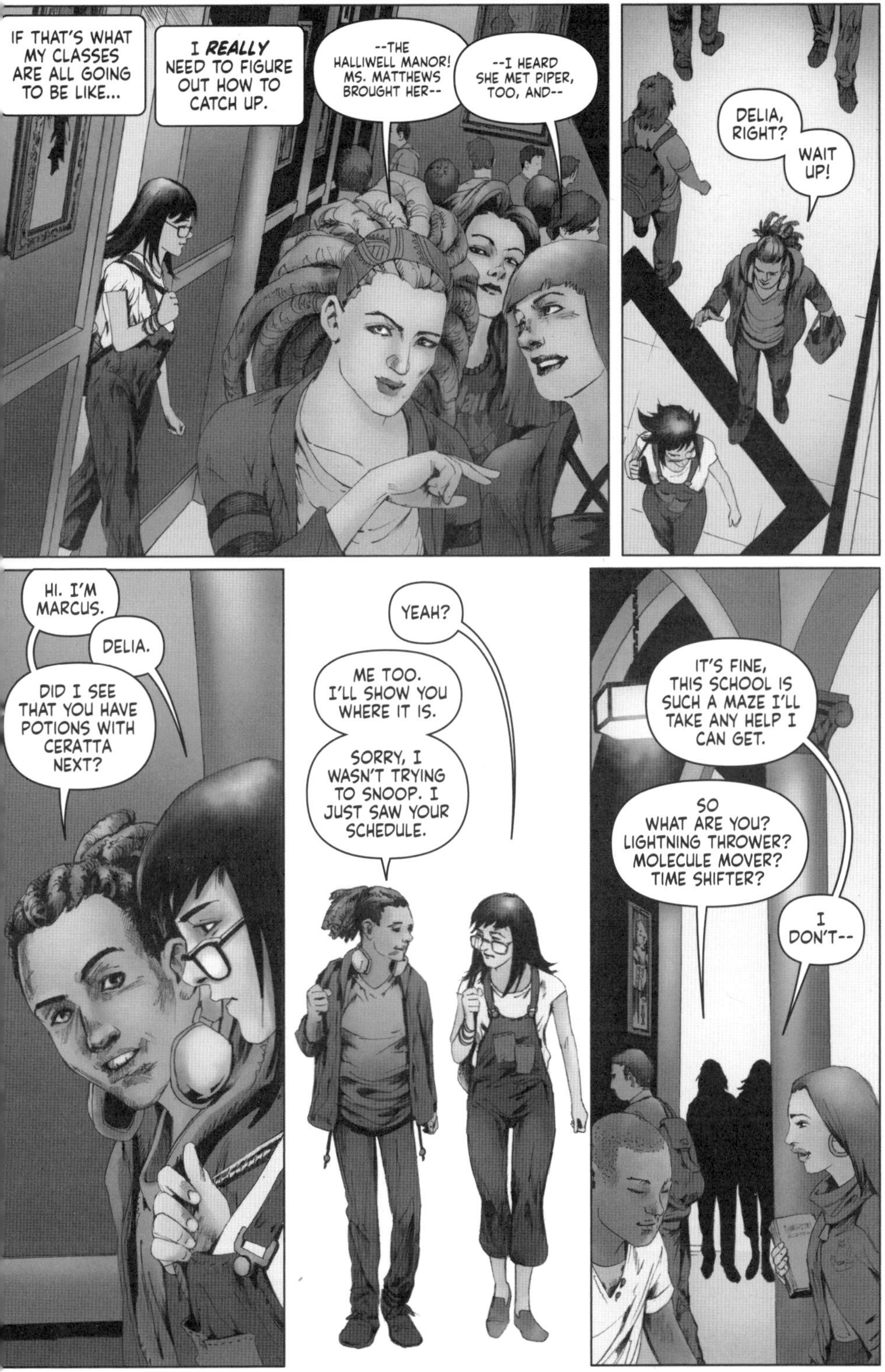
IF THAT'S WHAT MY CLASSES ARE ALL GOING TO BE LIKE...
I ***REALLY*** NEED TO FIGURE OUT HOW TO CATCH UP.
--THE HALLIWELL MANOR! MS. MATTHEWS BROUGHT HER--
--I HEARD SHE MET PIPER, TOO, AND--
DELIA, RIGHT?
WAIT UP!
HI. I'M MARCUS.
DELIA.
DID I SEE THAT YOU HAVE POTIONS WITH CERATTA NEXT?
YEAH?
ME TOO. I'LL SHOW YOU WHERE IT IS.
SORRY, I WASN'T TRYING TO SNOOP. I JUST SAW YOUR SCHEDULE.
IT'S FINE, THIS SCHOOL IS SUCH A MAZE I'LL TAKE ANY HELP I CAN GET.
SO WHAT ARE YOU? LIGHTNING THROWER? MOLECULE MOVER? TIME SHIFTER?
I DON'T--

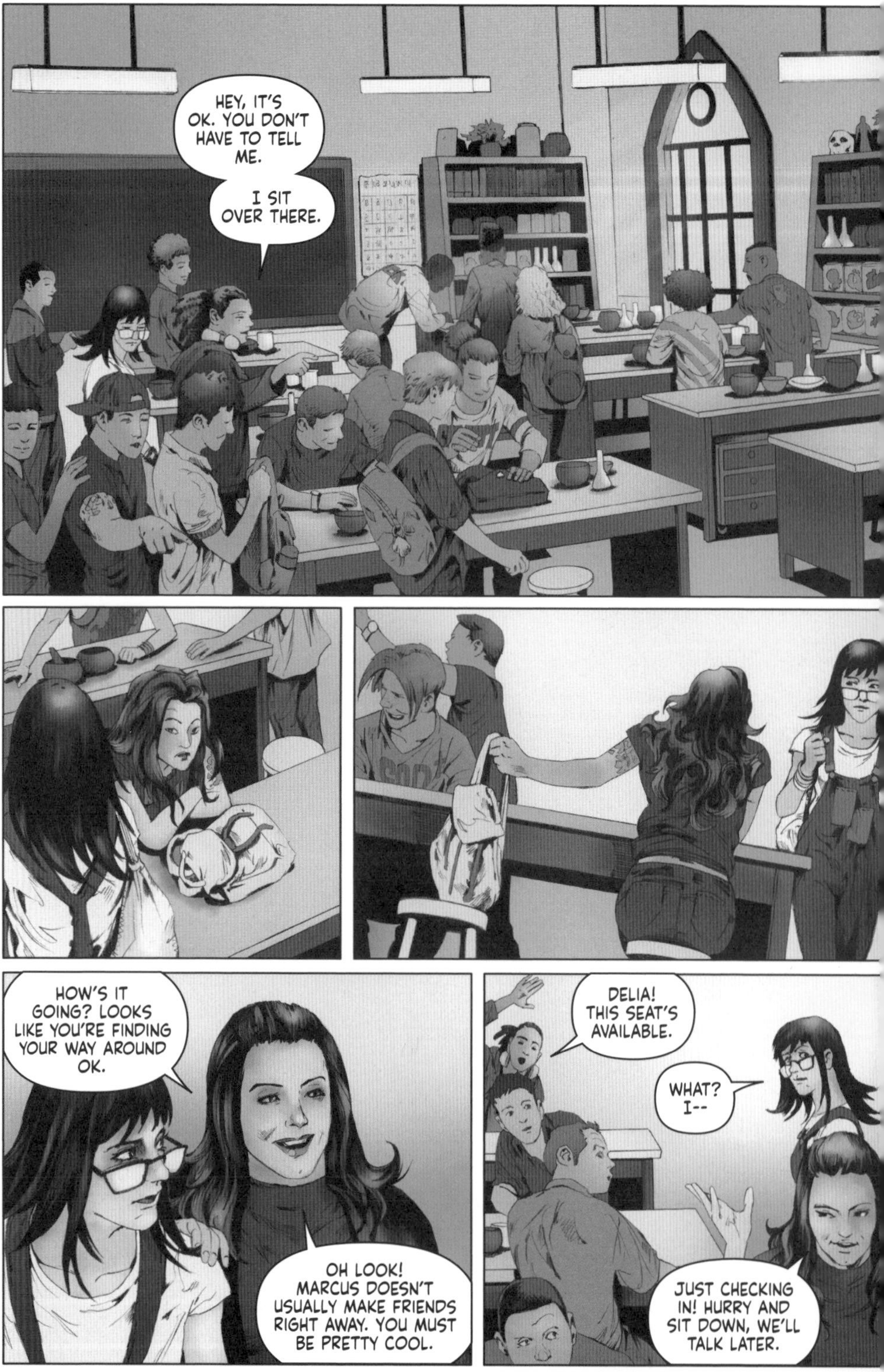
HEY, IT'S OK. YOU DON'T HAVE TO TELL ME.
I SIT OVER THERE.
HOW'S IT GOING? LOOKS LIKE YOU'RE FINDING YOUR WAY AROUND OK.
OH LOOK! MARCUS DOESN'T USUALLY MAKE FRIENDS RIGHT AWAY. YOU MUST BE PRETTY COOL.
DELIA! THIS SEAT'S AVAILABLE.
WHAT? I--
JUST CHECKING IN! HURRY AND SIT DOWN, WE'LL TALK LATER.

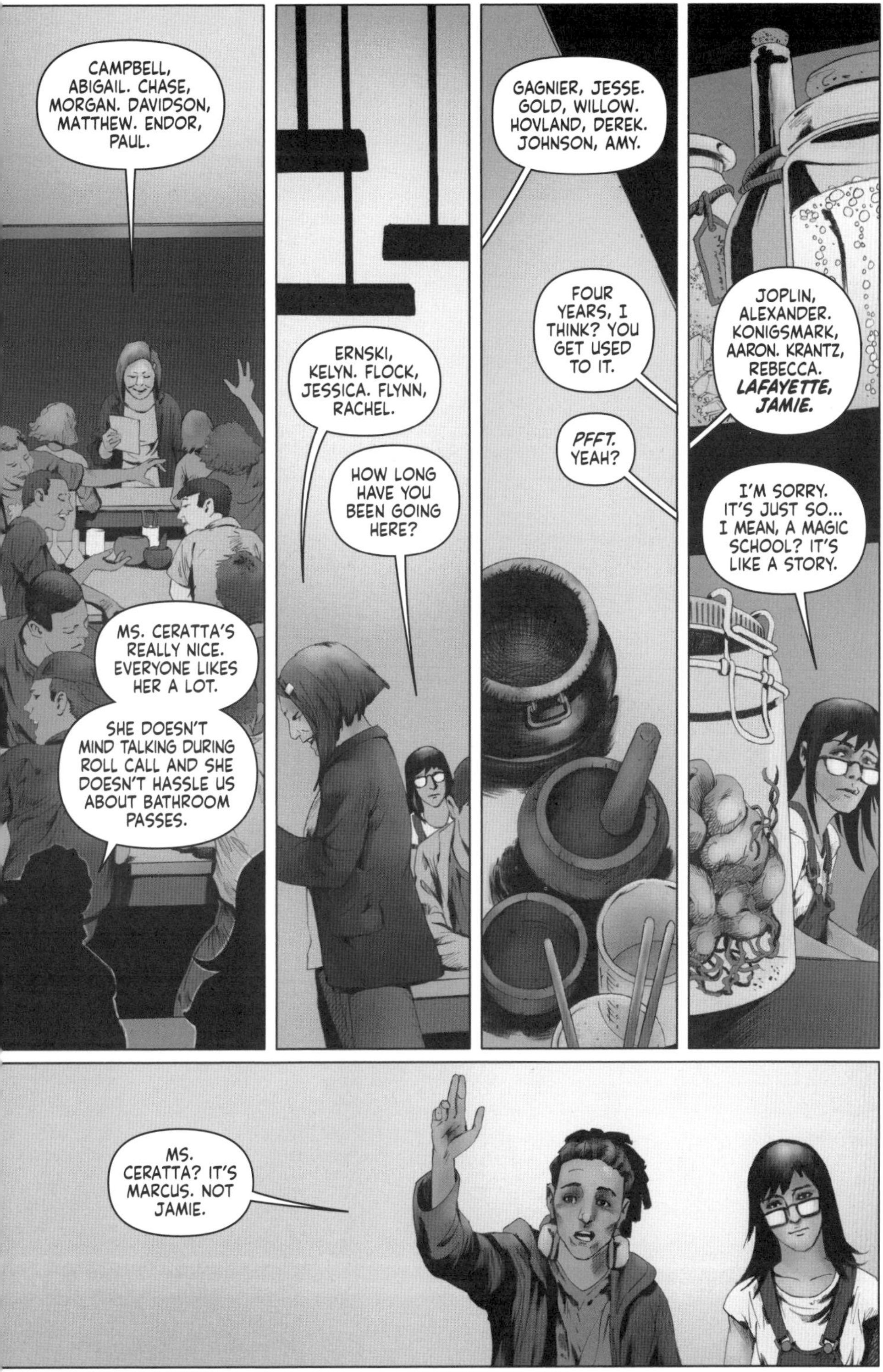
CAMPBELL, ABIGAIL. CHASE, MORGAN. DAVIDSON, MATTHEW. ENDOR, PAUL.
MS. CERATTA'S REALLY NICE. EVERYONE LIKES HER A LOT.
SHE DOESN'T MIND TALKING DURING ROLL CALL AND SHE DOESN'T HASSLE US ABOUT BATHROOM PASSES.
ERNSKI, KELYN. FLOCK, JESSICA. FLYNN, RACHEL.
HOW LONG HAVE YOU BEEN GOING HERE?
GAGNIER, JESSE. GOLD, WILLOW. HOVLAND, DEREK. JOHNSON, AMY.
FOUR YEARS, I THINK? YOU GET USED TO IT.
PFFT. YEAH?
JOPLIN, ALEXANDER. KONIGSMARK, AARON. KRANTZ, REBECCA. LAFAYETTE, JAMIE.
I'M SORRY. IT'S JUST SO... I MEAN, A MAGIC SCHOOL? IT'S LIKE A STORY.
MS. CERATTA? IT'S MARCUS. NOT JAMIE.

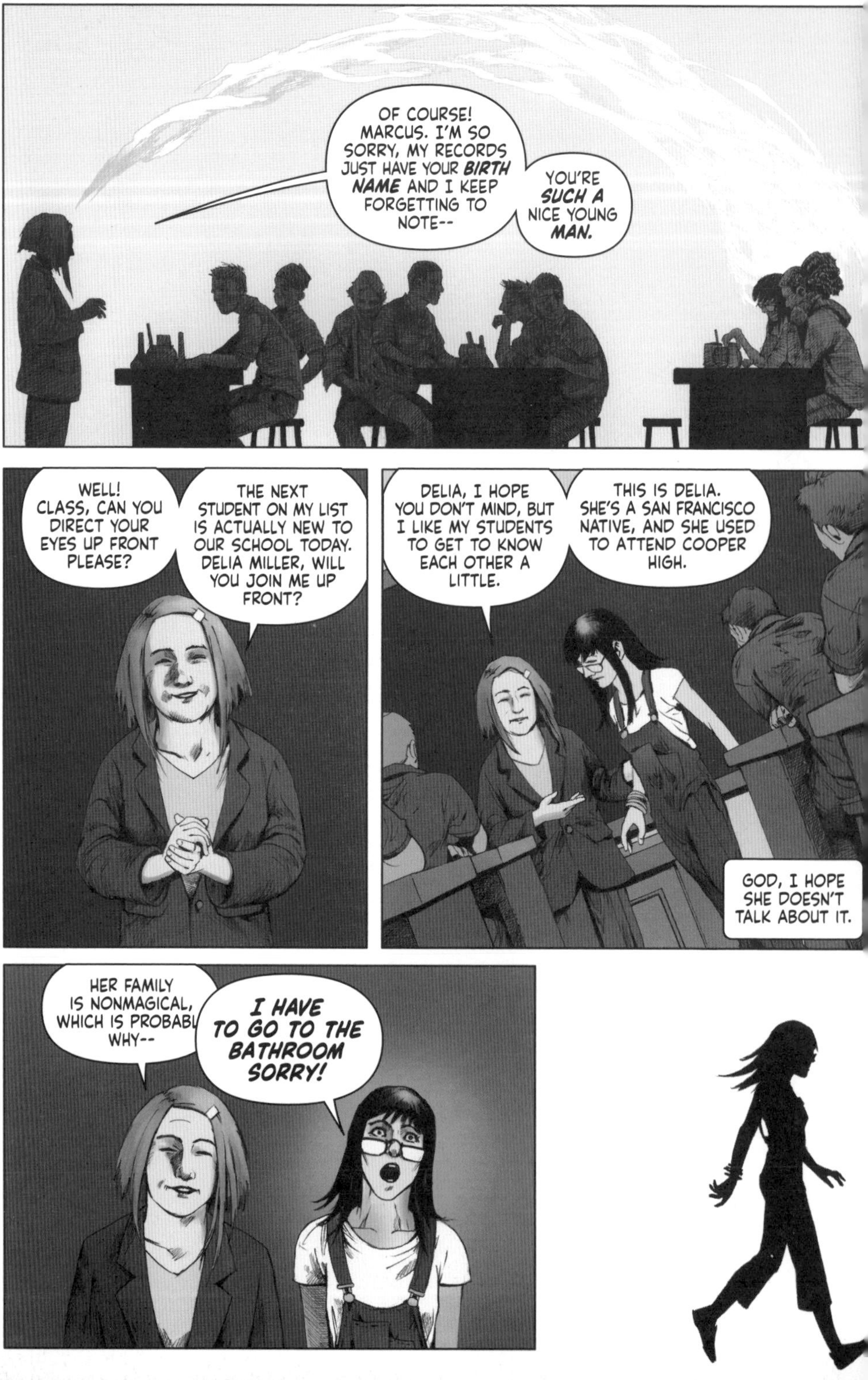
OF COURSE! MARCUS. I'M SO SORRY, MY RECORDS JUST HAVE YOUR **BIRTH NAME** AND I KEEP FORGETTING TO NOTE--
YOU'RE **SUCH A** NICE YOUNG **MAN.**
WELL! CLASS, CAN YOU DIRECT YOUR EYES UP FRONT PLEASE?
THE NEXT STUDENT ON MY LIST IS ACTUALLY NEW TO OUR SCHOOL TODAY. DELIA MILLER, WILL YOU JOIN ME UP FRONT?
DELIA, I HOPE YOU DON'T MIND, BUT I LIKE MY STUDENTS TO GET TO KNOW EACH OTHER A LITTLE.
THIS IS DELIA. SHE'S A SAN FRANCISCO NATIVE, AND SHE USED TO ATTEND COOPER HIGH.
GOD, I HOPE SHE DOESN'T TALK ABOUT IT.
HER FAMILY IS NONMAGICAL, WHICH IS PROBABL WHY--
I HAVE TO GO TO THE BATHROOM SORRY!

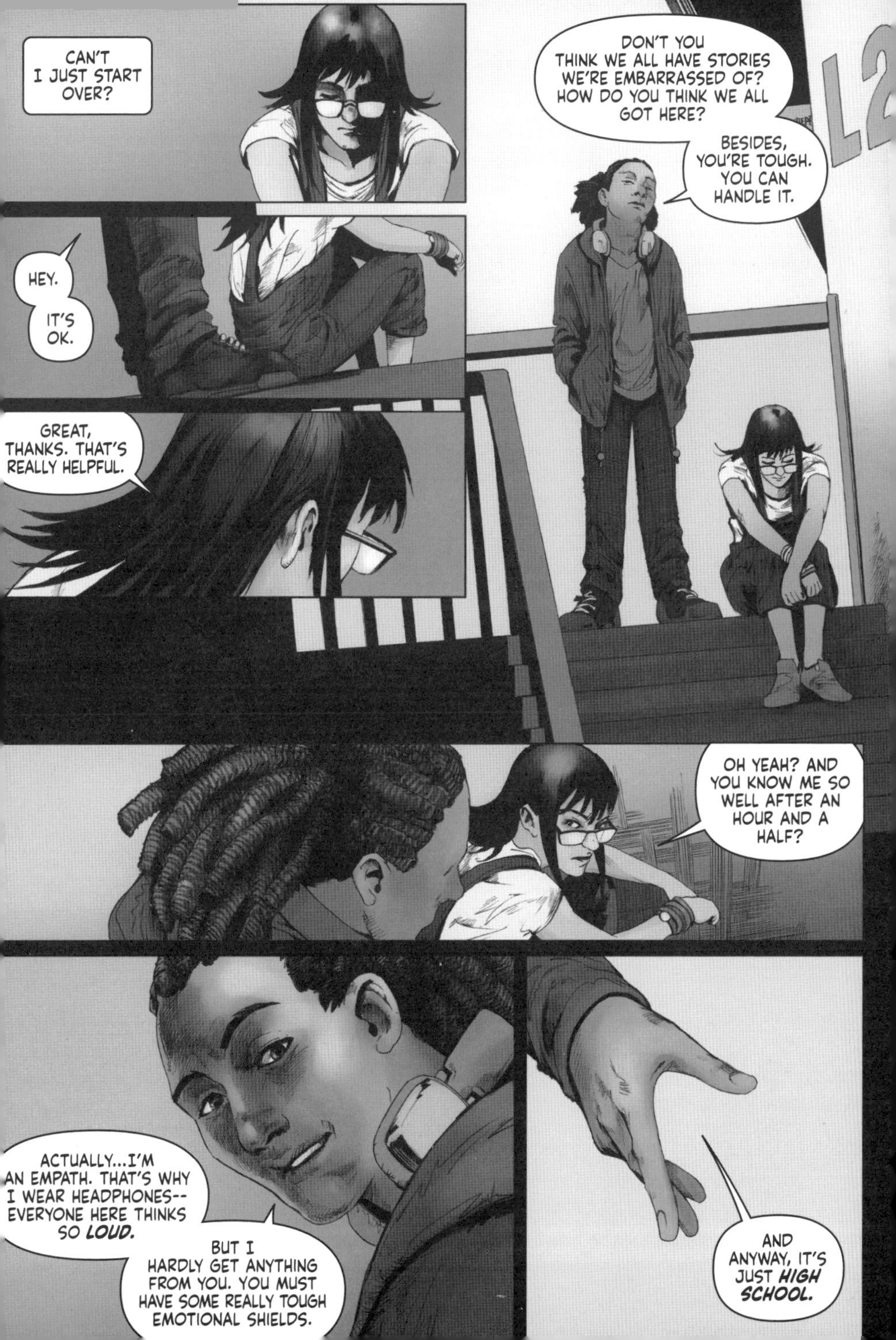
CAN'T I JUST START OVER?
HEY.
IT'S OK.
GREAT, THANKS. THAT'S REALLY HELPFUL.
DON'T YOU THINK WE ALL HAVE STORIES WE'RE EMBARRASSED OF? HOW DO YOU THINK WE ALL GOT HERE?
BESIDES, YOU'RE TOUGH. YOU CAN HANDLE IT.
OH YEAH? AND YOU KNOW ME SO WELL AFTER AN HOUR AND A HALF?
ACTUALLY...I'M AN EMPATH. THAT'S WHY I WEAR HEADPHONES--EVERYONE HERE THINKS SO ***LOUD.***
BUT I HARDLY GET ANYTHING FROM YOU. YOU MUST HAVE SOME REALLY TOUGH EMOTIONAL SHIELDS.
AND ANYWAY, IT'S JUST ***HIGH SCHOOL.***

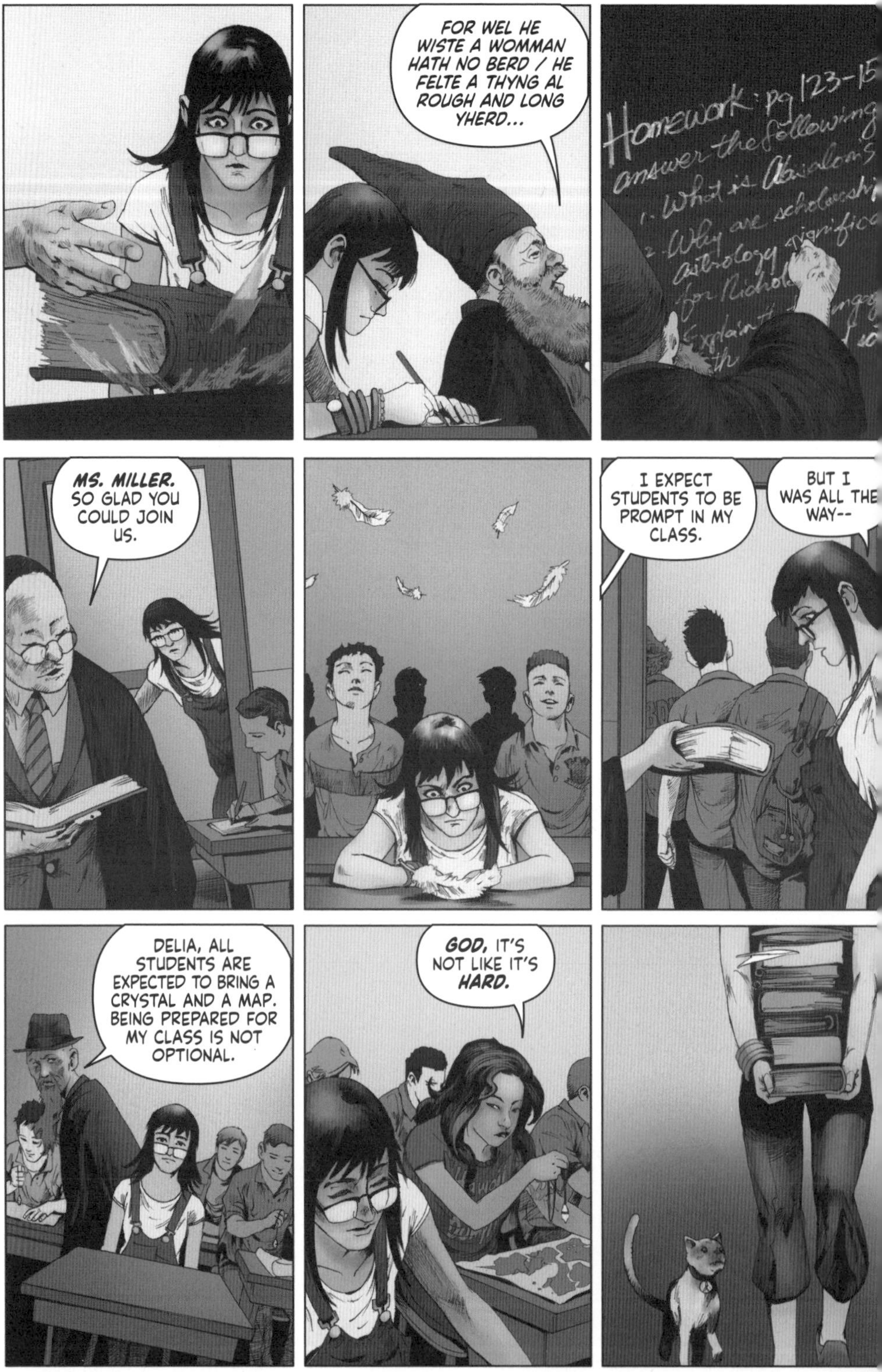
FOR WEL HE WISTE A WOMMAN HATH NO BERD / HE FELTE A THYNG AL ROUGH AND LONG YHERD...
Homework: pg 123-15
answer the following
MS. MILLER. SO GLAD YOU COULD JOIN US.
I EXPECT STUDENTS TO BE PROMPT IN MY CLASS.
BUT I WAS ALL THE WAY--
DELIA, ALL STUDENTS ARE EXPECTED TO BRING A CRYSTAL AND A MAP. BEING PREPARED FOR MY CLASS IS NOT OPTIONAL.
GOD, IT'S NOT LIKE IT'S HARD.

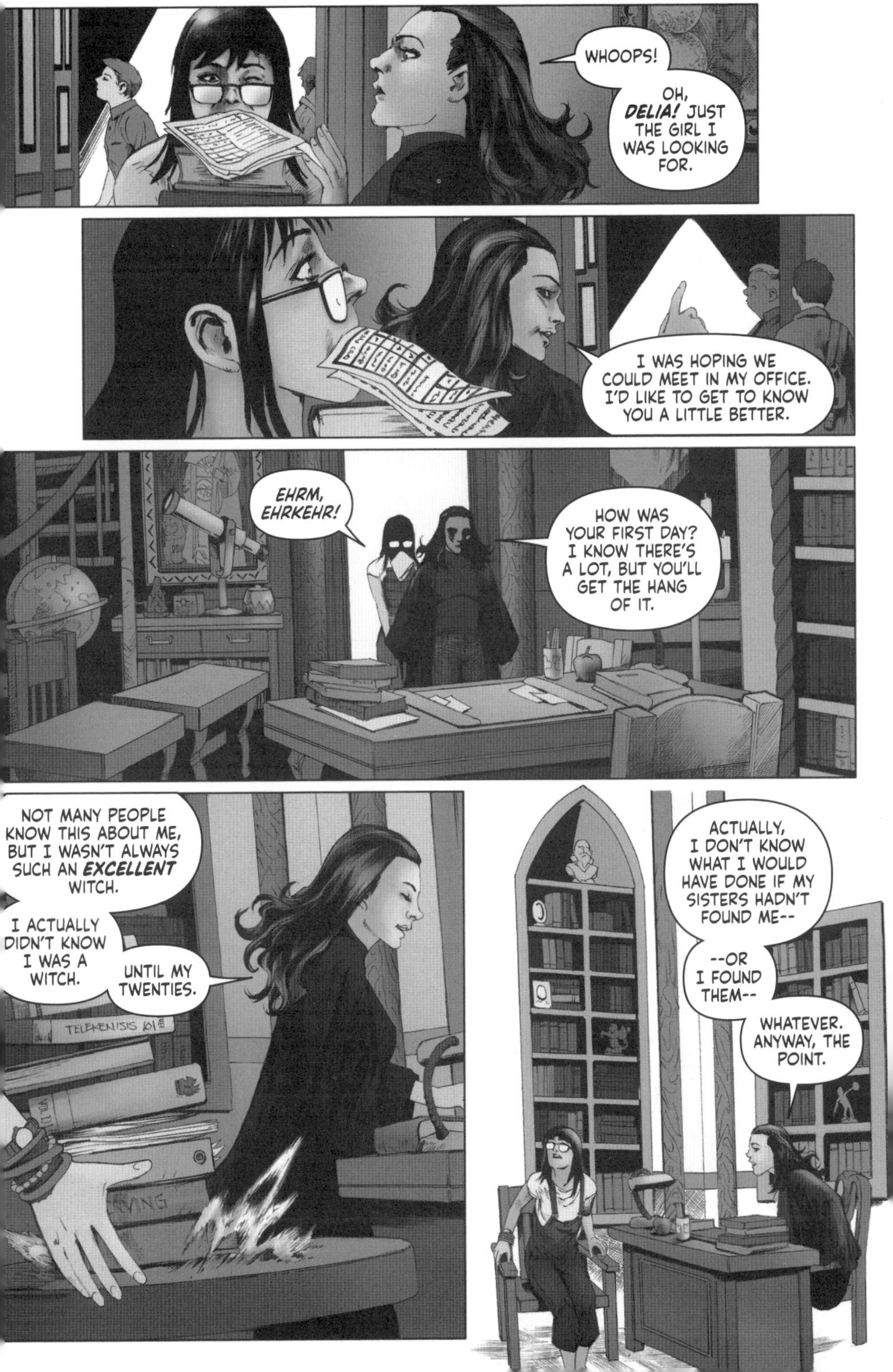
WHOOPS!
OH, *DELIA!* JUST THE GIRL I WAS LOOKING FOR.
I WAS HOPING WE COULD MEET IN MY OFFICE. I'D LIKE TO GET TO KNOW YOU A LITTLE BETTER.
EHRM, EHRKEHR!
HOW WAS YOUR FIRST DAY? I KNOW THERE'S A LOT, BUT YOU'LL GET THE HANG OF IT.
NOT MANY PEOPLE KNOW THIS ABOUT ME, BUT I WASN'T ALWAYS SUCH AN *EXCELLENT* WITCH.
I ACTUALLY DIDN'T KNOW I WAS A WITCH.
UNTIL MY TWENTIES.
TELEKENISIS 101
ACTUALLY, I DON'T KNOW WHAT I WOULD HAVE DONE IF MY SISTERS HADN'T FOUND ME--
--OR I FOUND THEM--
WHATEVER. ANYWAY, THE POINT.

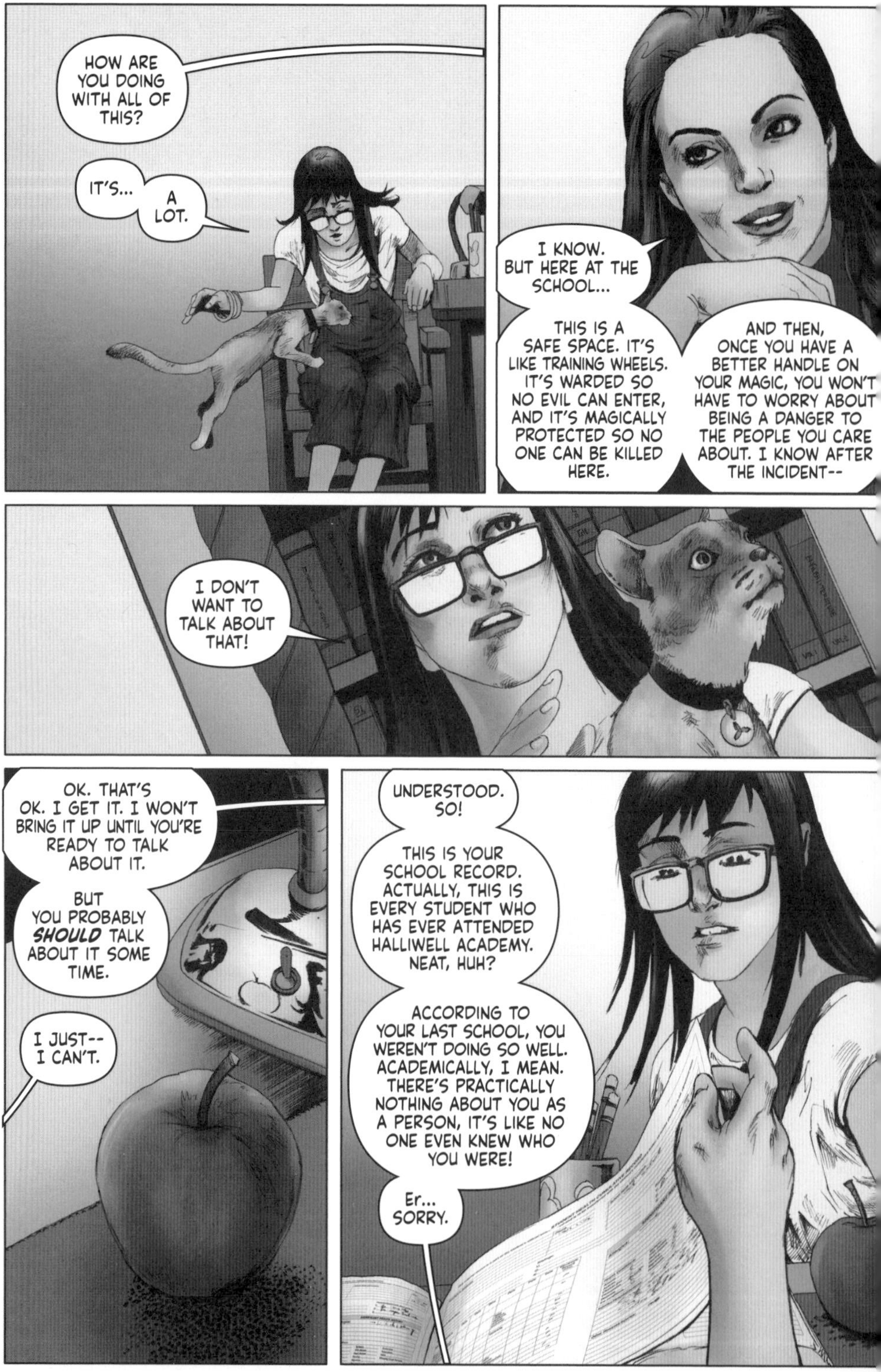
HOW ARE YOU DOING WITH ALL OF THIS?
IT'S...
A LOT.
I KNOW. BUT HERE AT THE SCHOOL...
THIS IS A SAFE SPACE. IT'S LIKE TRAINING WHEELS. IT'S WARDED SO NO EVIL CAN ENTER, AND IT'S MAGICALLY PROTECTED SO NO ONE CAN BE KILLED HERE.
AND THEN, ONCE YOU HAVE A BETTER HANDLE ON YOUR MAGIC, YOU WON'T HAVE TO WORRY ABOUT BEING A DANGER TO THE PEOPLE YOU CARE ABOUT. I KNOW AFTER THE INCIDENT--
I DON'T WANT TO TALK ABOUT THAT!
OK. THAT'S OK. I GET IT. I WON'T BRING IT UP UNTIL YOU'RE READY TO TALK ABOUT IT.
BUT YOU PROBABLY SHOULD TALK ABOUT IT SOME TIME.
I JUST-- I CAN'T.
UNDERSTOOD. SO!
THIS IS YOUR SCHOOL RECORD. ACTUALLY, THIS IS EVERY STUDENT WHO HAS EVER ATTENDED HALLIWELL ACADEMY. NEAT, HUH?
ACCORDING TO YOUR LAST SCHOOL, YOU WEREN'T DOING SO WELL. ACADEMICALLY, I MEAN. THERE'S PRACTICALLY NOTHING ABOUT YOU AS A PERSON, IT'S LIKE NO ONE EVEN KNEW WHO YOU WERE!
Er... SORRY.

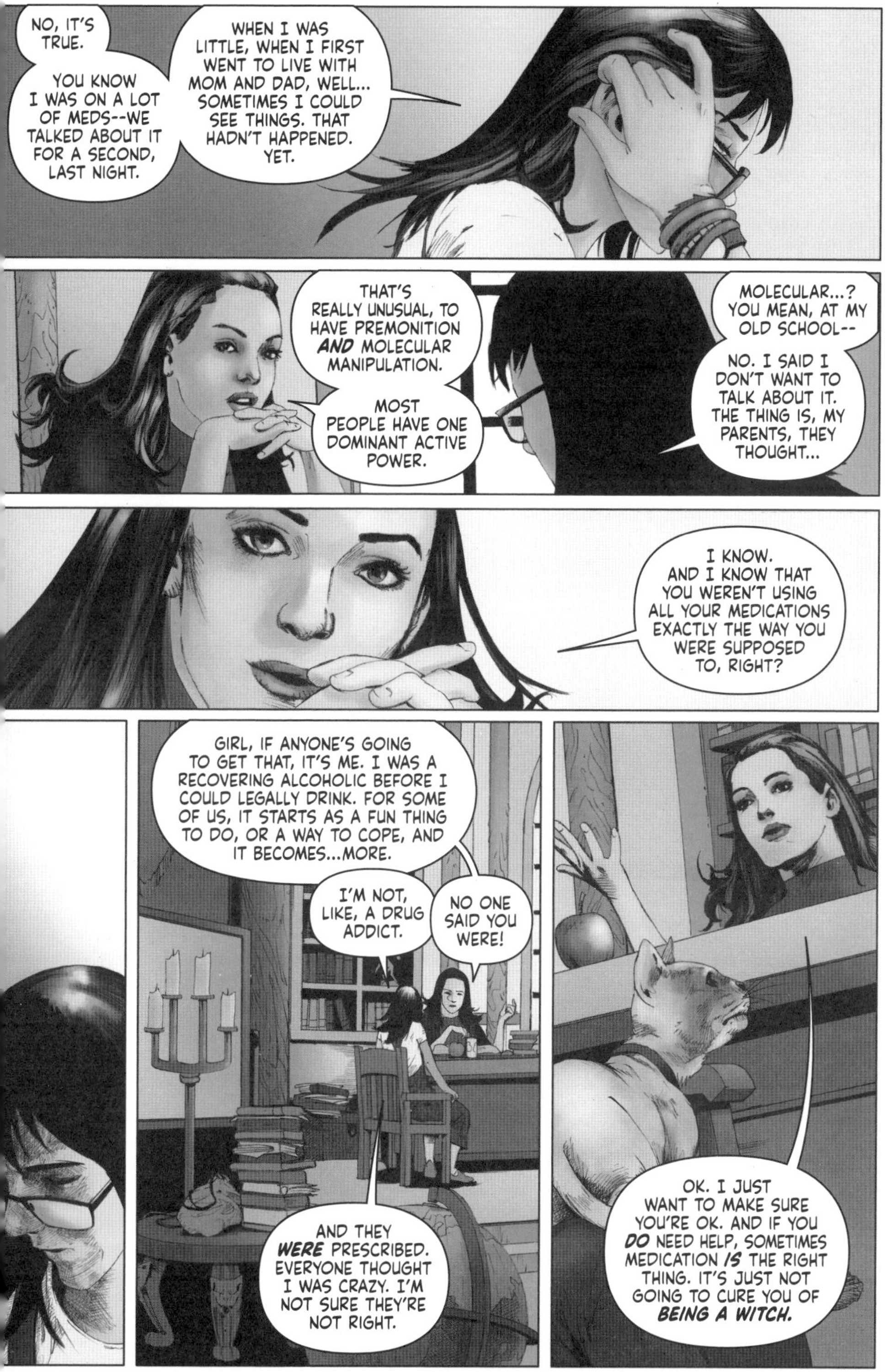
NO, IT'S TRUE.
YOU KNOW I WAS ON A LOT OF MEDS--WE TALKED ABOUT IT FOR A SECOND, LAST NIGHT.
WHEN I WAS LITTLE, WHEN I FIRST WENT TO LIVE WITH MOM AND DAD, WELL... SOMETIMES I COULD SEE THINGS. THAT HADN'T HAPPENED. YET.
THAT'S REALLY UNUSUAL, TO HAVE PREMONITION ***AND*** MOLECULAR MANIPULATION.
MOST PEOPLE HAVE ONE DOMINANT ACTIVE POWER.
MOLECULAR...? YOU MEAN, AT MY OLD SCHOOL--
NO. I SAID I DON'T WANT TO TALK ABOUT IT. THE THING IS, MY PARENTS, THEY THOUGHT...
I KNOW. AND I KNOW THAT YOU WEREN'T USING ALL YOUR MEDICATIONS EXACTLY THE WAY YOU WERE SUPPOSED TO, RIGHT?
GIRL, IF ANYONE'S GOING TO GET THAT, IT'S ME. I WAS A RECOVERING ALCOHOLIC BEFORE I COULD LEGALLY DRINK. FOR SOME OF US, IT STARTS AS A FUN THING TO DO, OR A WAY TO COPE, AND IT BECOMES...MORE.
I'M NOT, LIKE, A DRUG ADDICT.
NO ONE SAID YOU WERE!
AND THEY ***WERE*** PRESCRIBED. EVERYONE THOUGHT I WAS CRAZY. I'M NOT SURE THEY'RE NOT RIGHT.
OK. I JUST WANT TO MAKE SURE YOU'RE OK. AND IF YOU ***DO*** NEED HELP, SOMETIMES MEDICATION ***IS*** THE RIGHT THING. IT'S JUST NOT GOING TO CURE YOU OF ***BEING A WITCH.***

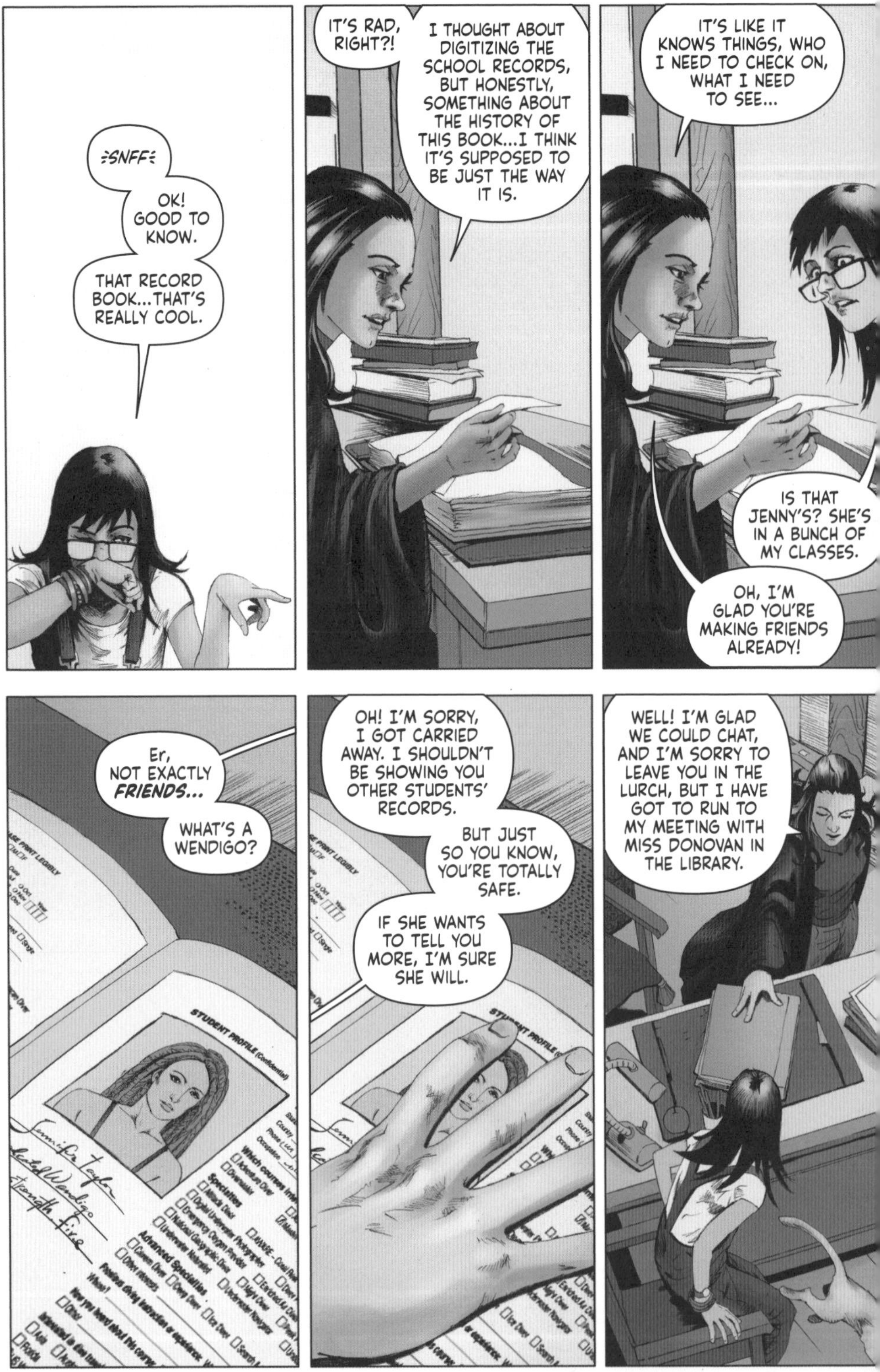

SNFF
OK! GOOD TO KNOW.
THAT RECORD BOOK...THAT'S REALLY COOL.
IT'S RAD, RIGHT?!
I THOUGHT ABOUT DIGITIZING THE SCHOOL RECORDS, BUT HONESTLY, SOMETHING ABOUT THE HISTORY OF THIS BOOK...I THINK IT'S SUPPOSED TO BE JUST THE WAY IT IS.
IT'S LIKE IT KNOWS THINGS, WHO I NEED TO CHECK ON, WHAT I NEED TO SEE...
IS THAT JENNY'S? SHE'S IN A BUNCH OF MY CLASSES.
OH, I'M GLAD YOU'RE MAKING FRIENDS ALREADY!
Er, NOT EXACTLY ***FRIENDS...***
WHAT'S A WENDIGO?
OH! I'M SORRY, I GOT CARRIED AWAY. I SHOULDN'T BE SHOWING YOU OTHER STUDENTS' RECORDS.
BUT JUST SO YOU KNOW, YOU'RE TOTALLY SAFE.
IF SHE WANTS TO TELL YOU MORE, I'M SURE SHE WILL.
WELL! I'M GLAD WE COULD CHAT, AND I'M SORRY TO LEAVE YOU IN THE LURCH, BUT I HAVE GOT TO RUN TO MY MEETING WITH MISS DONOVAN IN THE LIBRARY.

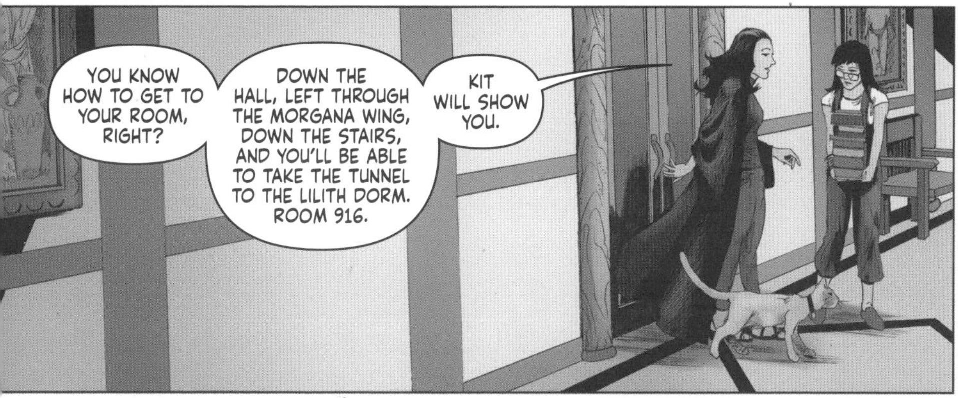
YOU KNOW HOW TO GET TO YOUR ROOM, RIGHT?
DOWN THE HALL, LEFT THROUGH THE MORGANA WING, DOWN THE STAIRS, AND YOU'LL BE ABLE TO TAKE THE TUNNEL TO THE LILITH DORM. ROOM 916.
KIT WILL SHOW YOU.
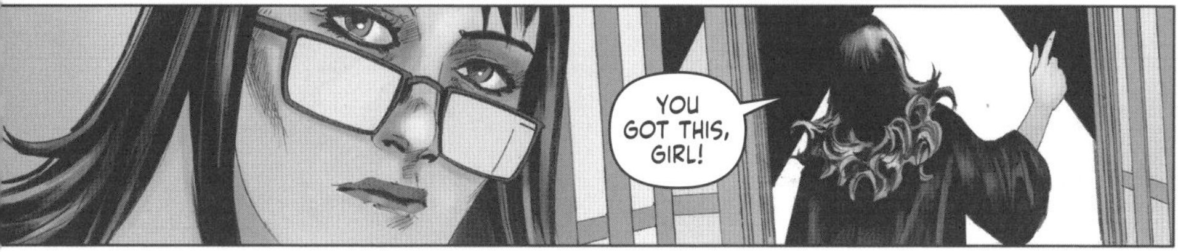
YOU GOT THIS, GIRL!
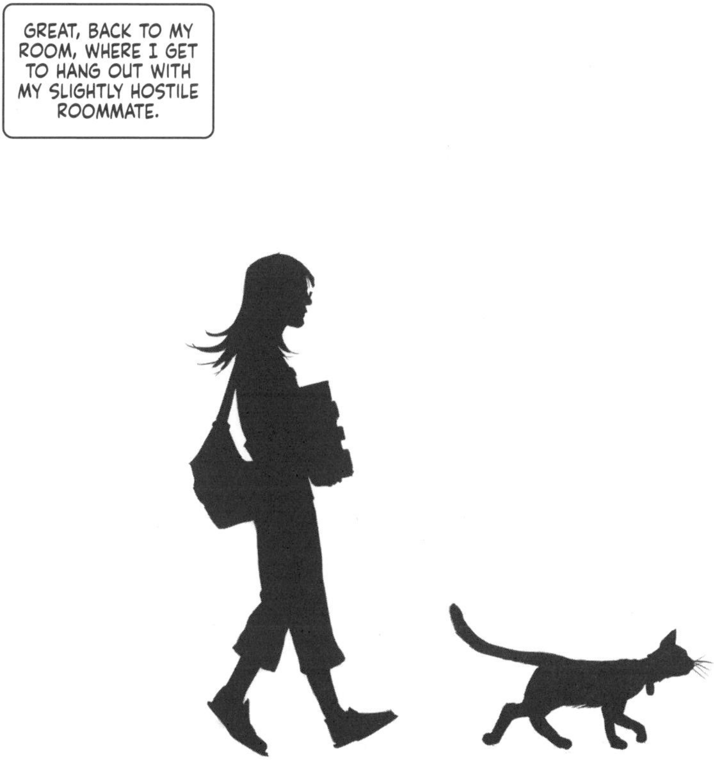
GREAT, BACK TO MY ROOM, WHERE I GET TO HANG OUT WITH MY SLIGHTLY HOSTILE ROOMMATE.

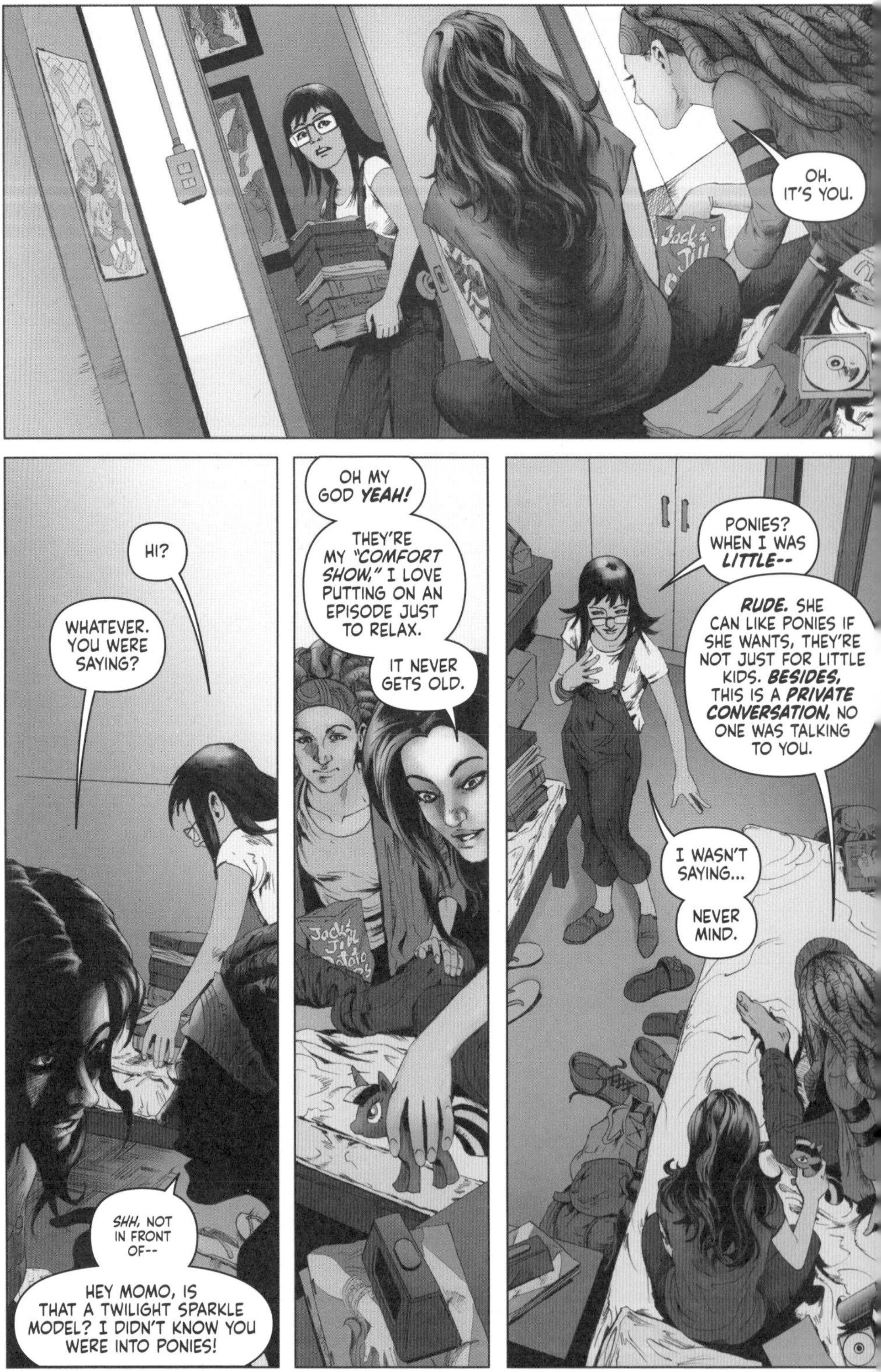
OH.
IT'S YOU.
HI?
WHATEVER. YOU WERE SAYING?
SHH, NOT IN FRONT OF--
HEY MOMO, IS THAT A TWILIGHT SPARKLE MODEL? I DIDN'T KNOW YOU WERE INTO PONIES!
OH MY GOD YEAH!
THEY'RE MY "COMFORT SHOW," I LOVE PUTTING ON AN EPISODE JUST TO RELAX.
IT NEVER GETS OLD.
PONIES? WHEN I WAS LITTLE--
RUDE. SHE CAN LIKE PONIES IF SHE WANTS, THEY'RE NOT JUST FOR LITTLE KIDS. BESIDES, THIS IS A PRIVATE CONVERSATION, NO ONE WAS TALKING TO YOU.
I WASN'T SAYING...
NEVER MIND.

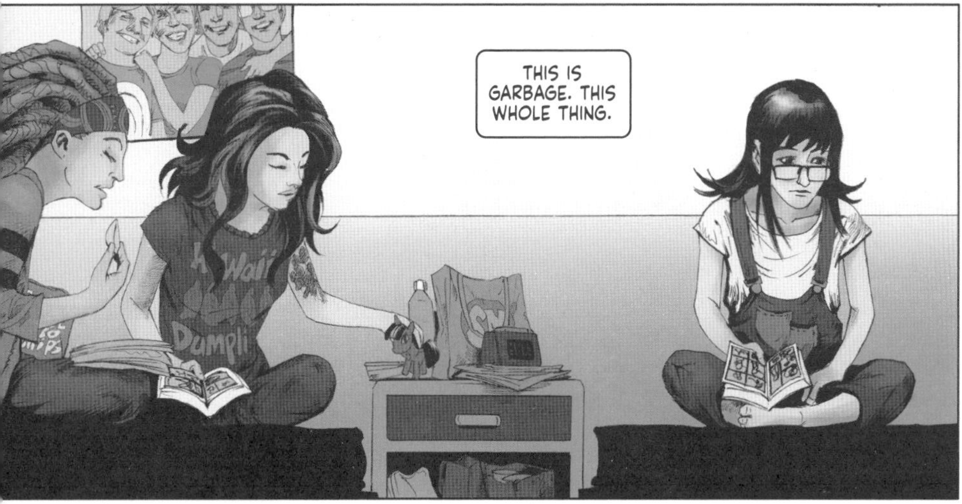
THIS IS GARBAGE. THIS WHOLE THING.

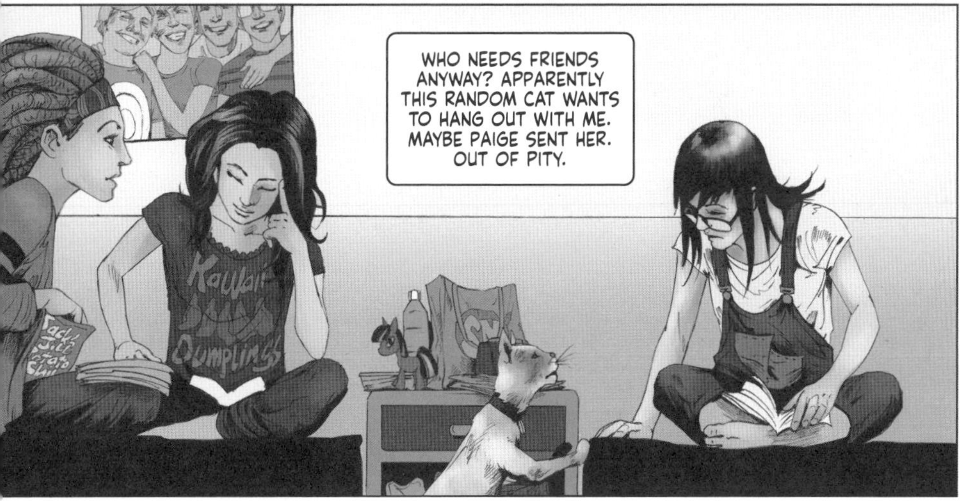
WHO NEEDS FRIENDS ANYWAY? APPARENTLY THIS RANDOM CAT WANTS TO HANG OUT WITH ME. MAYBE PAIGE SENT HER. OUT OF PITY.

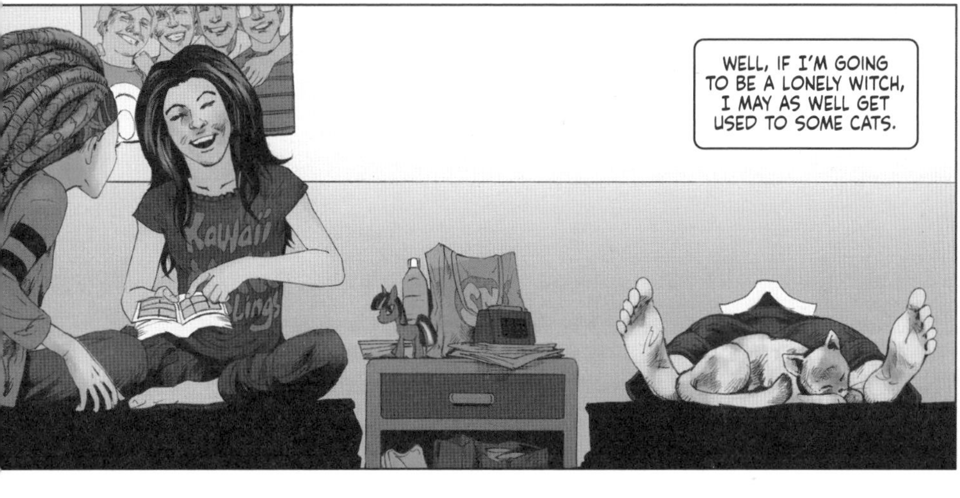
WELL, IF I'M GOING TO BE A LONELY WITCH, I MAY AS WELL GET USED TO SOME CATS.

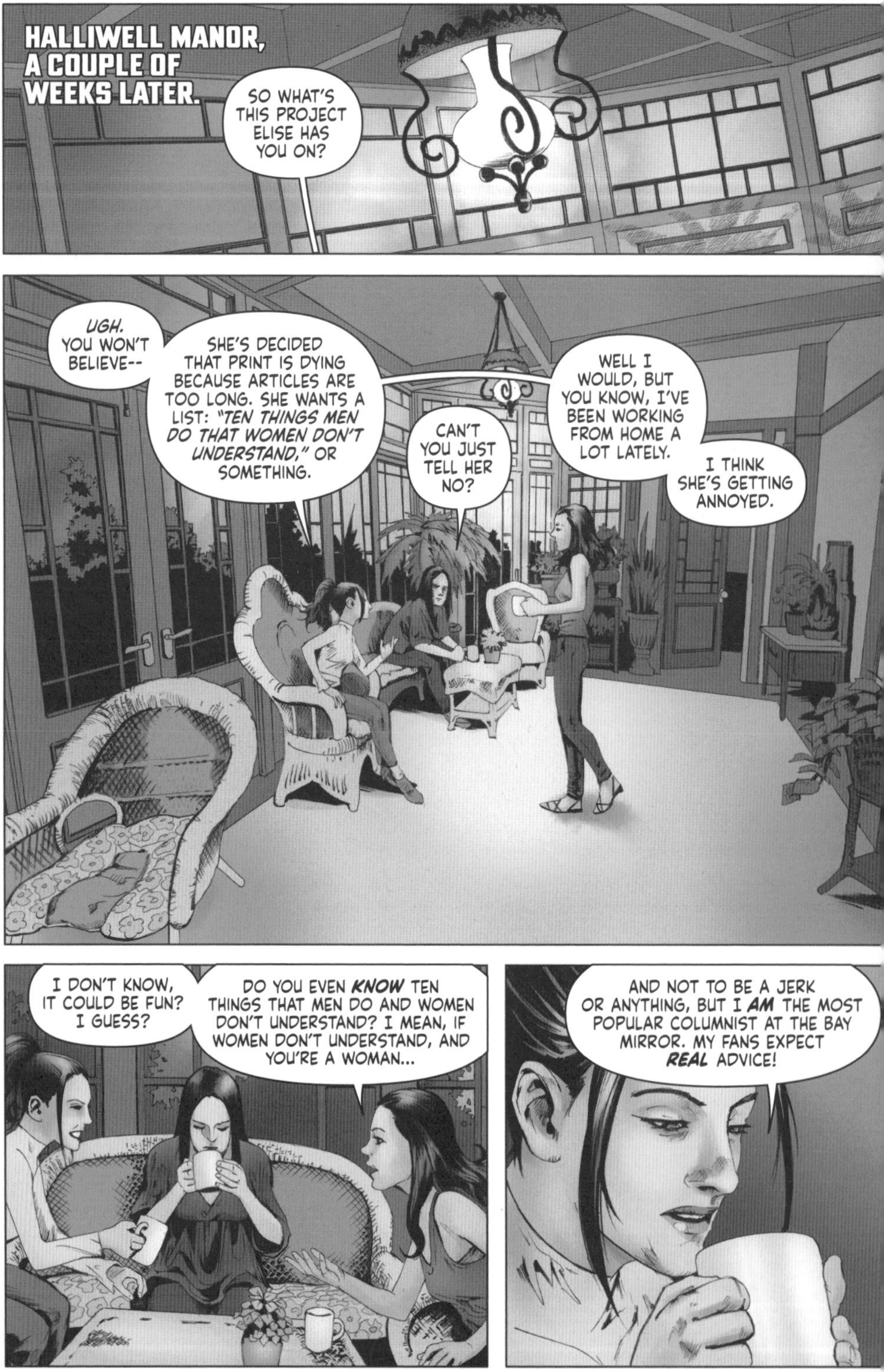
HALLIWELL MANOR, A COUPLE OF WEEKS LATER.
SO WHAT'S THIS PROJECT ELISE HAS YOU ON?
UGH. YOU WON'T BELIEVE--
SHE'S DECIDED THAT PRINT IS DYING BECAUSE ARTICLES ARE TOO LONG. SHE WANTS A LIST: "TEN THINGS MEN DO THAT WOMEN DON'T UNDERSTAND," OR SOMETHING.
CAN'T YOU JUST TELL HER NO?
WELL I WOULD, BUT YOU KNOW, I'VE BEEN WORKING FROM HOME A LOT LATELY.
I THINK SHE'S GETTING ANNOYED.
I DON'T KNOW, IT COULD BE FUN? I GUESS?
DO YOU EVEN KNOW TEN THINGS THAT MEN DO AND WOMEN DON'T UNDERSTAND? I MEAN, IF WOMEN DON'T UNDERSTAND, AND YOU'RE A WOMAN...
AND NOT TO BE A JERK OR ANYTHING, BUT I AM THE MOST POPULAR COLUMNIST AT THE BAY MIRROR. MY FANS EXPECT REAL ADVICE!

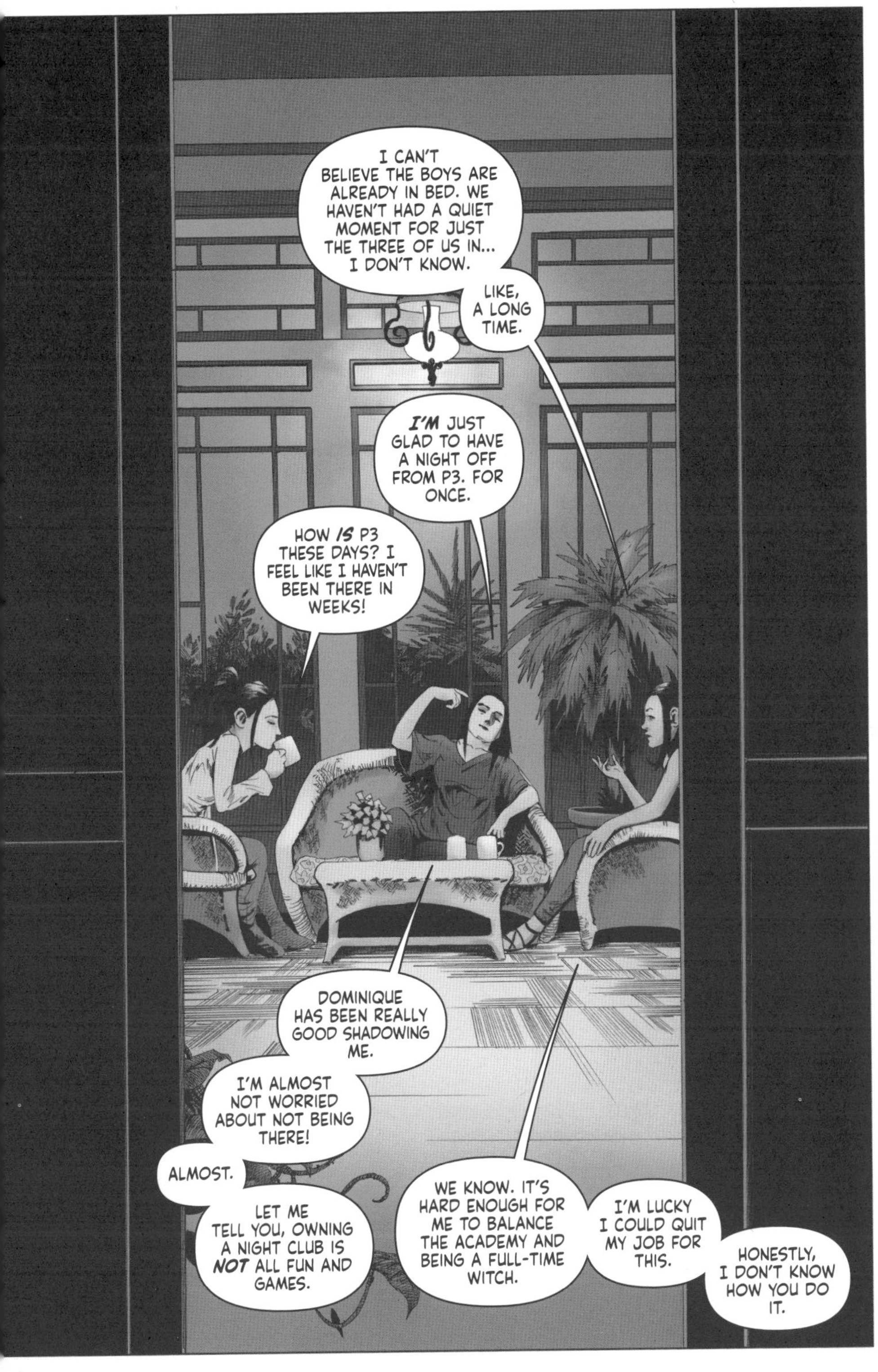
I CAN'T BELIEVE THE BOYS ARE ALREADY IN BED. WE HAVEN'T HAD A QUIET MOMENT FOR JUST THE THREE OF US IN... I DON'T KNOW.
LIKE, A LONG TIME.
I'M JUST GLAD TO HAVE A NIGHT OFF FROM P3. FOR ONCE.
HOW *IS* P3 THESE DAYS? I FEEL LIKE I HAVEN'T BEEN THERE IN WEEKS!
DOMINIQUE HAS BEEN REALLY GOOD SHADOWING ME.
I'M ALMOST NOT WORRIED ABOUT NOT BEING THERE!
ALMOST.
LET ME TELL YOU, OWNING A NIGHT CLUB IS *NOT* ALL FUN AND GAMES.
WE KNOW. IT'S HARD ENOUGH FOR ME TO BALANCE THE ACADEMY AND BEING A FULL-TIME WITCH.
I'M LUCKY I COULD QUIT MY JOB FOR THIS.
HONESTLY, I DON'T KNOW HOW YOU DO IT.

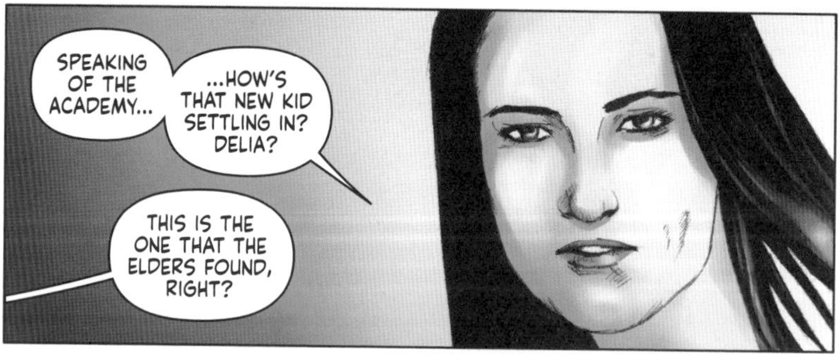
SPEAKING OF THE ACADEMY...
...HOW'S THAT NEW KID SETTLING IN? DELIA?
THIS IS THE ONE THAT THE ELDERS FOUND, RIGHT?

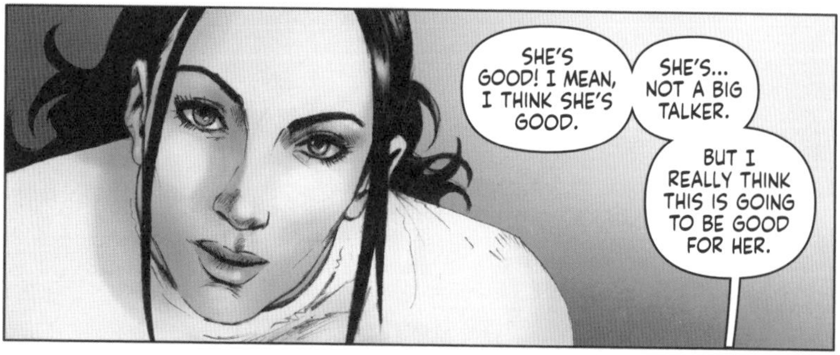
SHE'S GOOD! I MEAN, I THINK SHE'S GOOD.
SHE'S... NOT A BIG TALKER.
BUT I REALLY THINK THIS IS GOING TO BE GOOD FOR HER.

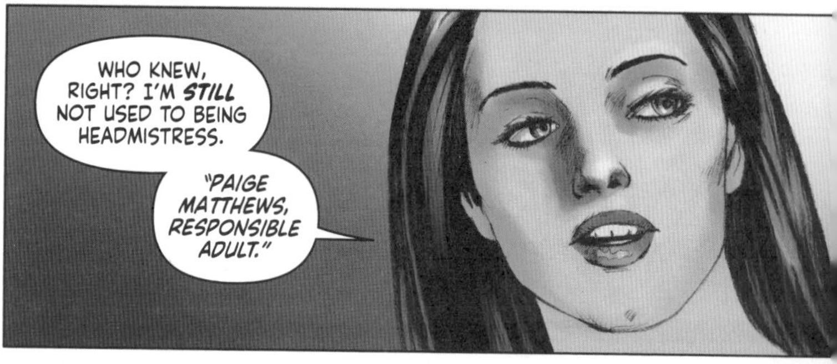
WHO KNEW, RIGHT? I'M ***STILL*** NOT USED TO BEING HEADMISTRESS.
"PAIGE MATTHEWS, RESPONSIBLE ADULT."

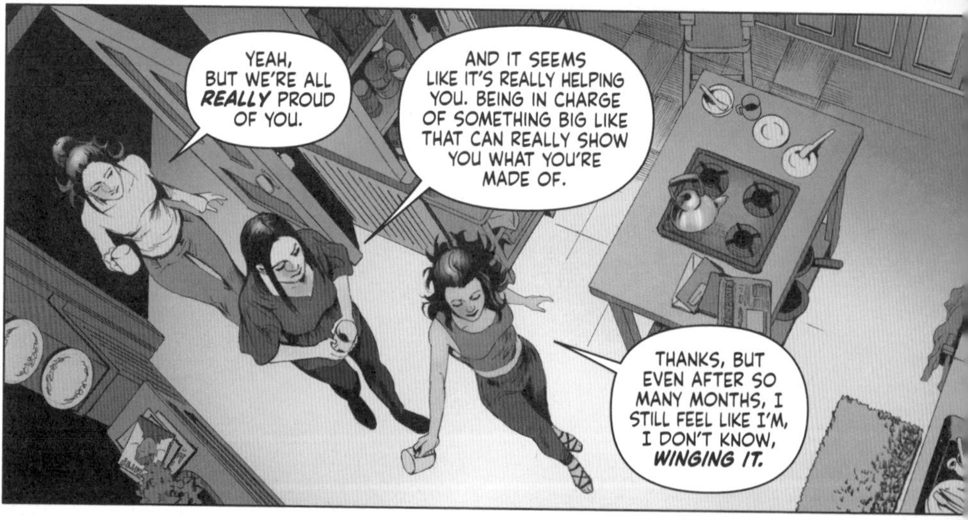
YEAH, BUT WE'RE ALL ***REALLY*** PROUD OF YOU.
AND IT SEEMS LIKE IT'S REALLY HELPING YOU. BEING IN CHARGE OF SOMETHING BIG LIKE THAT CAN REALLY SHOW YOU WHAT YOU'RE MADE OF.
THANKS, BUT EVEN AFTER SO MANY MONTHS, I STILL FEEL LIKE I'M, I DON'T KNOW, ***WINGING IT.***

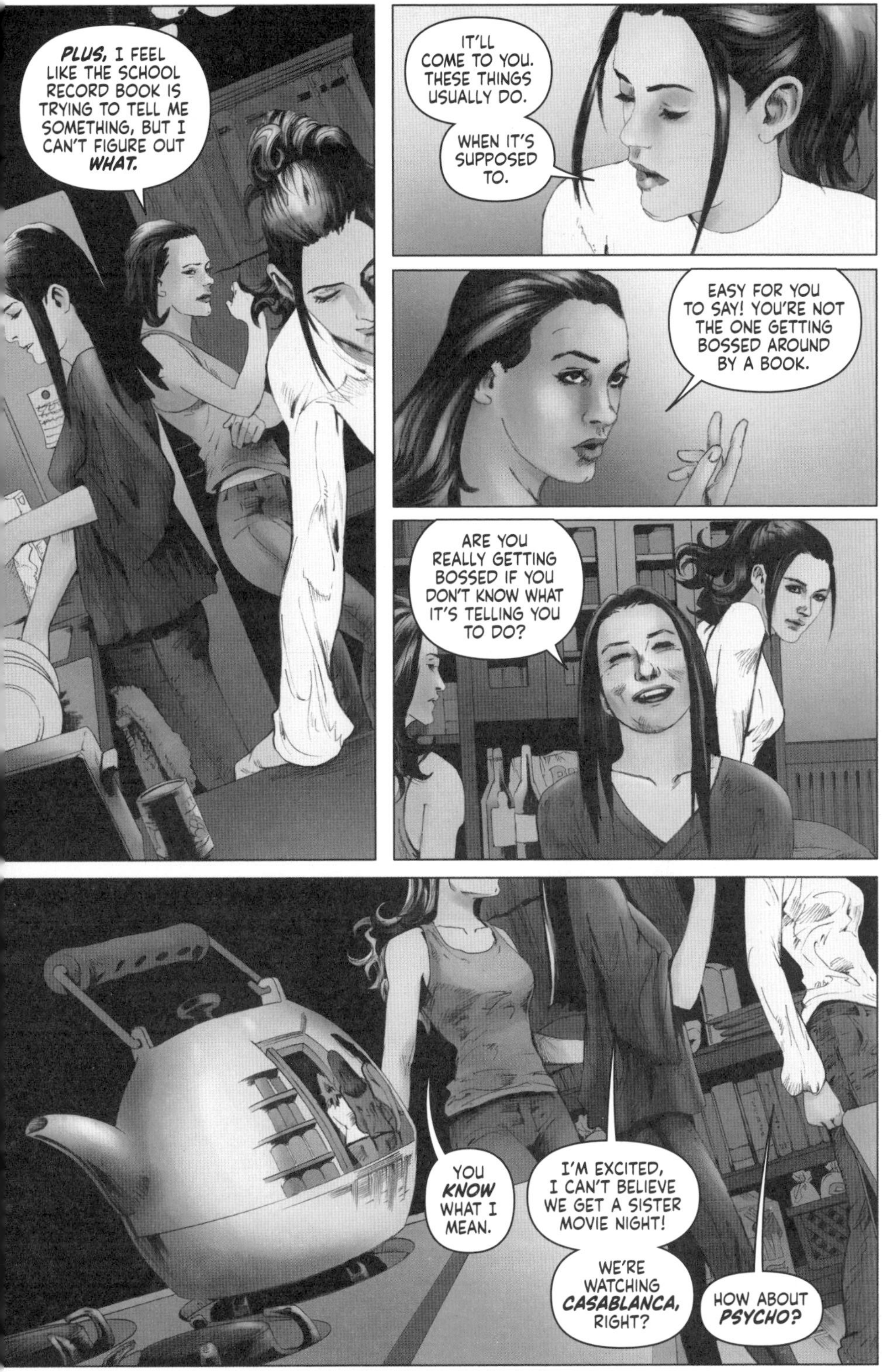
PLUS, I FEEL LIKE THE SCHOOL RECORD BOOK IS TRYING TO TELL ME SOMETHING, BUT I CAN'T FIGURE OUT WHAT.
IT'LL COME TO YOU. THESE THINGS USUALLY DO.
WHEN IT'S SUPPOSED TO.
EASY FOR YOU TO SAY! YOU'RE NOT THE ONE GETTING BOSSED AROUND BY A BOOK.
ARE YOU REALLY GETTING BOSSED IF YOU DON'T KNOW WHAT IT'S TELLING YOU TO DO?
YOU KNOW WHAT I MEAN.
I'M EXCITED, I CAN'T BELIEVE WE GET A SISTER MOVIE NIGHT!
WE'RE WATCHING CASABLANCA, RIGHT?
HOW ABOUT PSYCHO?

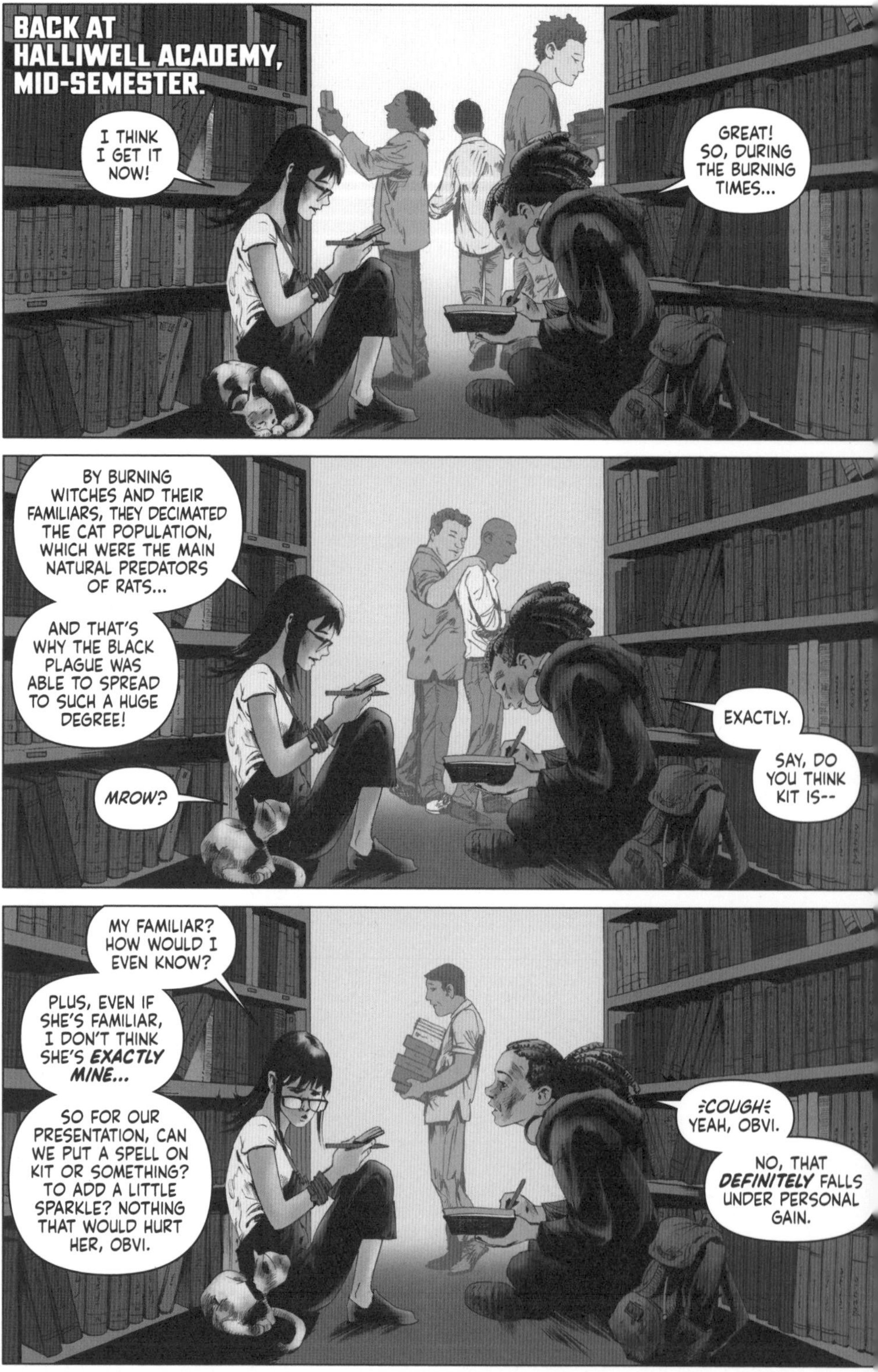
BACK AT HALLIWELL ACADEMY, MID-SEMESTER.
I THINK I GET IT NOW!
GREAT! SO, DURING THE BURNING TIMES...
BY BURNING WITCHES AND THEIR FAMILIARS, THEY DECIMATED THE CAT POPULATION, WHICH WERE THE MAIN NATURAL PREDATORS OF RATS...
AND THAT'S WHY THE BLACK PLAGUE WAS ABLE TO SPREAD TO SUCH A HUGE DEGREE!
MROW?
EXACTLY.
SAY, DO YOU THINK KIT IS--
MY FAMILIAR? HOW WOULD I EVEN KNOW?
PLUS, EVEN IF SHE'S FAMILIAR, I DON'T THINK SHE'S EXACTLY MINE...
SO FOR OUR PRESENTATION, CAN WE PUT A SPELL ON KIT OR SOMETHING? TO ADD A LITTLE SPARKLE? NOTHING THAT WOULD HURT HER, OBVI.
COUGH YEAH, OBVI.
NO, THAT DEFINITELY FALLS UNDER PERSONAL GAIN.

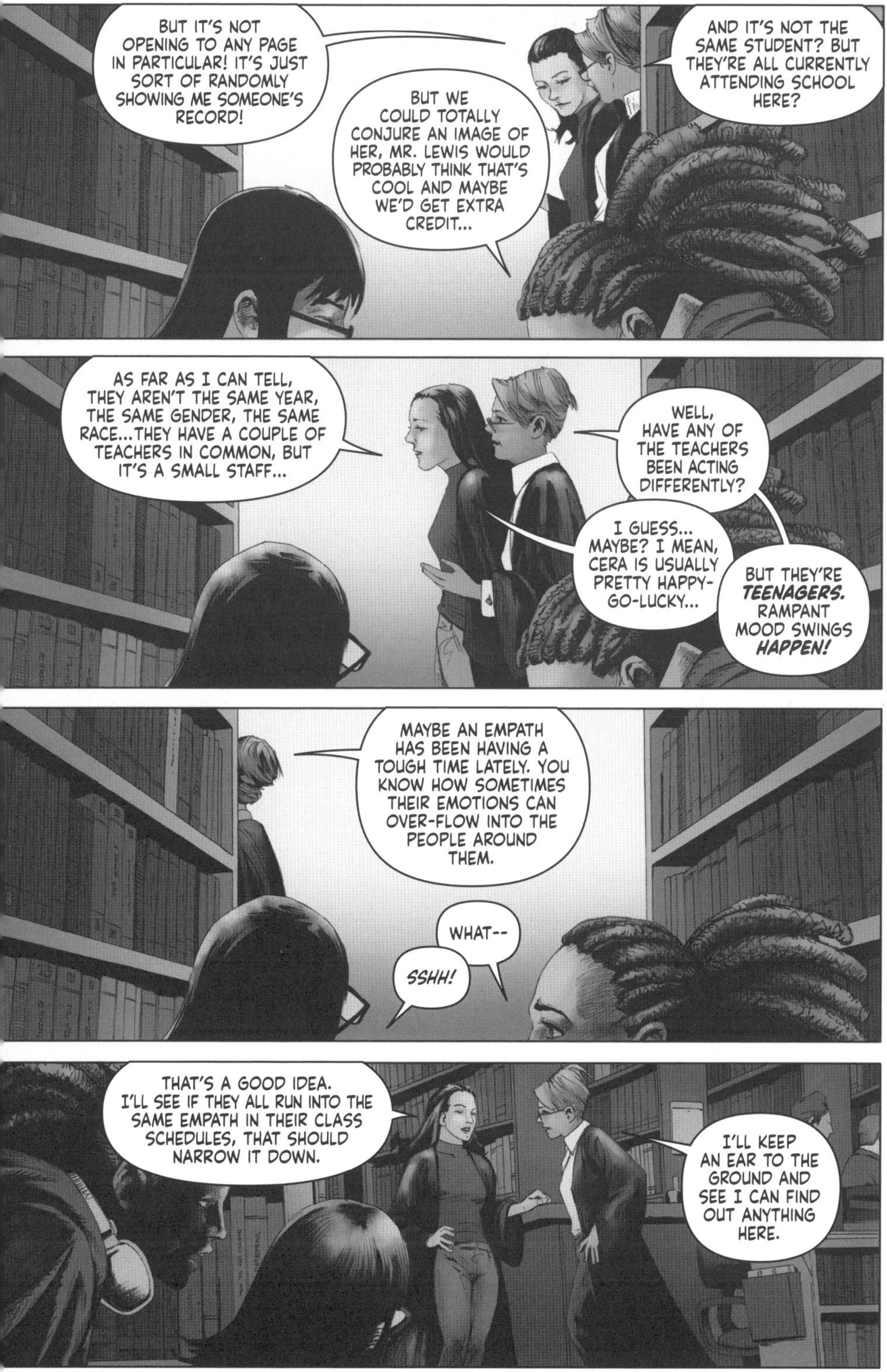
BUT IT'S NOT OPENING TO ANY PAGE IN PARTICULAR! IT'S JUST SORT OF RANDOMLY SHOWING ME SOMEONE'S RECORD!
BUT WE COULD TOTALLY CONJURE AN IMAGE OF HER, MR. LEWIS WOULD PROBABLY THINK THAT'S COOL AND MAYBE WE'D GET EXTRA CREDIT...
AND IT'S NOT THE SAME STUDENT? BUT THEY'RE ALL CURRENTLY ATTENDING SCHOOL HERE?
AS FAR AS I CAN TELL, THEY AREN'T THE SAME YEAR, THE SAME GENDER, THE SAME RACE...THEY HAVE A COUPLE OF TEACHERS IN COMMON, BUT IT'S A SMALL STAFF...
WELL, HAVE ANY OF THE TEACHERS BEEN ACTING DIFFERENTLY?
I GUESS... MAYBE? I MEAN, CERA IS USUALLY PRETTY HAPPY-GO-LUCKY...
BUT THEY'RE ***TEENAGERS.*** RAMPANT MOOD SWINGS ***HAPPEN!***
MAYBE AN EMPATH HAS BEEN HAVING A TOUGH TIME LATELY. YOU KNOW HOW SOMETIMES THEIR EMOTIONS CAN OVER-FLOW INTO THE PEOPLE AROUND THEM.
WHAT--
SSHH!
THAT'S A GOOD IDEA. I'LL SEE IF THEY ALL RUN INTO THE SAME EMPATH IN THEIR CLASS SCHEDULES, THAT SHOULD NARROW IT DOWN.
I'LL KEEP AN EAR TO THE GROUND AND SEE I CAN FIND OUT ANYTHING HERE.

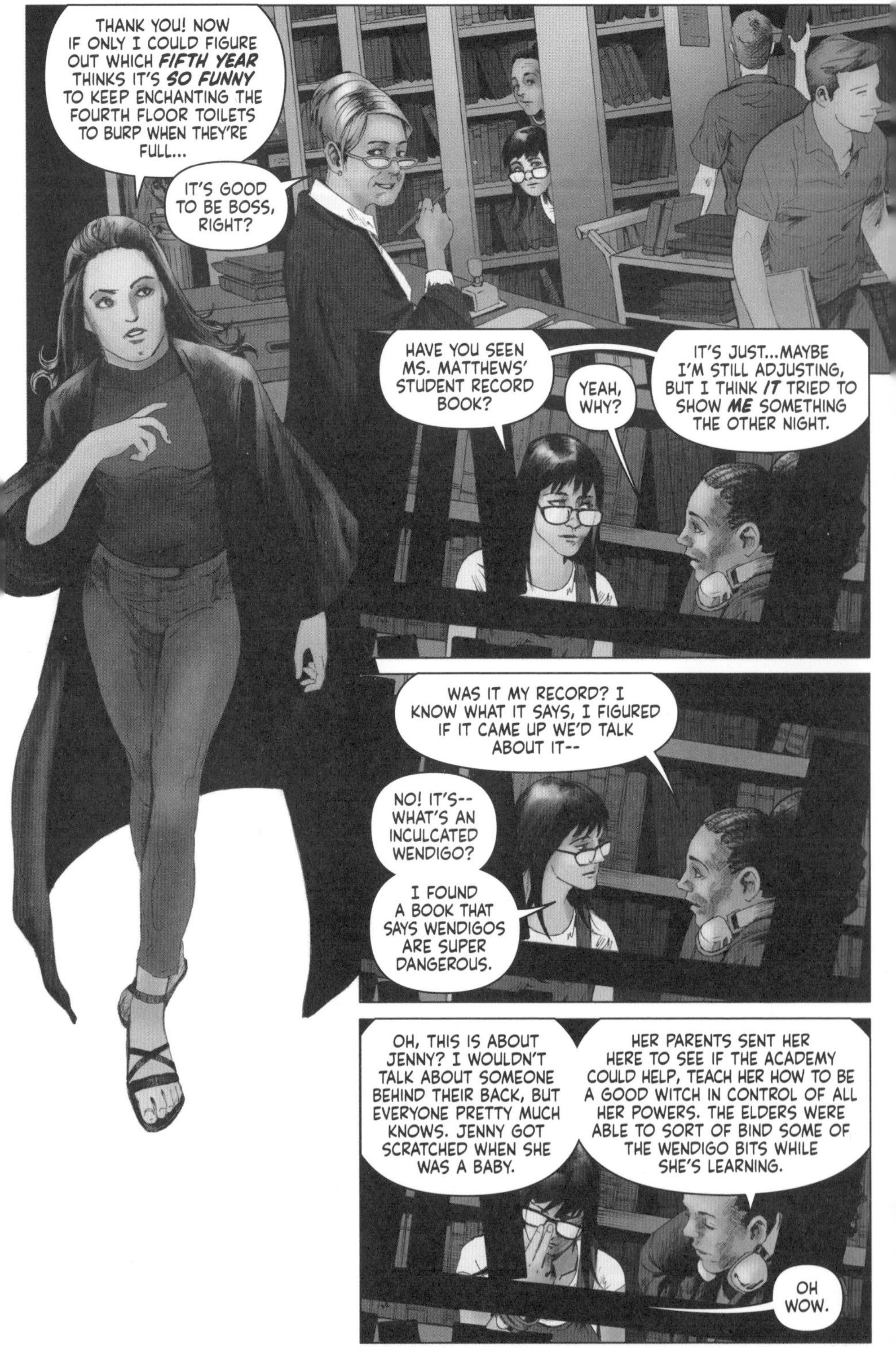
THANK YOU! NOW IF ONLY I COULD FIGURE OUT WHICH *FIFTH YEAR* THINKS IT'S *SO FUNNY* TO KEEP ENCHANTING THE FOURTH FLOOR TOILETS TO BURP WHEN THEY'RE FULL...
IT'S GOOD TO BE BOSS, RIGHT?
HAVE YOU SEEN MS. MATTHEWS' STUDENT RECORD BOOK?
YEAH, WHY?
IT'S JUST...MAYBE I'M STILL ADJUSTING, BUT I THINK *IT* TRIED TO SHOW *ME* SOMETHING THE OTHER NIGHT.
WAS IT MY RECORD? I KNOW WHAT IT SAYS, I FIGURED IF IT CAME UP WE'D TALK ABOUT IT--
NO! IT'S-- WHAT'S AN INCULCATED WENDIGO?
I FOUND A BOOK THAT SAYS WENDIGOS ARE SUPER DANGEROUS.
OH, THIS IS ABOUT JENNY? I WOULDN'T TALK ABOUT SOMEONE BEHIND THEIR BACK, BUT EVERYONE PRETTY MUCH KNOWS. JENNY GOT SCRATCHED WHEN SHE WAS A BABY.
HER PARENTS SENT HER HERE TO SEE IF THE ACADEMY COULD HELP, TEACH HER HOW TO BE A GOOD WITCH IN CONTROL OF ALL HER POWERS. THE ELDERS WERE ABLE TO SORT OF BIND SOME OF THE WENDIGO BITS WHILE SHE'S LEARNING.
OH WOW.

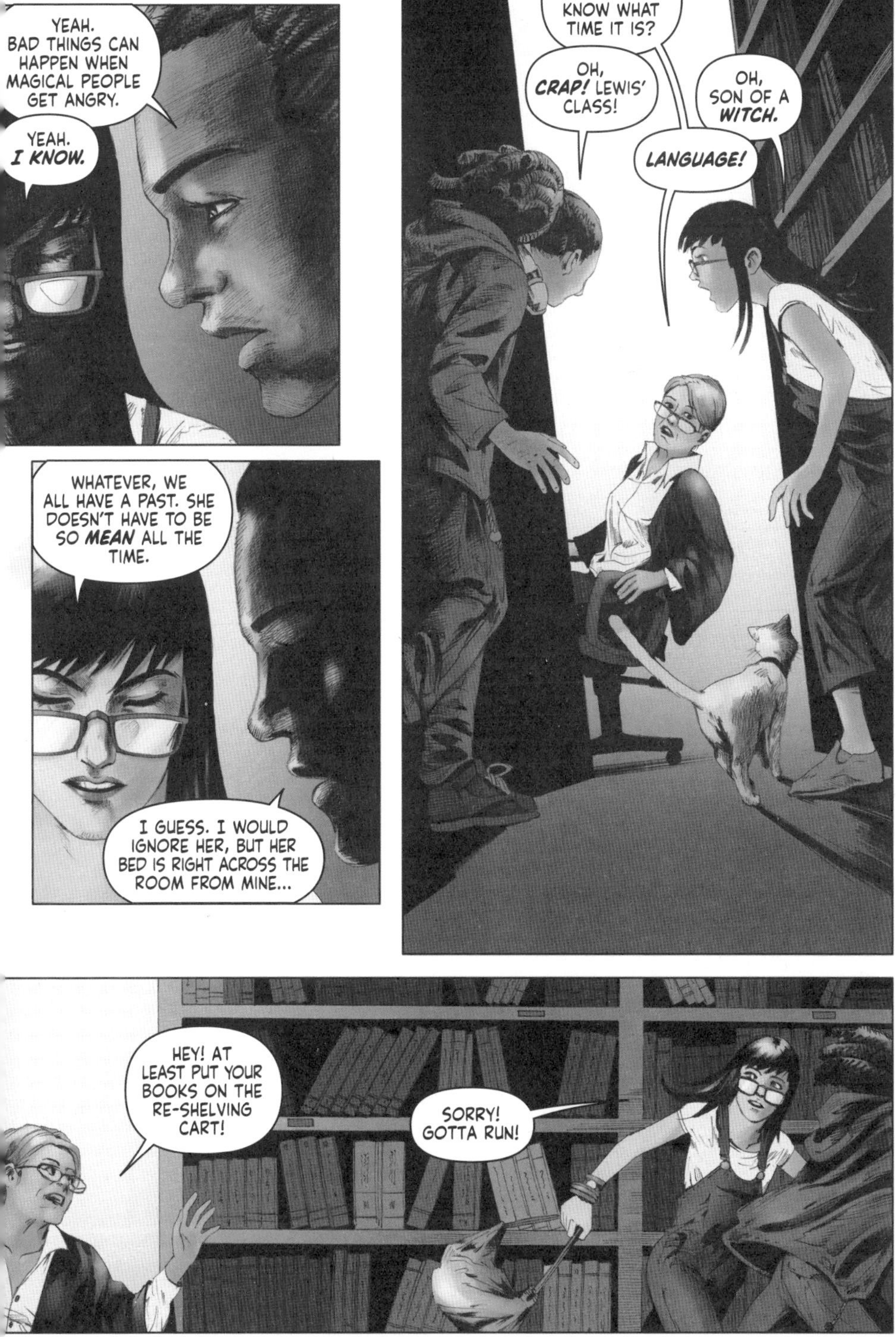
YEAH. BAD THINGS CAN HAPPEN WHEN MAGICAL PEOPLE GET ANGRY.
YEAH. ***I KNOW.***
WHATEVER, WE ALL HAVE A PAST. SHE DOESN'T HAVE TO BE SO ***MEAN*** ALL THE TIME.
I GUESS. I WOULD IGNORE HER, BUT HER BED IS RIGHT ACROSS THE ROOM FROM MINE...
HEY! DO YOU GUYS KNOW WHAT TIME IT IS?
OH, ***CRAP!*** LEWIS' CLASS!
OH, SON OF A ***WITCH.***
LANGUAGE!
HEY! AT LEAST PUT YOUR BOOKS ON THE RE-SHELVING CART!
SORRY! GOTTA RUN!

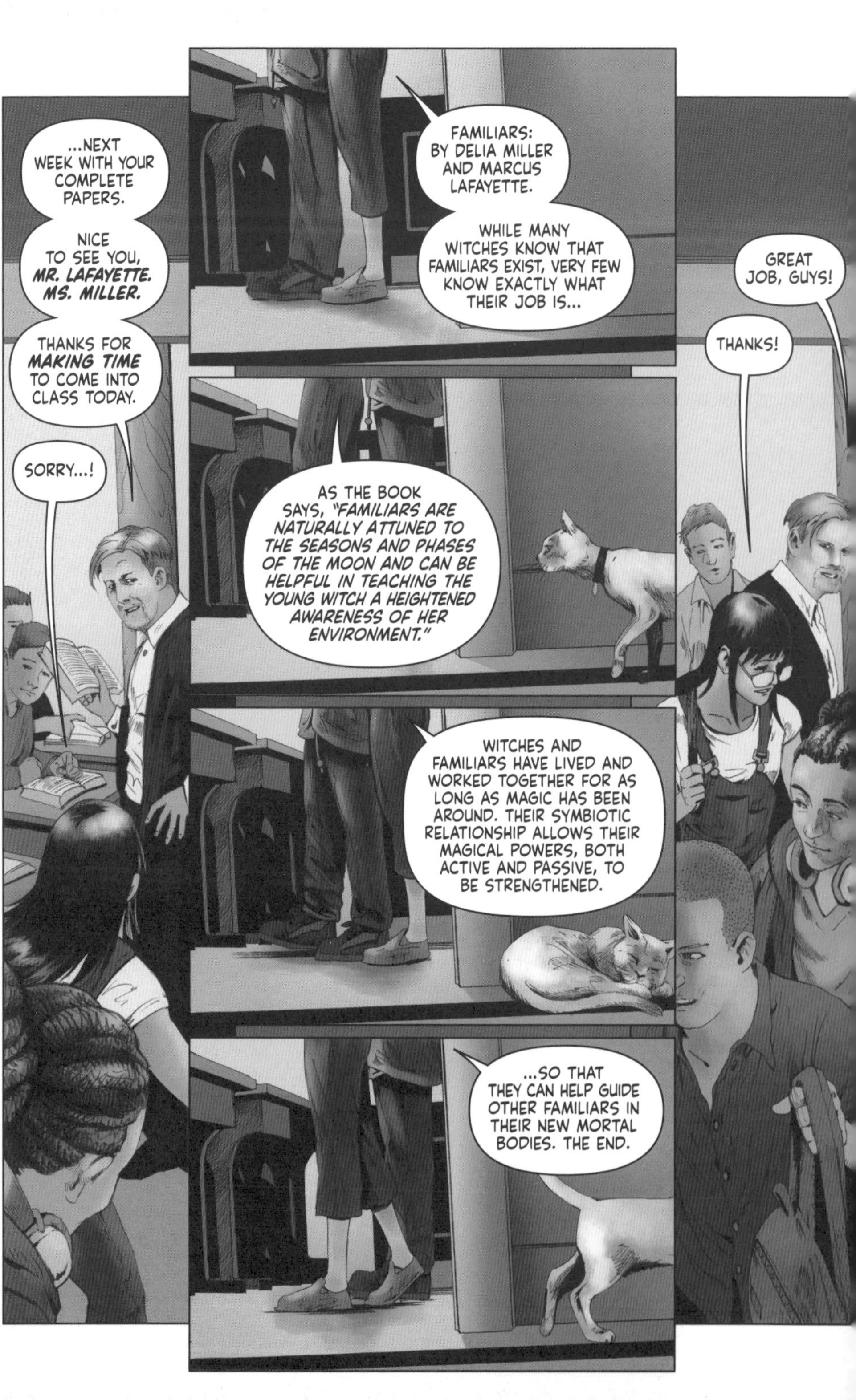
...NEXT WEEK WITH YOUR COMPLETE PAPERS.
NICE TO SEE YOU, **MR. LAFAYETTE. MS. MILLER.**
THANKS FOR **MAKING TIME** TO COME INTO CLASS TODAY.
SORRY...!
FAMILIARS: BY DELIA MILLER AND MARCUS LAFAYETTE.
WHILE MANY WITCHES KNOW THAT FAMILIARS EXIST, VERY FEW KNOW EXACTLY WHAT THEIR JOB IS...
AS THE BOOK SAYS, *"FAMILIARS ARE NATURALLY ATTUNED TO THE SEASONS AND PHASES OF THE MOON AND CAN BE HELPFUL IN TEACHING THE YOUNG WITCH A HEIGHTENED AWARENESS OF HER ENVIRONMENT."*
WITCHES AND FAMILIARS HAVE LIVED AND WORKED TOGETHER FOR AS LONG AS MAGIC HAS BEEN AROUND. THEIR SYMBIOTIC RELATIONSHIP ALLOWS THEIR MAGICAL POWERS, BOTH ACTIVE AND PASSIVE, TO BE STRENGTHENED.
...SO THAT THEY CAN HELP GUIDE OTHER FAMILIARS IN THEIR NEW MORTAL BODIES. THE END.
GREAT JOB, GUYS!
THANKS!

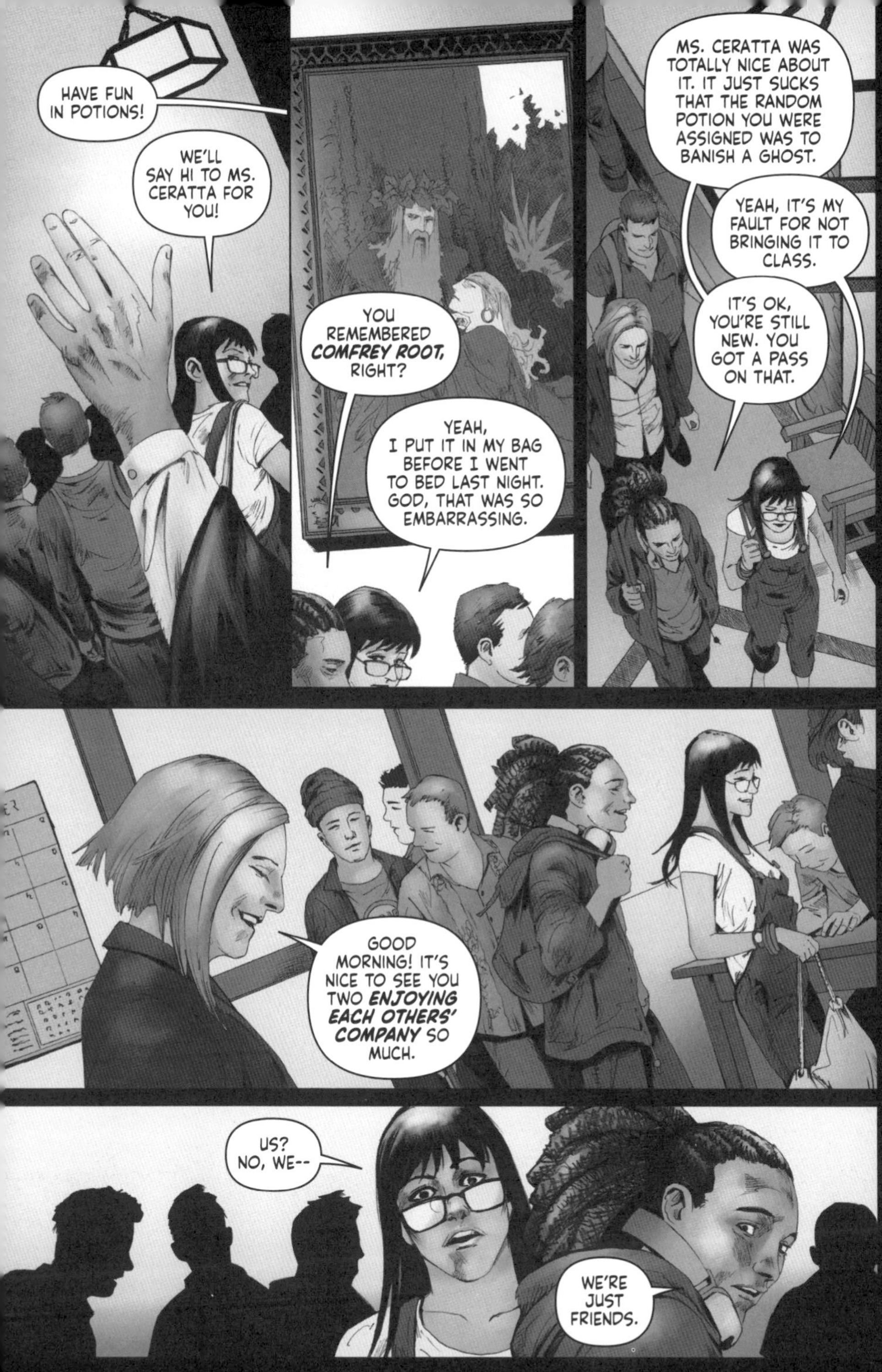
HAVE FUN IN POTIONS!
WE'LL SAY HI TO MS. CERATTA FOR YOU!
YOU REMEMBERED **COMFREY ROOT,** RIGHT?
YEAH, I PUT IT IN MY BAG BEFORE I WENT TO BED LAST NIGHT. GOD, THAT WAS SO EMBARRASSING.
MS. CERATTA WAS TOTALLY NICE ABOUT IT. IT JUST SUCKS THAT THE RANDOM POTION YOU WERE ASSIGNED WAS TO BANISH A GHOST.
YEAH, IT'S MY FAULT FOR NOT BRINGING IT TO CLASS.
IT'S OK, YOU'RE STILL NEW. YOU GOT A PASS ON THAT.
GOOD MORNING! IT'S NICE TO SEE YOU TWO ***ENJOYING EACH OTHERS' COMPANY*** SO MUCH.
US? NO, WE--
WE'RE JUST FRIENDS.

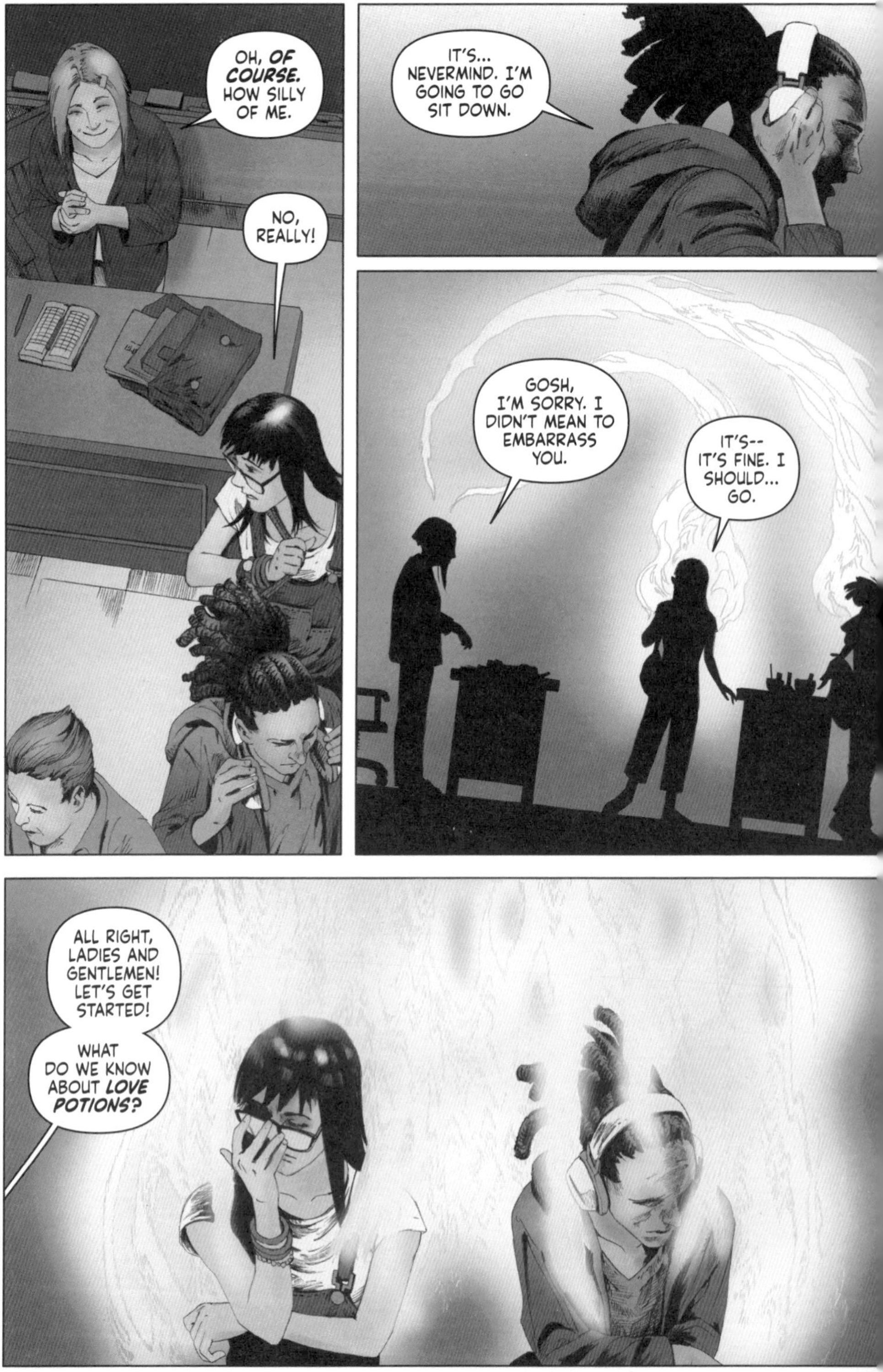
OH, ***OF COURSE.*** HOW SILLY OF ME.
NO, REALLY!
IT'S... NEVERMIND. I'M GOING TO GO SIT DOWN.
GOSH, I'M SORRY. I DIDN'T MEAN TO EMBARRASS YOU.
IT'S-- IT'S FINE. I SHOULD... GO.
ALL RIGHT, LADIES AND GENTLEMEN! LET'S GET STARTED!
WHAT DO WE KNOW ABOUT ***LOVE POTIONS?***

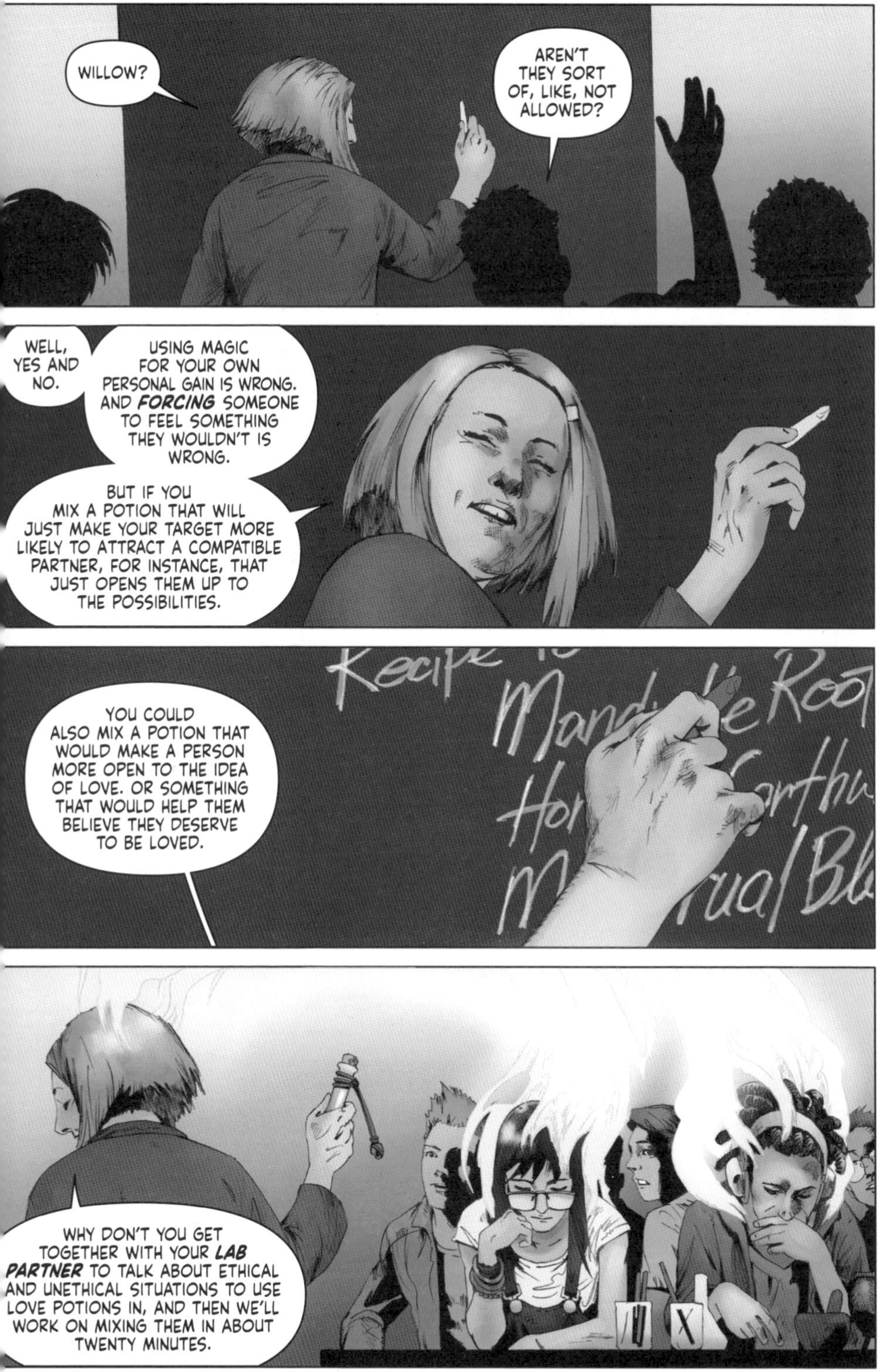
WILLOW?
AREN'T THEY SORT OF, LIKE, NOT ALLOWED?
WELL, YES AND NO.
USING MAGIC FOR YOUR OWN PERSONAL GAIN IS WRONG. AND ***FORCING*** SOMEONE TO FEEL SOMETHING THEY WOULDN'T IS WRONG.
BUT IF YOU MIX A POTION THAT WILL JUST MAKE YOUR TARGET MORE LIKELY TO ATTRACT A COMPATIBLE PARTNER, FOR INSTANCE, THAT JUST OPENS THEM UP TO THE POSSIBILITIES.
YOU COULD ALSO MIX A POTION THAT WOULD MAKE A PERSON MORE OPEN TO THE IDEA OF LOVE. OR SOMETHING THAT WOULD HELP THEM BELIEVE THEY DESERVE TO BE LOVED.
WHY DON'T YOU GET TOGETHER WITH YOUR ***LAB PARTNER*** TO TALK ABOUT ETHICAL AND UNETHICAL SITUATIONS TO USE LOVE POTIONS IN, AND THEN WE'LL WORK ON MIXING THEM IN ABOUT TWENTY MINUTES.

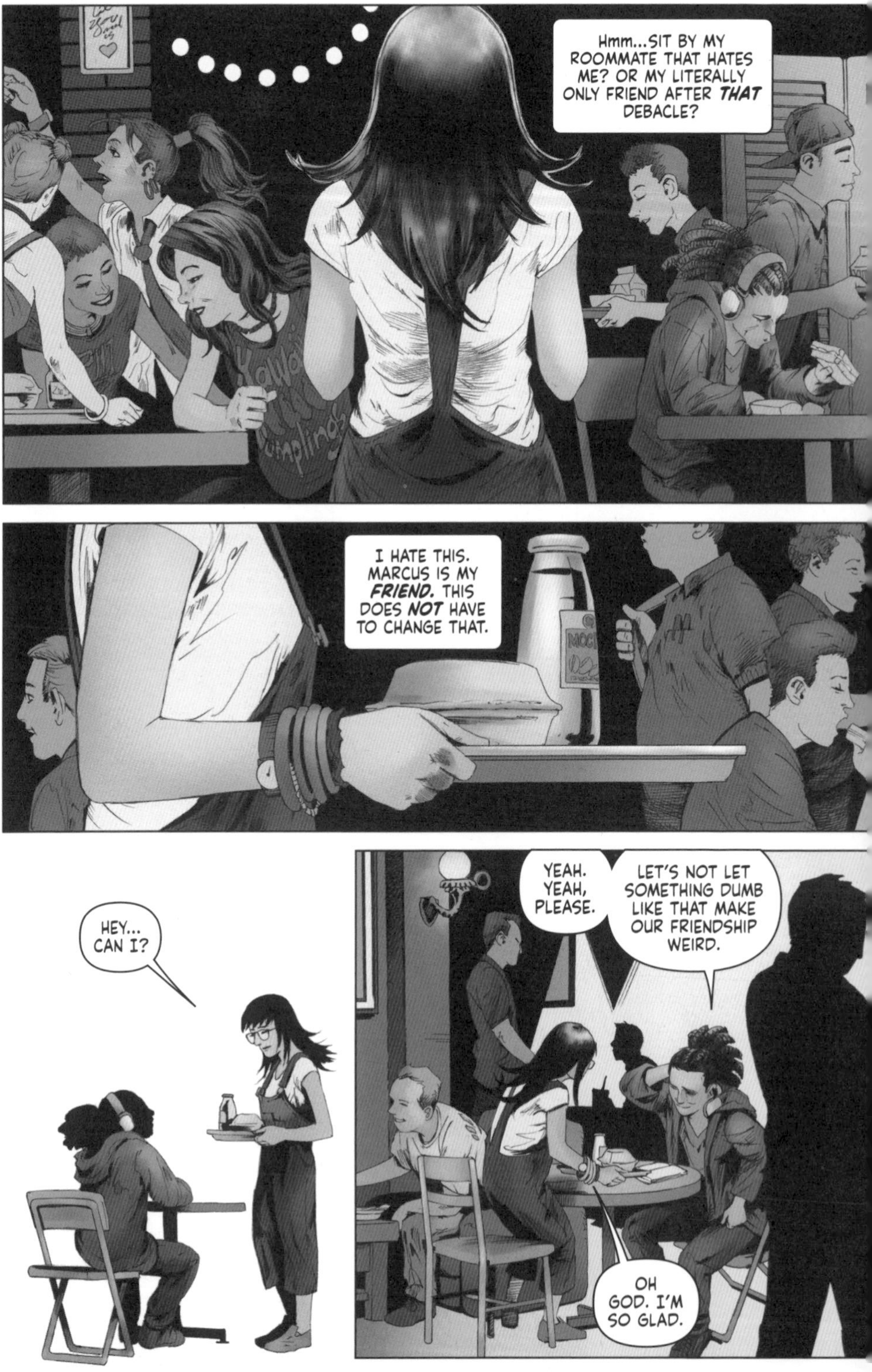
Hmm...SIT BY MY ROOMMATE THAT HATES ME? OR MY LITERALLY ONLY FRIEND AFTER *THAT* DEBACLE?
I HATE THIS. MARCUS IS MY *FRIEND.* THIS DOES *NOT* HAVE TO CHANGE THAT.
HEY... CAN I?
YEAH. YEAH, PLEASE.
LET'S NOT LET SOMETHING DUMB LIKE THAT MAKE OUR FRIENDSHIP WEIRD.
OH GOD. I'M SO GLAD.

IT'S JUST *DUMB*, RIGHT?

THERE'S NO REASON FOR EITHER OF US TO WORRY ABOUT IT. RIGHT?

EXACTLY. YOU'RE A GOOD FRIEND AND I DON'T--

OH NO!

NO USE CRYING OVER SPILT MILK!

OH GOD. YOU'RE THE *WORST*.

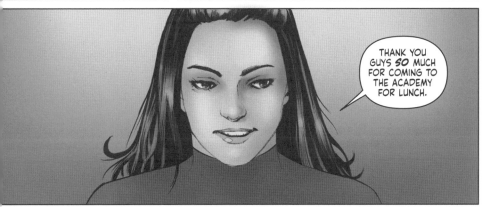

THANK YOU GUYS *SO* MUCH FOR COMING TO THE ACADEMY FOR LUNCH.

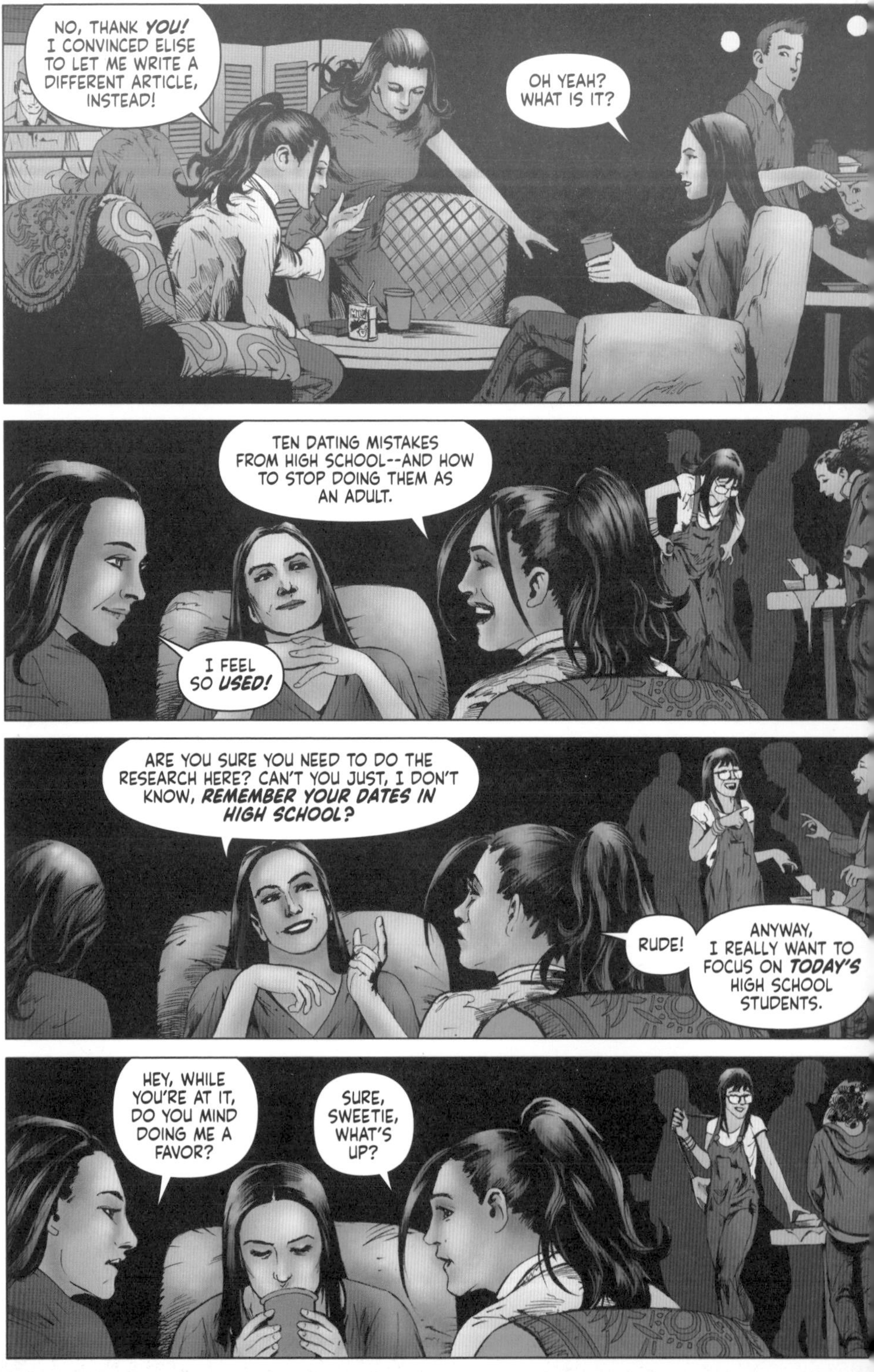
NO, THANK YOU! I CONVINCED ELISE TO LET ME WRITE A DIFFERENT ARTICLE, INSTEAD!
OH YEAH? WHAT IS IT?
TEN DATING MISTAKES FROM HIGH SCHOOL--AND HOW TO STOP DOING THEM AS AN ADULT.
I FEEL SO USED!
ARE YOU SURE YOU NEED TO DO THE RESEARCH HERE? CAN'T YOU JUST, I DON'T KNOW, REMEMBER YOUR DATES IN HIGH SCHOOL?
RUDE!
ANYWAY, I REALLY WANT TO FOCUS ON TODAY'S HIGH SCHOOL STUDENTS.
HEY, WHILE YOU'RE AT IT, DO YOU MIND DOING ME A FAVOR?
SURE, SWEETIE, WHAT'S UP?

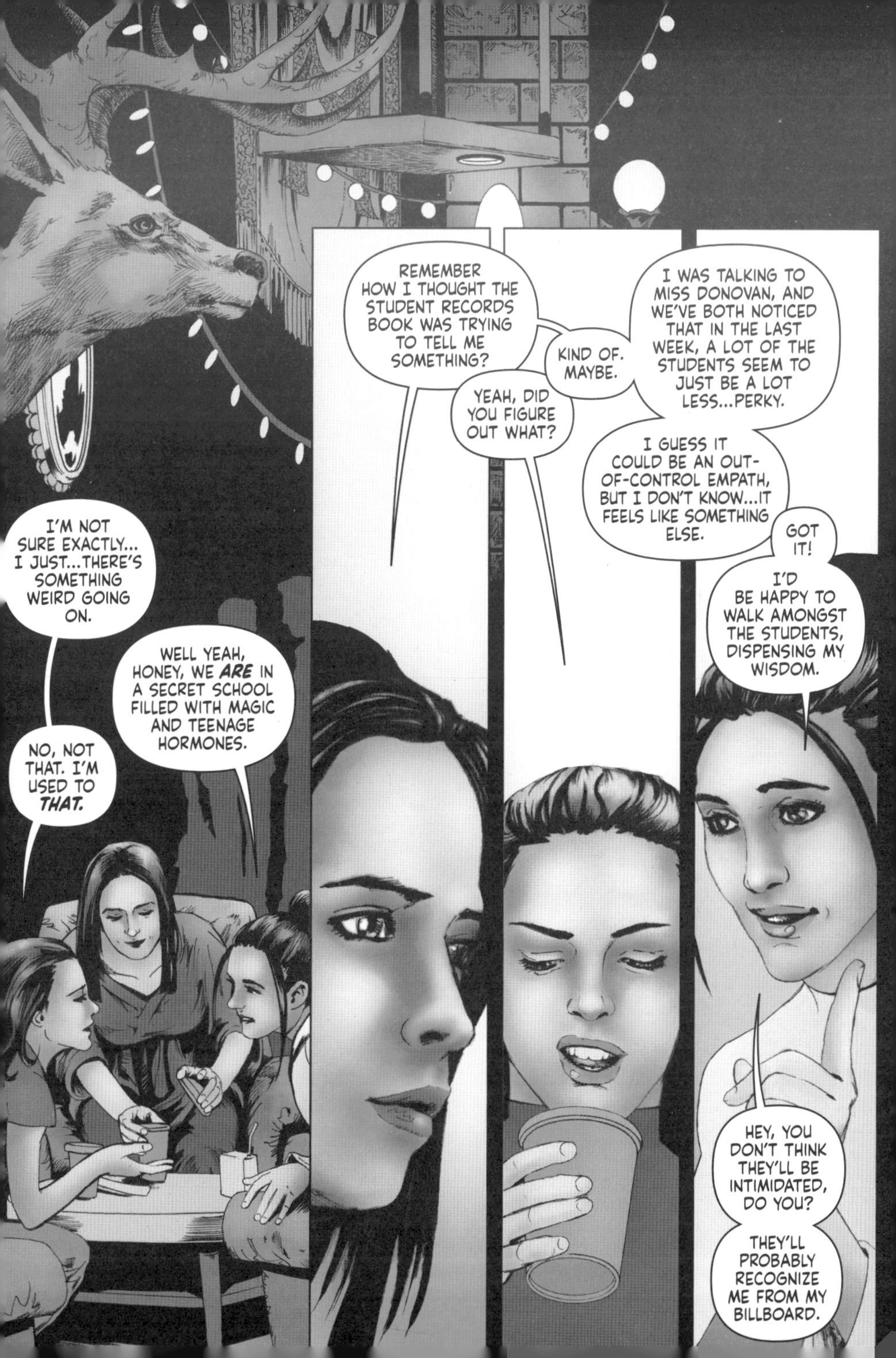
I'M NOT SURE EXACTLY... I JUST...THERE'S SOMETHING WEIRD GOING ON.
WELL YEAH, HONEY, WE *ARE* IN A SECRET SCHOOL FILLED WITH MAGIC AND TEENAGE HORMONES.
NO, NOT THAT. I'M USED TO *THAT.*
REMEMBER HOW I THOUGHT THE STUDENT RECORDS BOOK WAS TRYING TO TELL ME SOMETHING?
KIND OF. MAYBE.
YEAH, DID YOU FIGURE OUT WHAT?
I WAS TALKING TO MISS DONOVAN, AND WE'VE BOTH NOTICED THAT IN THE LAST WEEK, A LOT OF THE STUDENTS SEEM TO JUST BE A LOT LESS...PERKY.
I GUESS IT COULD BE AN OUT-OF-CONTROL EMPATH, BUT I DON'T KNOW...IT FEELS LIKE SOMETHING ELSE.
GOT IT!
I'D BE HAPPY TO WALK AMONGST THE STUDENTS, DISPENSING MY WISDOM.
HEY, YOU DON'T THINK THEY'LL BE INTIMIDATED, DO YOU?
THEY'LL PROBABLY RECOGNIZE ME FROM MY BILLBOARD.

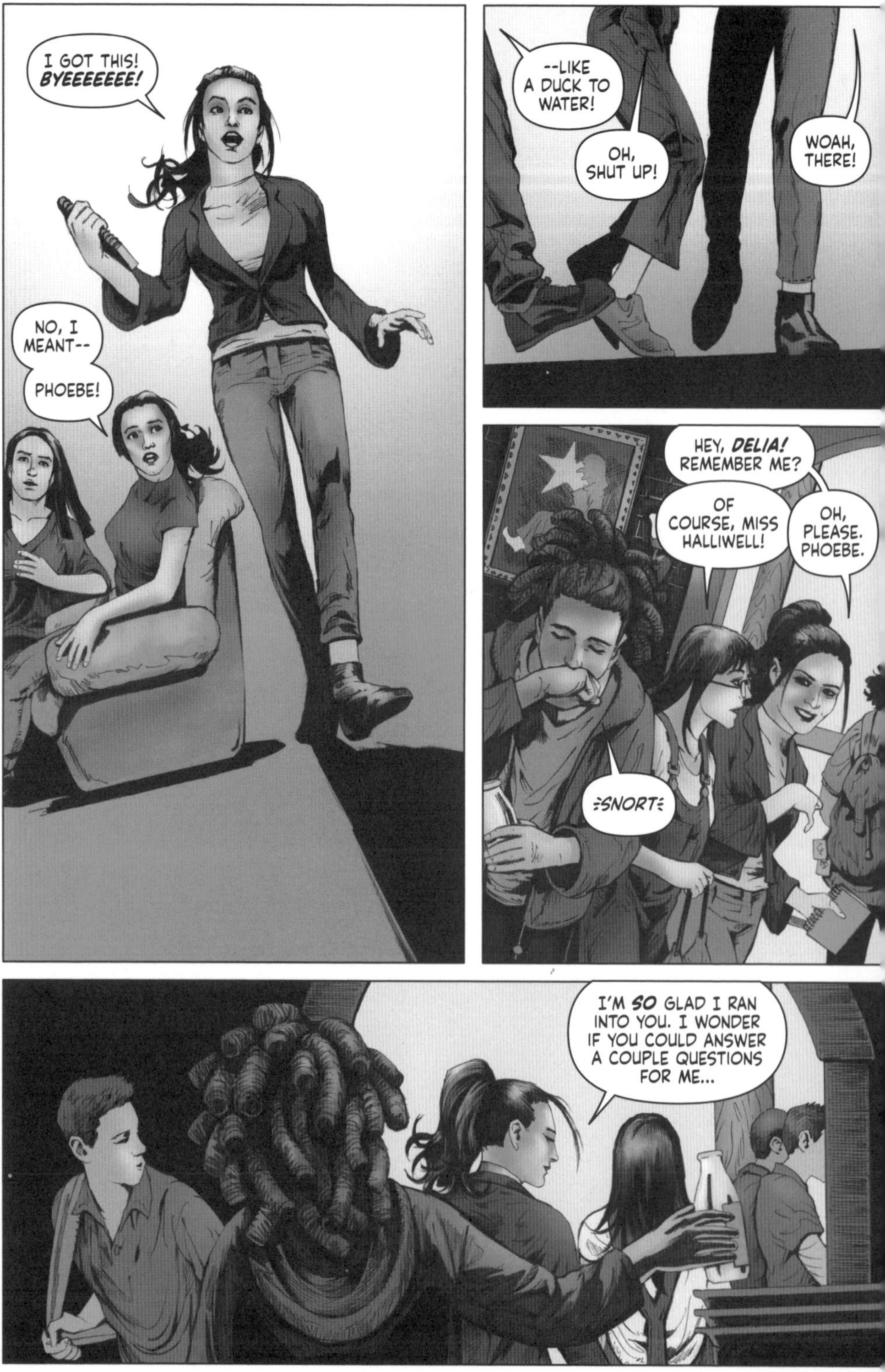

I GOT THIS! BYEEEEEEE!
NO, I MEANT--
PHOEBE!
--LIKE A DUCK TO WATER!
OH, SHUT UP!
WOAH, THERE!
HEY, DELIA! REMEMBER ME?
OF COURSE, MISS HALLIWELL!
OH, PLEASE. PHOEBE.
SNORT
I'M SO GLAD I RAN INTO YOU. I WONDER IF YOU COULD ANSWER A COUPLE QUESTIONS FOR ME...

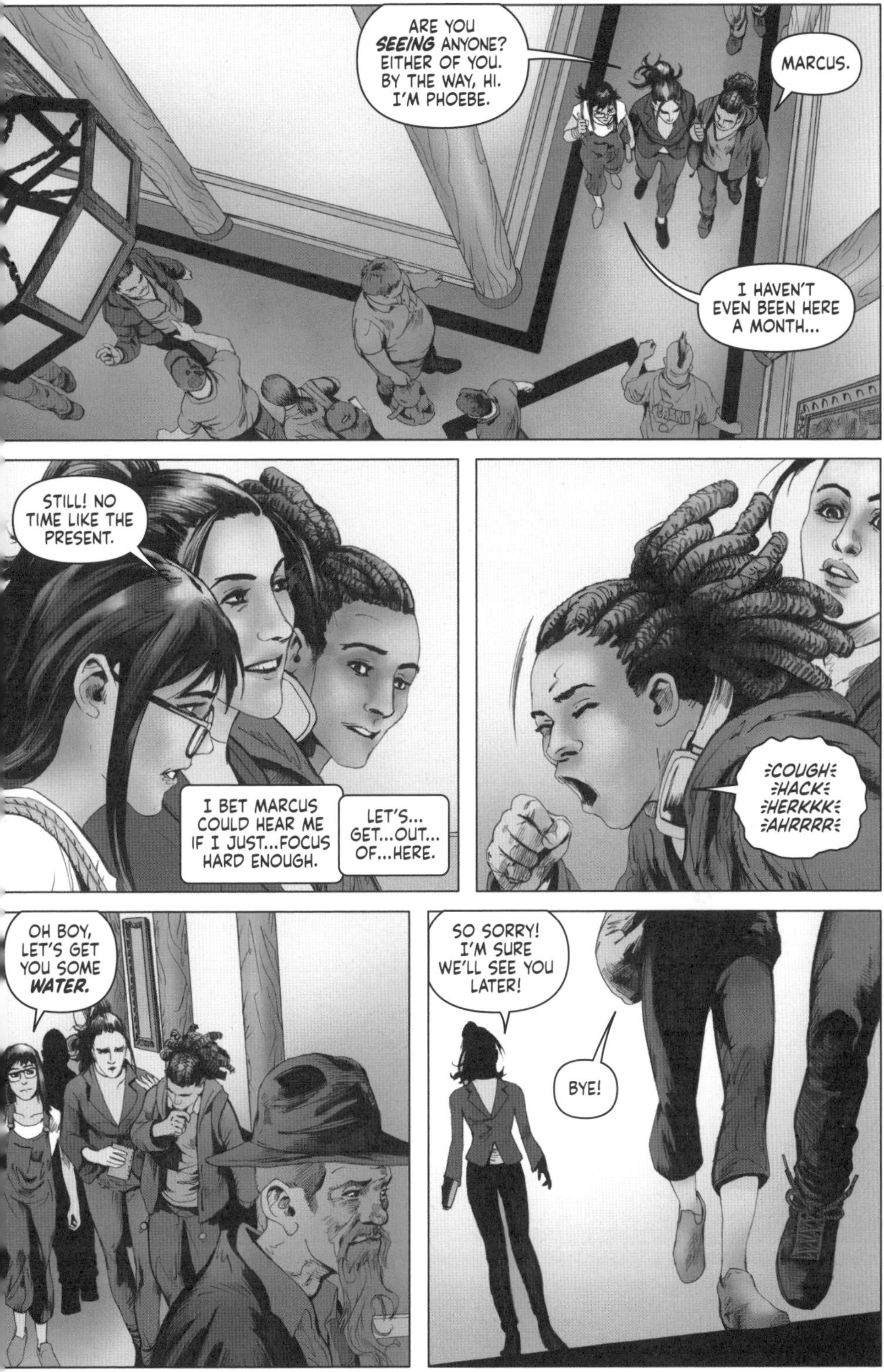
ARE YOU SEEING ANYONE? EITHER OF YOU. BY THE WAY, HI. I'M PHOEBE.
MARCUS.
I HAVEN'T EVEN BEEN HERE A MONTH...
STILL! NO TIME LIKE THE PRESENT.
I BET MARCUS COULD HEAR ME IF I JUST...FOCUS HARD ENOUGH.
LET'S... GET...OUT... OF...HERE.
COUGH HACK HERKKK AHRRRR
OH BOY, LET'S GET YOU SOME WATER.
SO SORRY! I'M SURE WE'LL SEE YOU LATER!
BYE!

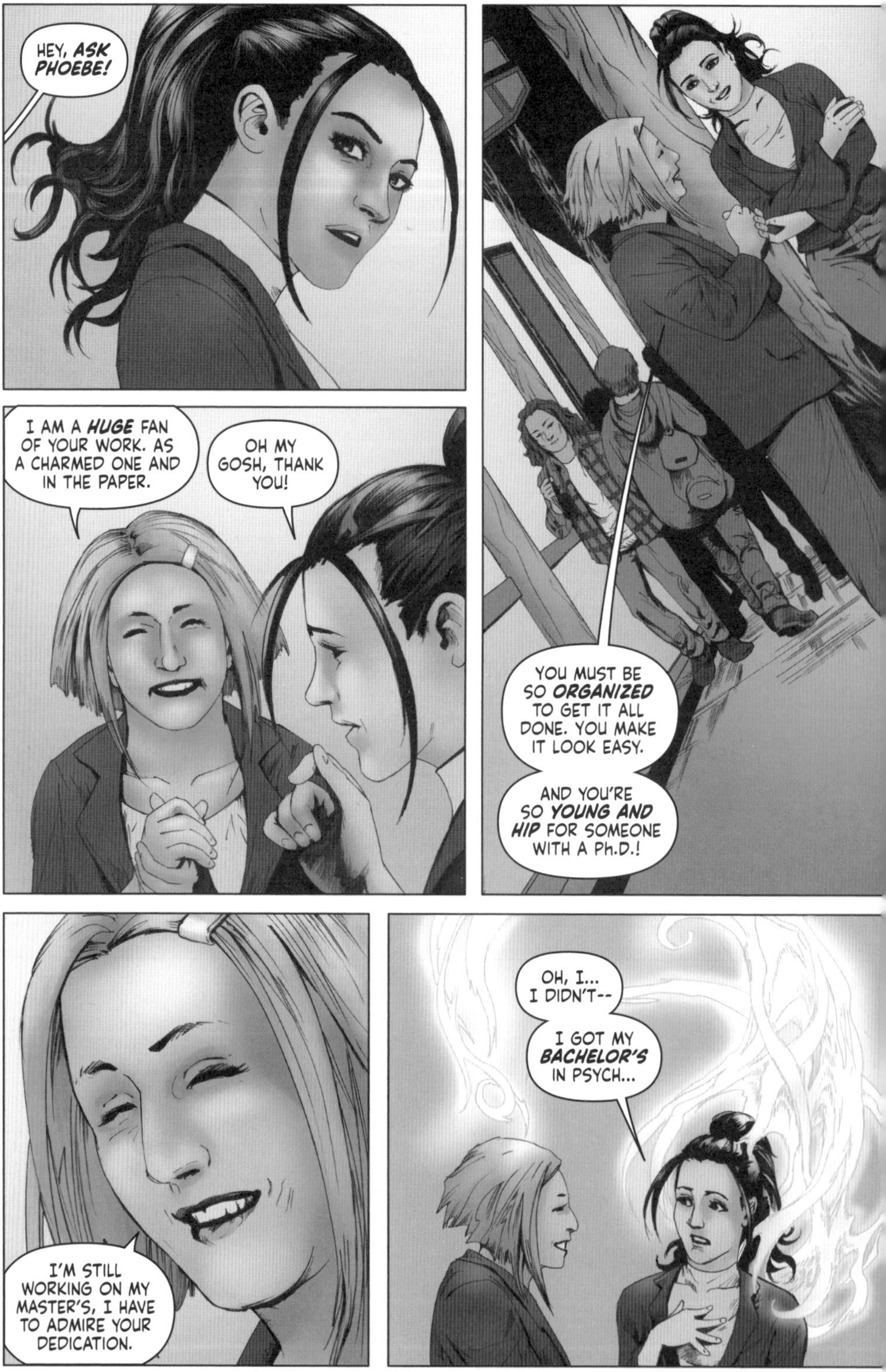
HEY, ASK PHOEBE!
I AM A HUGE FAN OF YOUR WORK. AS A CHARMED ONE AND IN THE PAPER.
OH MY GOSH, THANK YOU!
YOU MUST BE SO ORGANIZED TO GET IT ALL DONE. YOU MAKE IT LOOK EASY.
AND YOU'RE SO YOUNG AND HIP FOR SOMEONE WITH A Ph.D.!
I'M STILL WORKING ON MY MASTER'S, I HAVE TO ADMIRE YOUR DEDICATION.
OH, I... I DIDN'T--
I GOT MY BACHELOR'S IN PSYCH...

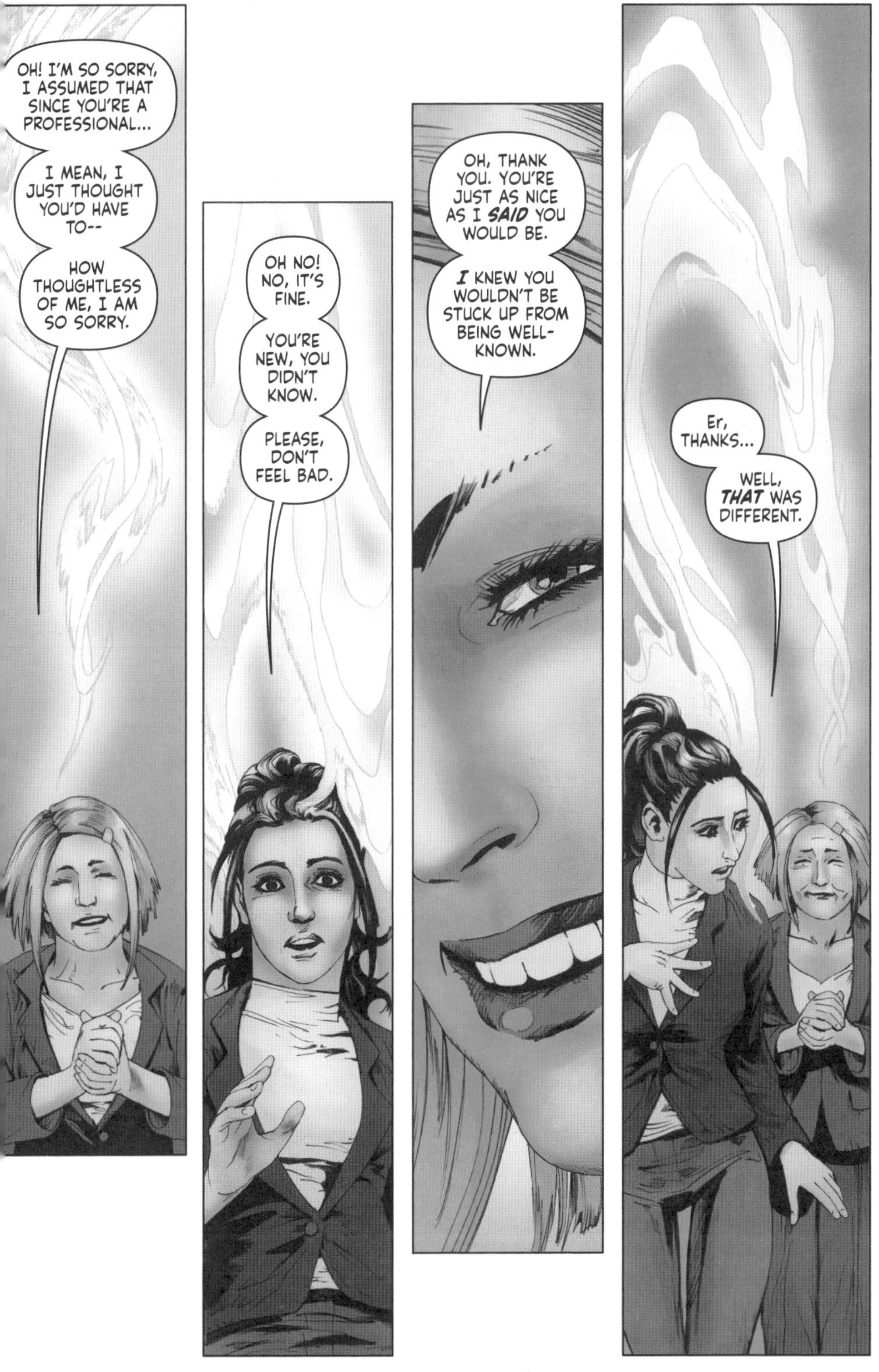
OH! I'M SO SORRY, I ASSUMED THAT SINCE YOU'RE A PROFESSIONAL...
I MEAN, I JUST THOUGHT YOU'D HAVE TO--
HOW THOUGHTLESS OF ME, I AM SO SORRY.
OH NO! NO, IT'S FINE.
YOU'RE NEW, YOU DIDN'T KNOW.
PLEASE, DON'T FEEL BAD.
OH, THANK YOU. YOU'RE JUST AS NICE AS I ***SAID*** YOU WOULD BE.
I KNEW YOU WOULDN'T BE STUCK UP FROM BEING WELL-KNOWN.
Er, THANKS...
WELL, ***THAT*** WAS DIFFERENT.

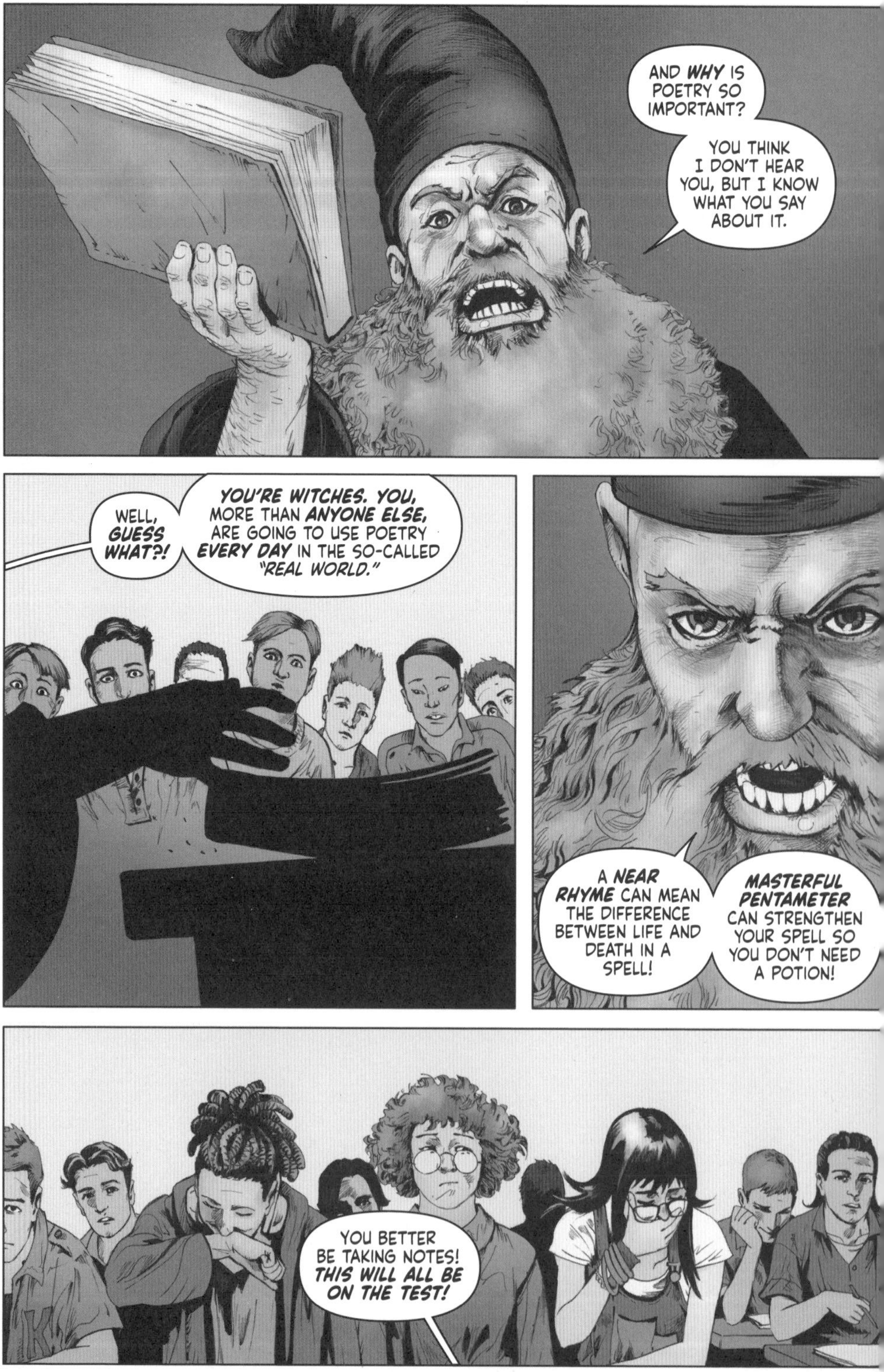

AND **WHY** IS POETRY SO IMPORTANT?
YOU THINK I DON'T HEAR YOU, BUT I KNOW WHAT YOU SAY ABOUT IT.
WELL, ***GUESS WHAT?!***
YOU'RE WITCHES. YOU, MORE THAN ***ANYONE ELSE,*** ARE GOING TO USE POETRY ***EVERY DAY*** IN THE SO-CALLED *"REAL WORLD."*
A ***NEAR RHYME*** CAN MEAN THE DIFFERENCE BETWEEN LIFE AND DEATH IN A SPELL!
MASTERFUL PENTAMETER CAN STRENGTHEN YOUR SPELL SO YOU DON'T NEED A POTION!
YOU BETTER BE TAKING NOTES! ***THIS WILL ALL BE ON THE TEST!***

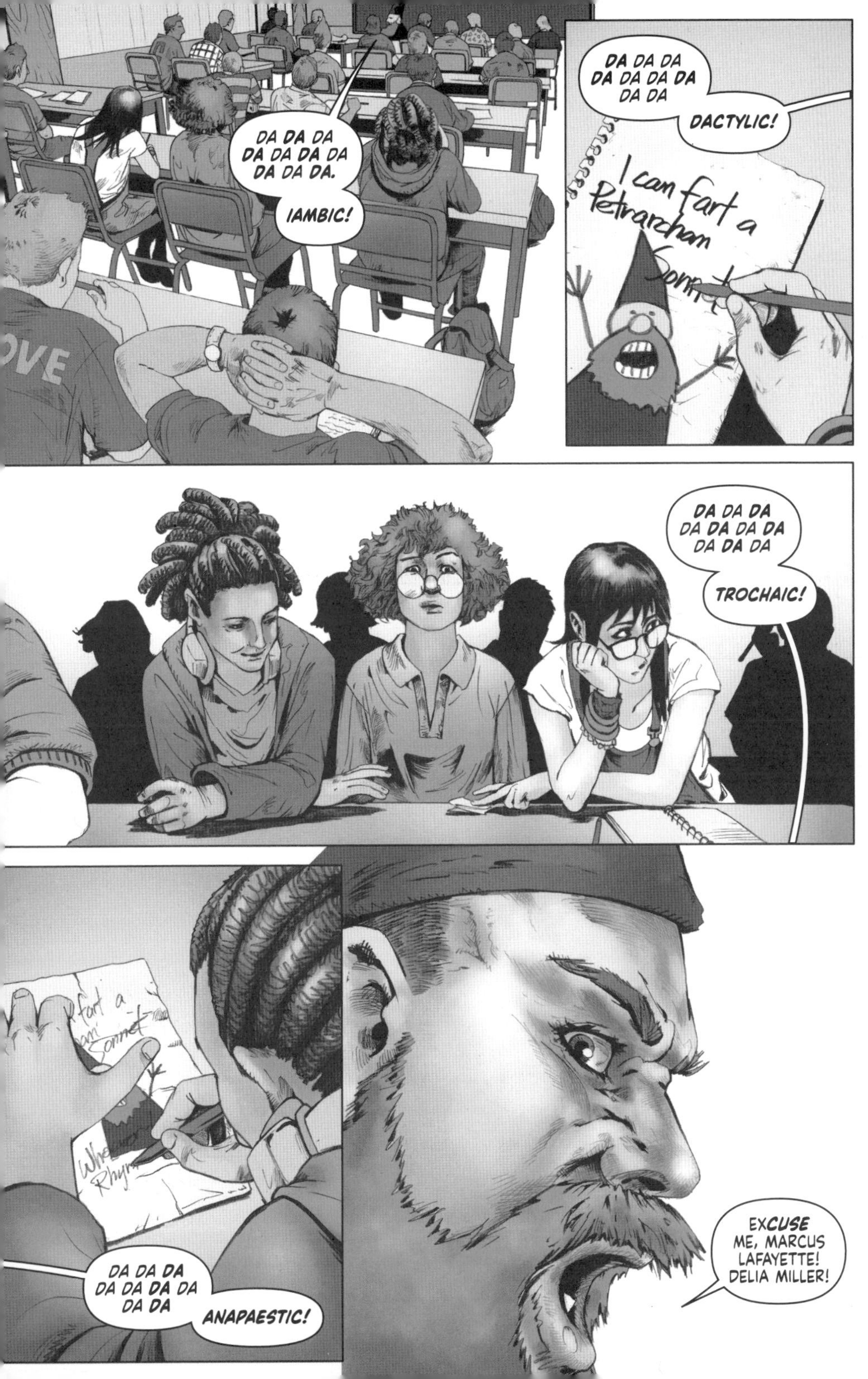
DA DA DA DA DA DA DA DA DA DA.
IAMBIC!
DA DA DA DA DA DA DA DA DA
DACTYLIC!
I can fart a Petrarchan
DA DA DA DA DA DA DA DA DA DA
TROCHAIC!
DA DA DA DA DA DA DA DA DA
ANAPAESTIC!
EXCUSE ME, MARCUS LAFAYETTE! DELIA MILLER!

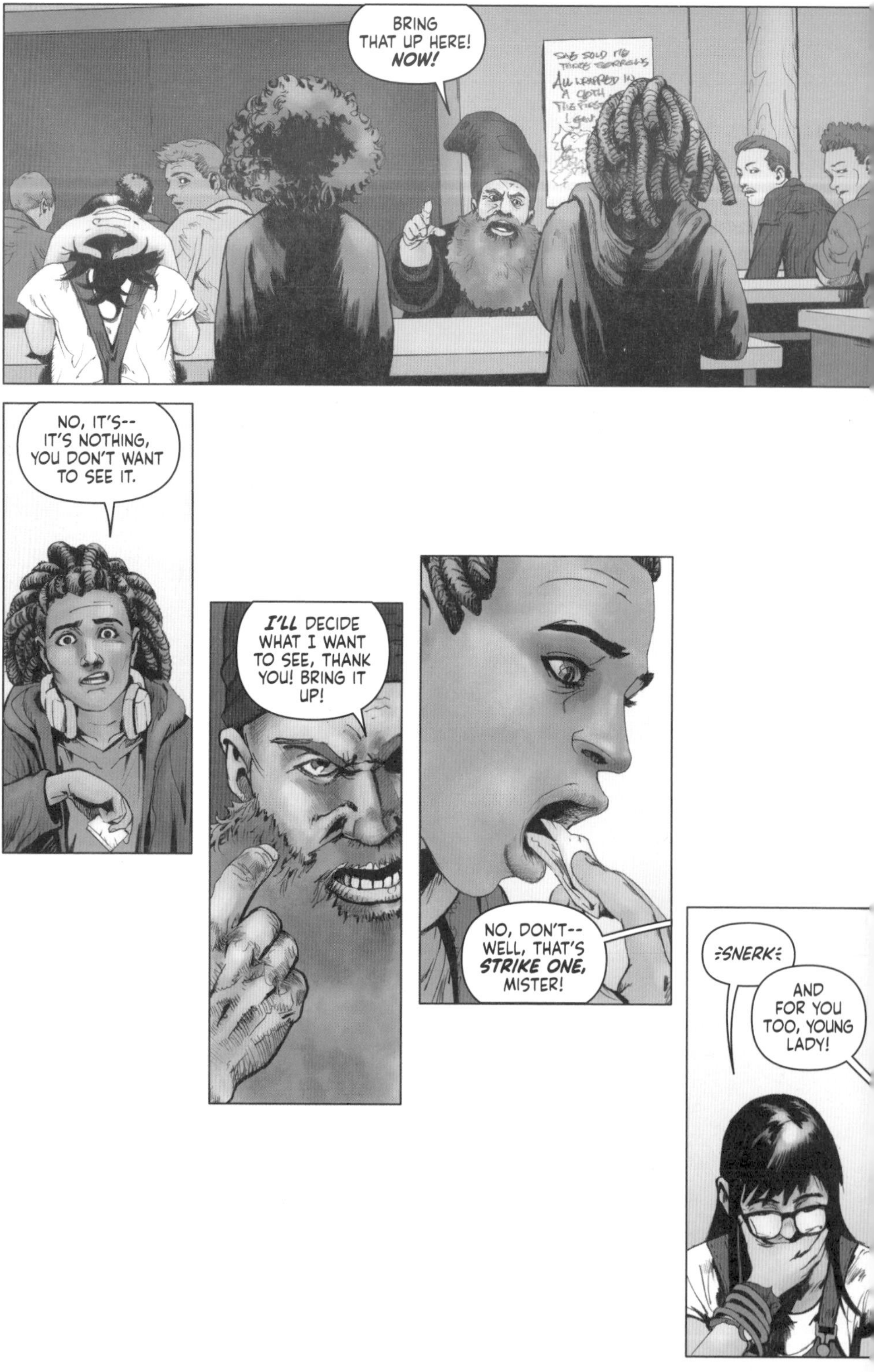
BRING THAT UP HERE! **NOW!**
NO, IT'S-- IT'S NOTHING, YOU DON'T WANT TO SEE IT.
I'LL DECIDE WHAT I WANT TO SEE, THANK YOU! BRING IT UP!
NO, DON'T-- WELL, THAT'S ***STRIKE ONE,*** MISTER!
=SNERK=
AND FOR YOU TOO, YOUNG LADY!

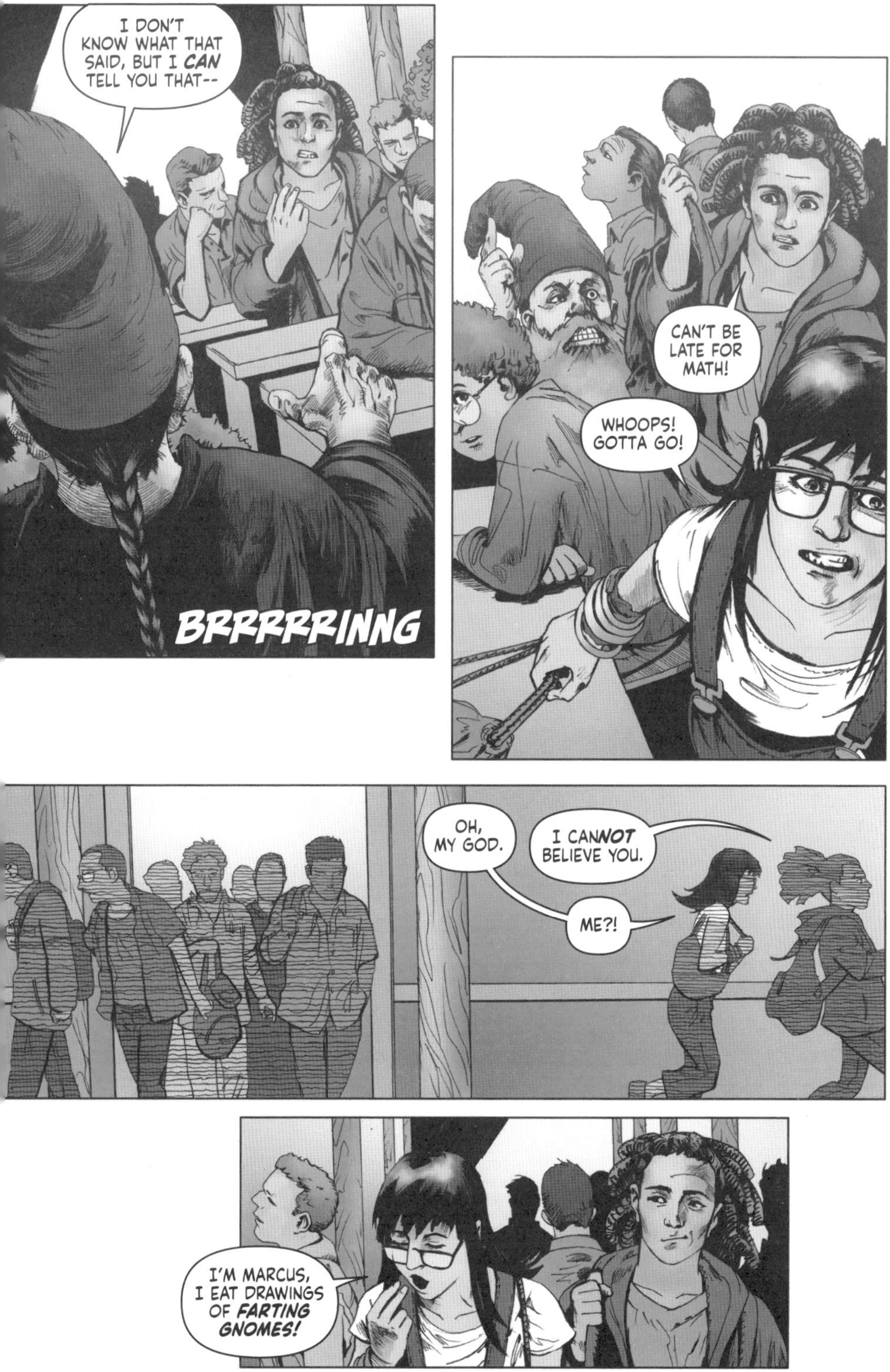

I DON'T KNOW WHAT THAT SAID, BUT I CAN TELL YOU THAT--
BRRRRRINNG
CAN'T BE LATE FOR MATH!
WHOOPS! GOTTA GO!
OH, MY GOD.
I CANNOT BELIEVE YOU.
ME?!
I'M MARCUS, I EAT DRAWINGS OF FARTING GNOMES!

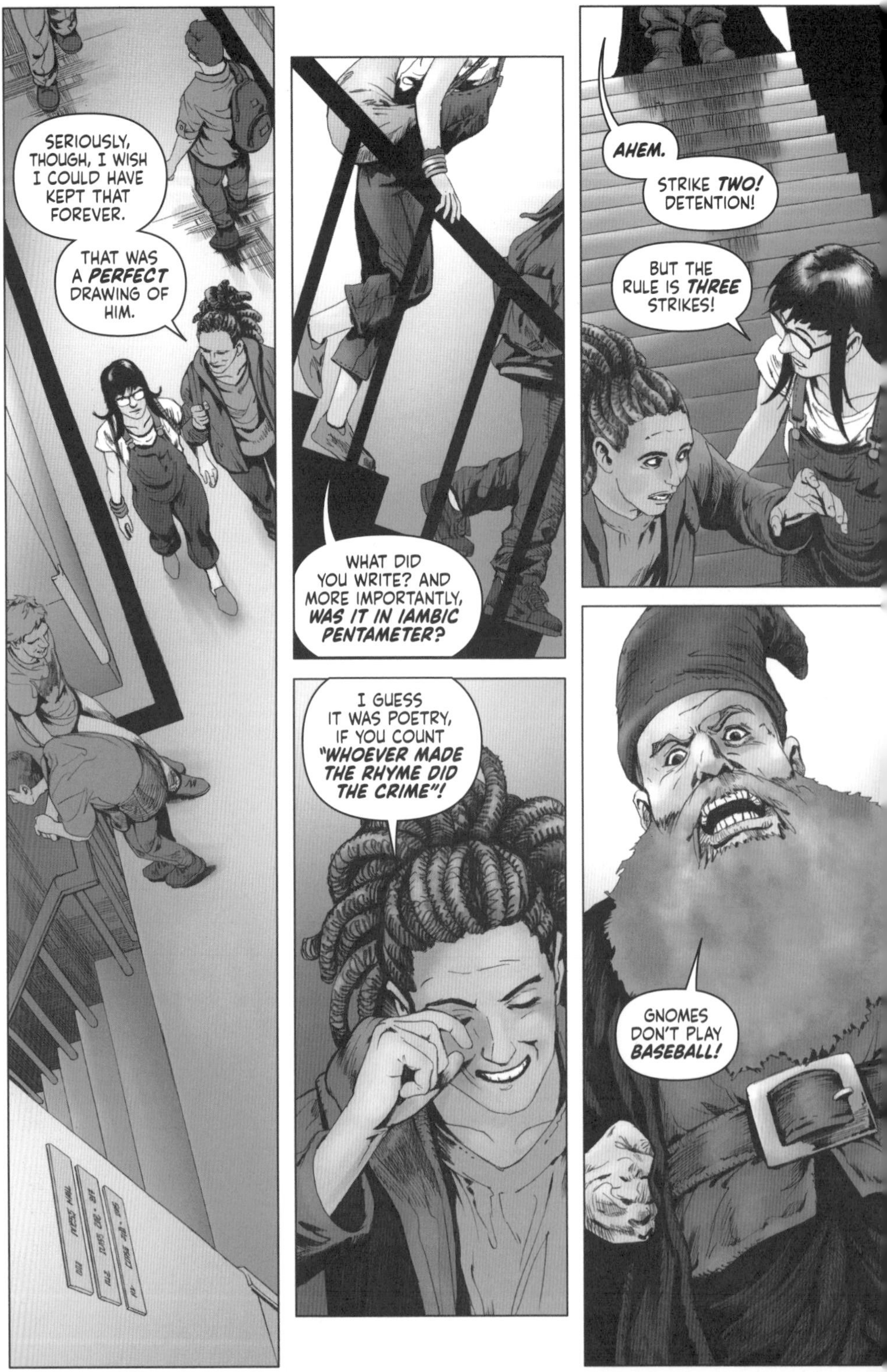
SERIOUSLY, THOUGH, I WISH I COULD HAVE KEPT THAT FOREVER.
THAT WAS A *PERFECT* DRAWING OF HIM.
WHAT DID YOU WRITE? AND MORE IMPORTANTLY, *WAS IT IN IAMBIC PENTAMETER?*
I GUESS IT WAS POETRY, IF YOU COUNT *"WHOEVER MADE THE RHYME DID THE CRIME"!*
AHEM.
STRIKE *TWO!* DETENTION!
BUT THE RULE IS *THREE* STRIKES!
GNOMES DON'T PLAY *BASEBALL!*

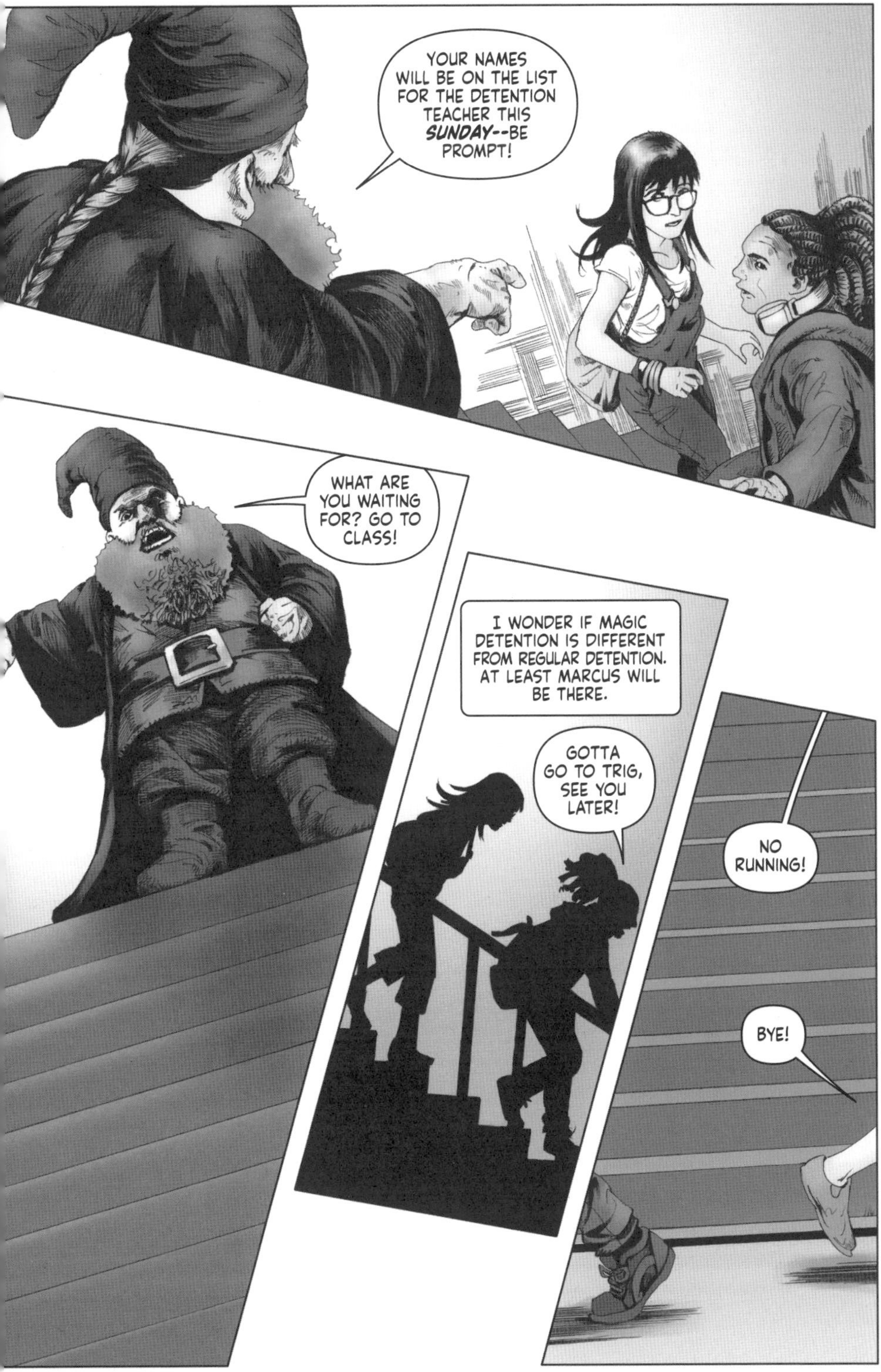
YOUR NAMES WILL BE ON THE LIST FOR THE DETENTION TEACHER THIS **SUNDAY**--BE PROMPT!
WHAT ARE YOU WAITING FOR? GO TO CLASS!
I WONDER IF MAGIC DETENTION IS DIFFERENT FROM REGULAR DETENTION. AT LEAST MARCUS WILL BE THERE.
GOTTA GO TO TRIG, SEE YOU LATER!
NO RUNNING!
BYE!

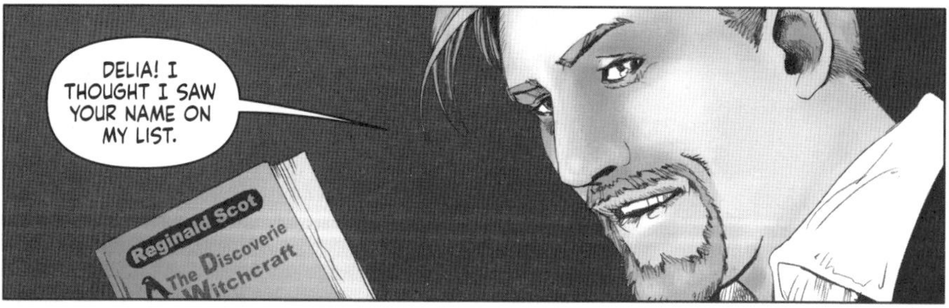
DELIA! I THOUGHT I SAW YOUR NAME ON MY LIST.
Reginald Scot
The Discoverie of Witchcraft

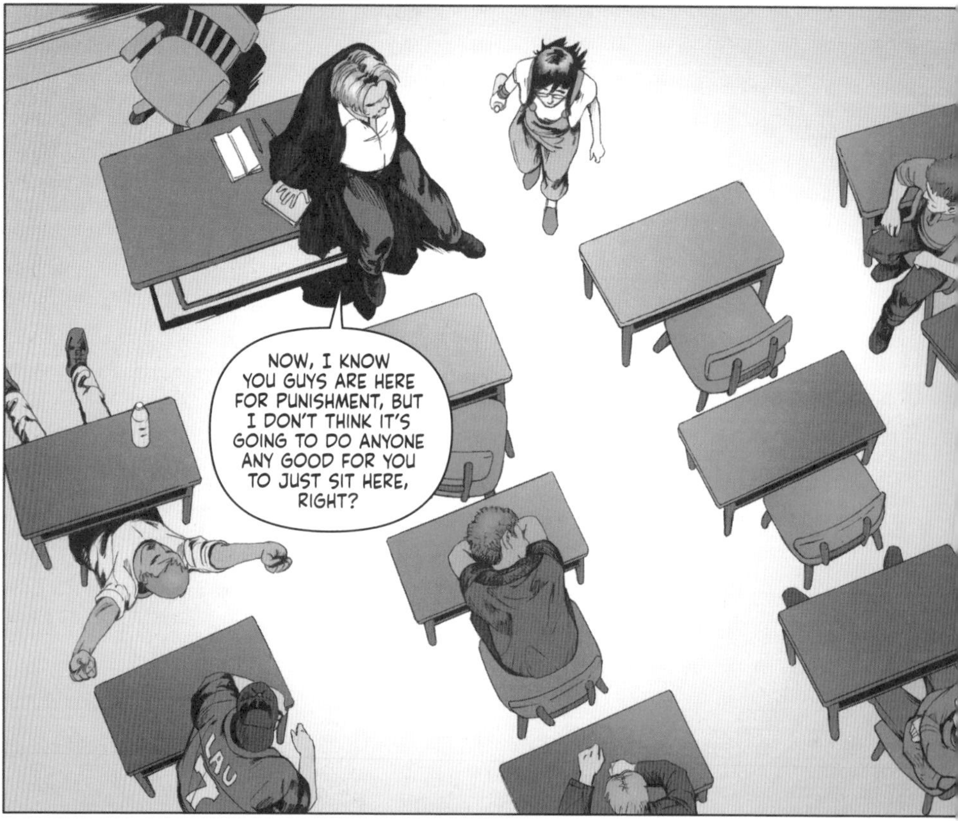
NOW, I KNOW YOU GUYS ARE HERE FOR PUNISHMENT, BUT I DON'T THINK IT'S GOING TO DO ANYONE ANY GOOD FOR YOU TO JUST SIT HERE, RIGHT?
LAU

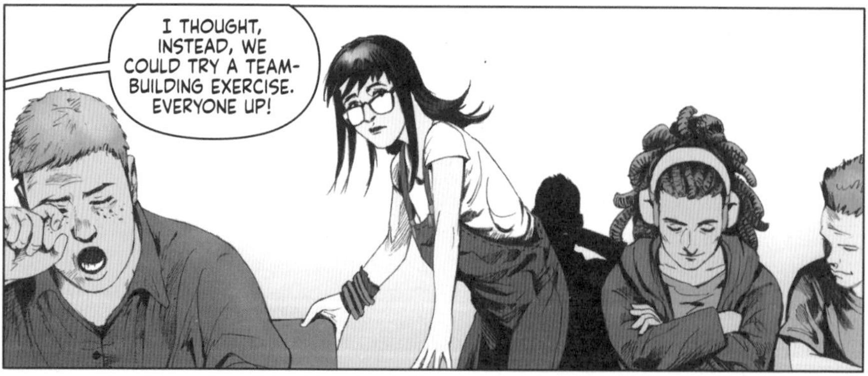
I THOUGHT, INSTEAD, WE COULD TRY A TEAM-BUILDING EXERCISE. EVERYONE UP!

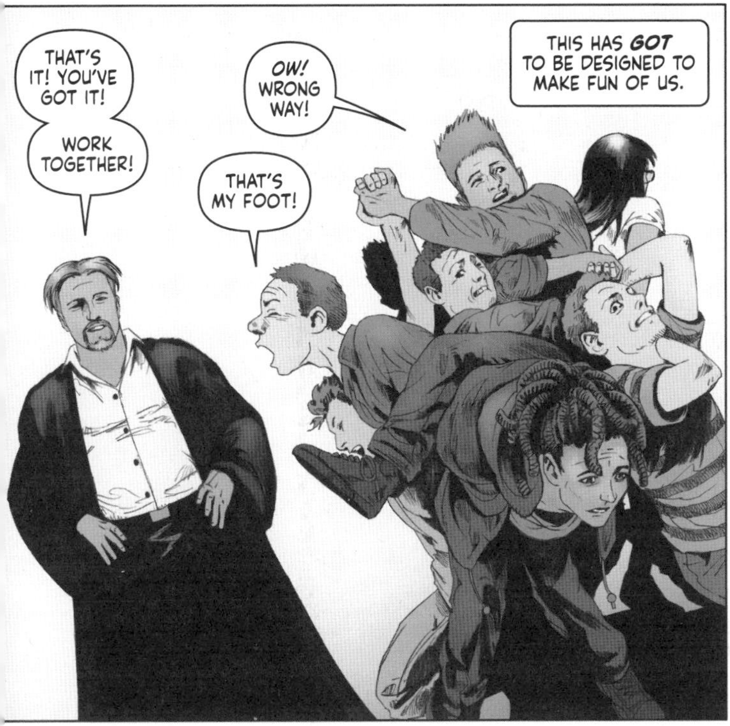
THAT'S IT! YOU'VE GOT IT!
WORK TOGETHER!
OW! WRONG WAY!
THAT'S MY FOOT!
THIS HAS *GOT* TO BE DESIGNED TO MAKE FUN OF US.

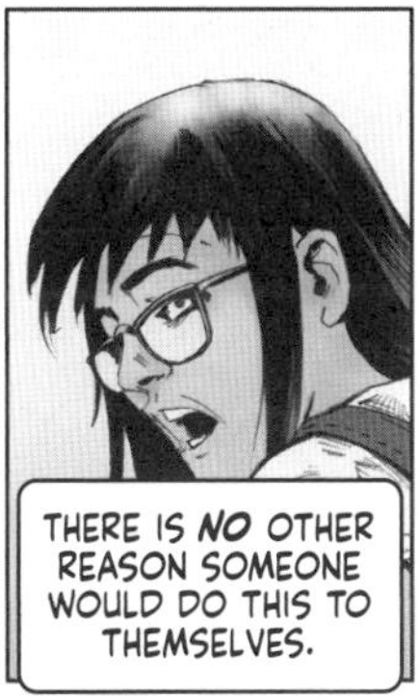
THERE IS *NO* OTHER REASON SOMEONE WOULD DO THIS TO THEMSELVES.

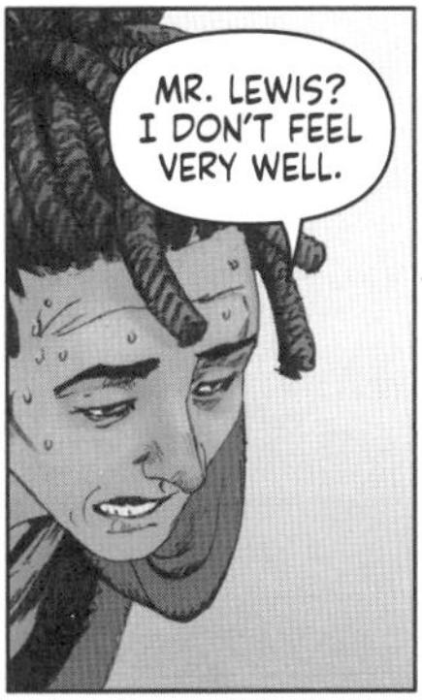
MR. LEWIS? I DON'T FEEL VERY WELL.

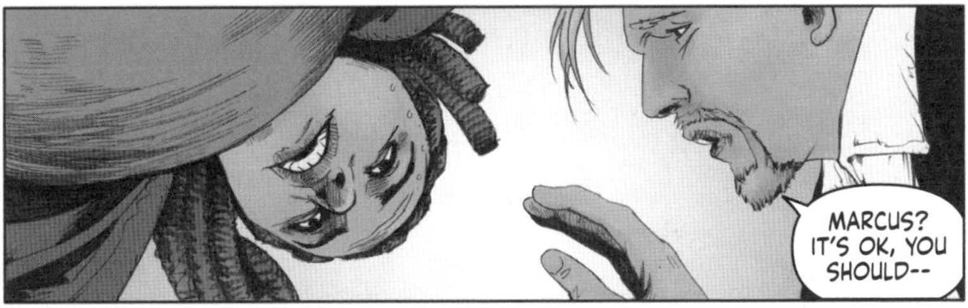
MARCUS? IT'S OK, YOU SHOULD--

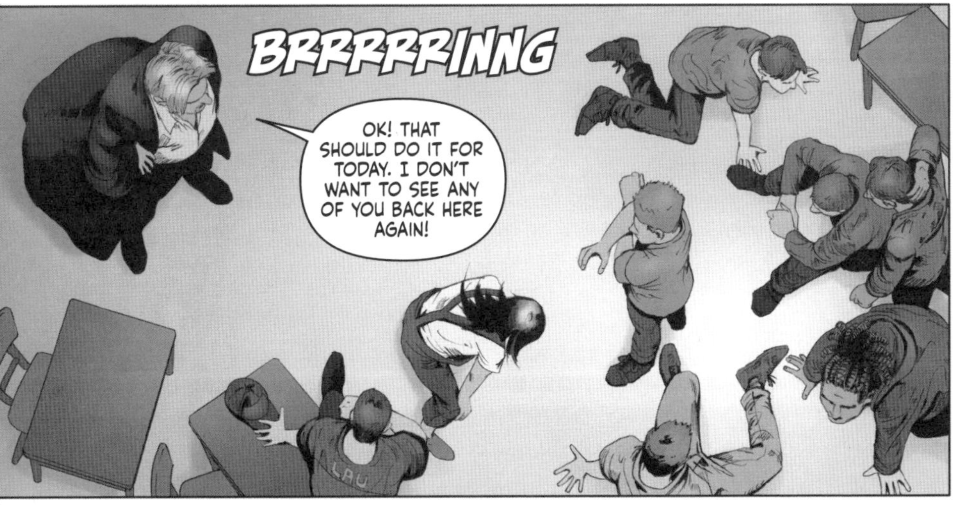
BRRRRRINNG
OK! THAT SHOULD DO IT FOR TODAY. I DON'T WANT TO SEE ANY OF YOU BACK HERE AGAIN!
LAU

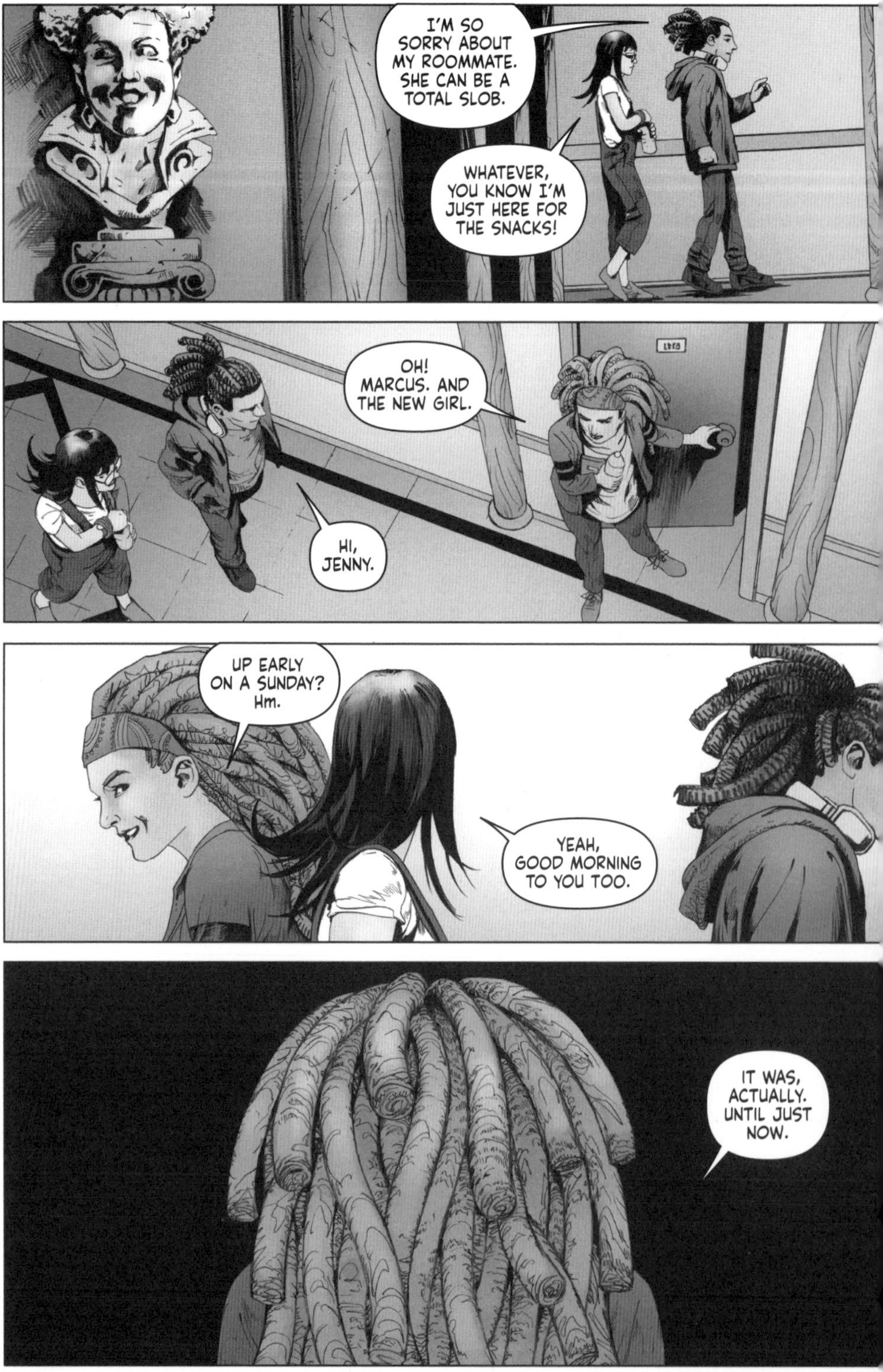
I'M SO SORRY ABOUT MY ROOMMATE. SHE CAN BE A TOTAL SLOB.
WHATEVER, YOU KNOW I'M JUST HERE FOR THE SNACKS!
OH! MARCUS. AND THE NEW GIRL.
HI, JENNY.
UP EARLY ON A SUNDAY? Hm.
YEAH, GOOD MORNING TO YOU TOO.
IT WAS, ACTUALLY. UNTIL JUST NOW.

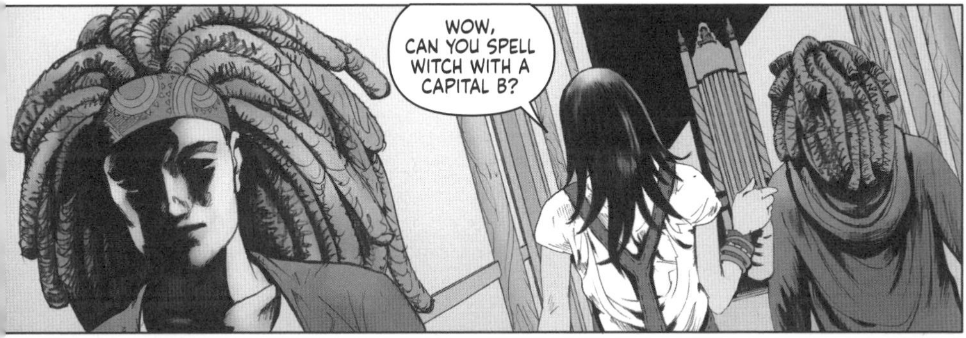
WOW, CAN YOU SPELL WITCH WITH A CAPITAL B?

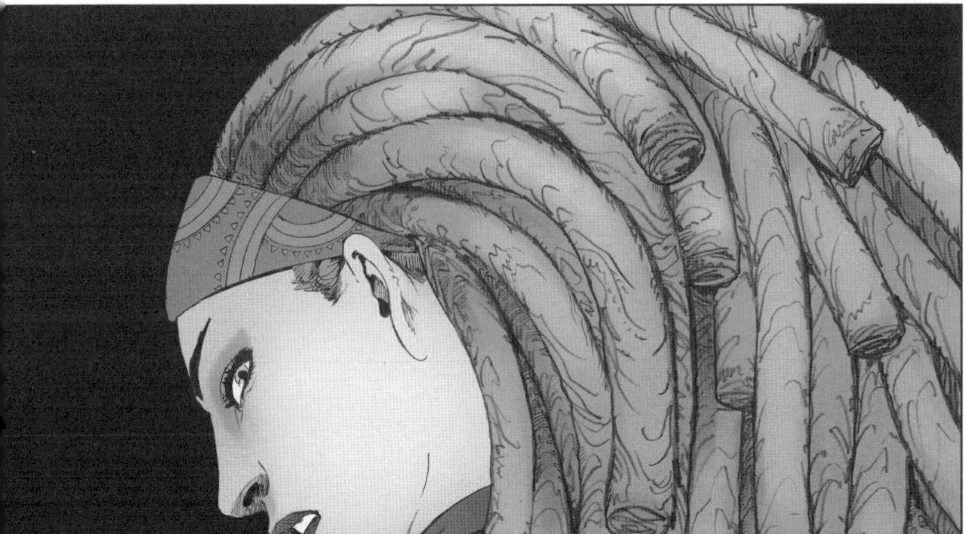
AS IN, FEMALE DOG? DID SOMEONE TELL YOU--

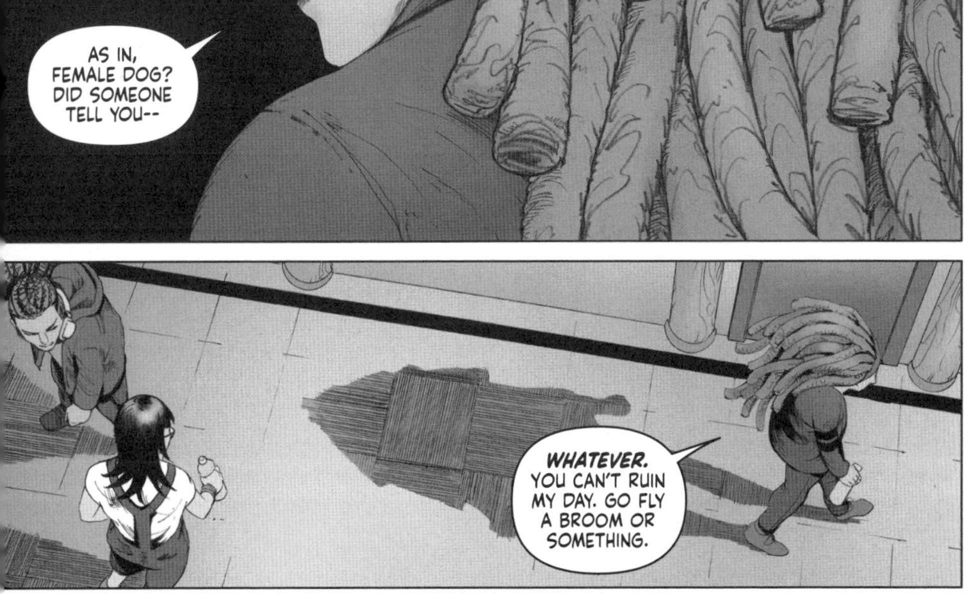
WHATEVER. YOU CAN'T RUIN MY DAY. GO FLY A BROOM OR SOMETHING.

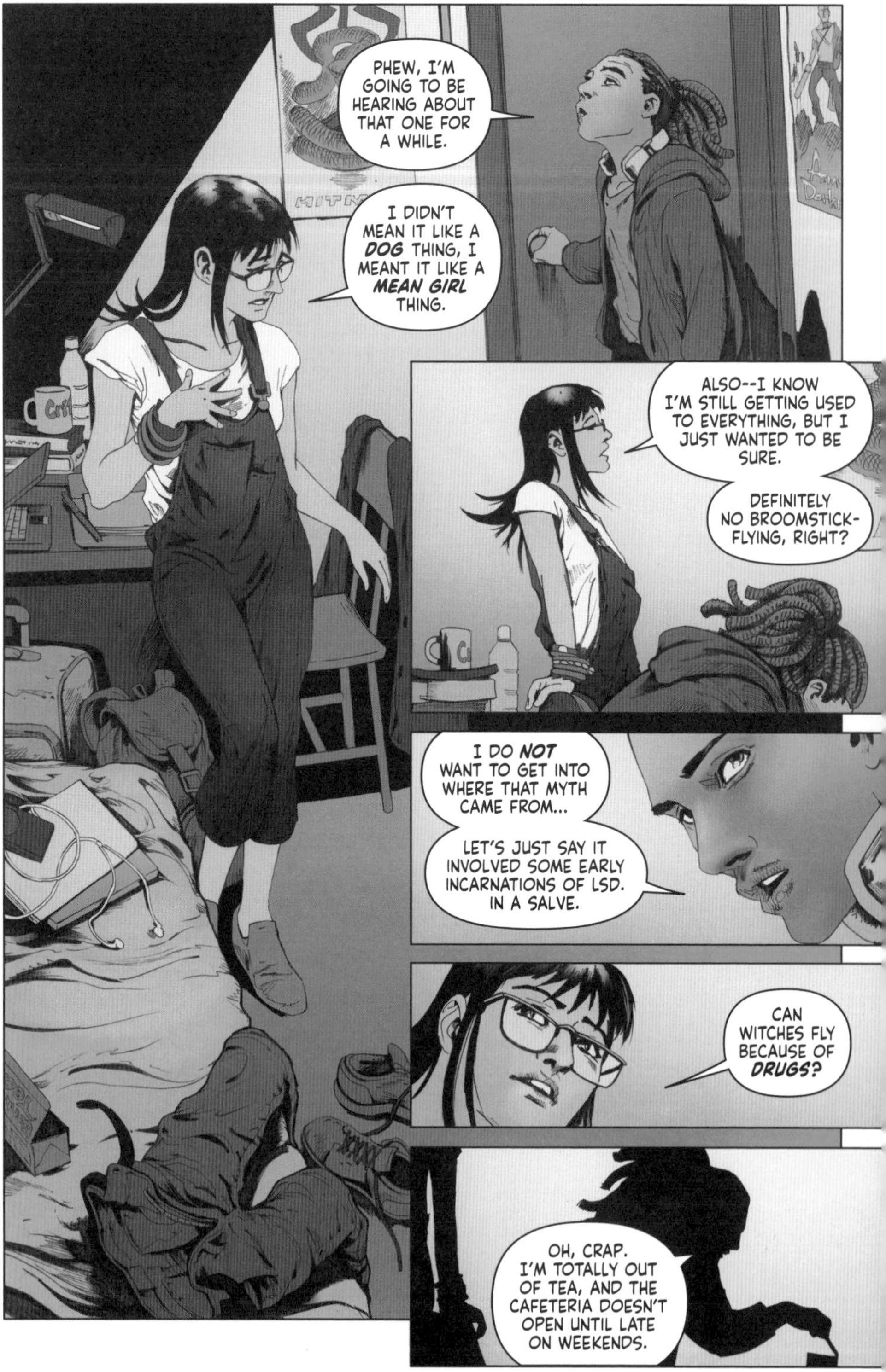
PHEW, I'M GOING TO BE HEARING ABOUT THAT ONE FOR A WHILE.
I DIDN'T MEAN IT LIKE A **DOG** THING, I MEANT IT LIKE A **MEAN GIRL** THING.
ALSO--I KNOW I'M STILL GETTING USED TO EVERYTHING, BUT I JUST WANTED TO BE SURE.
DEFINITELY NO BROOMSTICK-FLYING, RIGHT?
I DO **NOT** WANT TO GET INTO WHERE THAT MYTH CAME FROM...
LET'S JUST SAY IT INVOLVED SOME EARLY INCARNATIONS OF LSD. IN A SALVE.
CAN WITCHES FLY BECAUSE OF **DRUGS?**
OH, CRAP. I'M TOTALLY OUT OF TEA, AND THE CAFETERIA DOESN'T OPEN UNTIL LATE ON WEEKENDS.

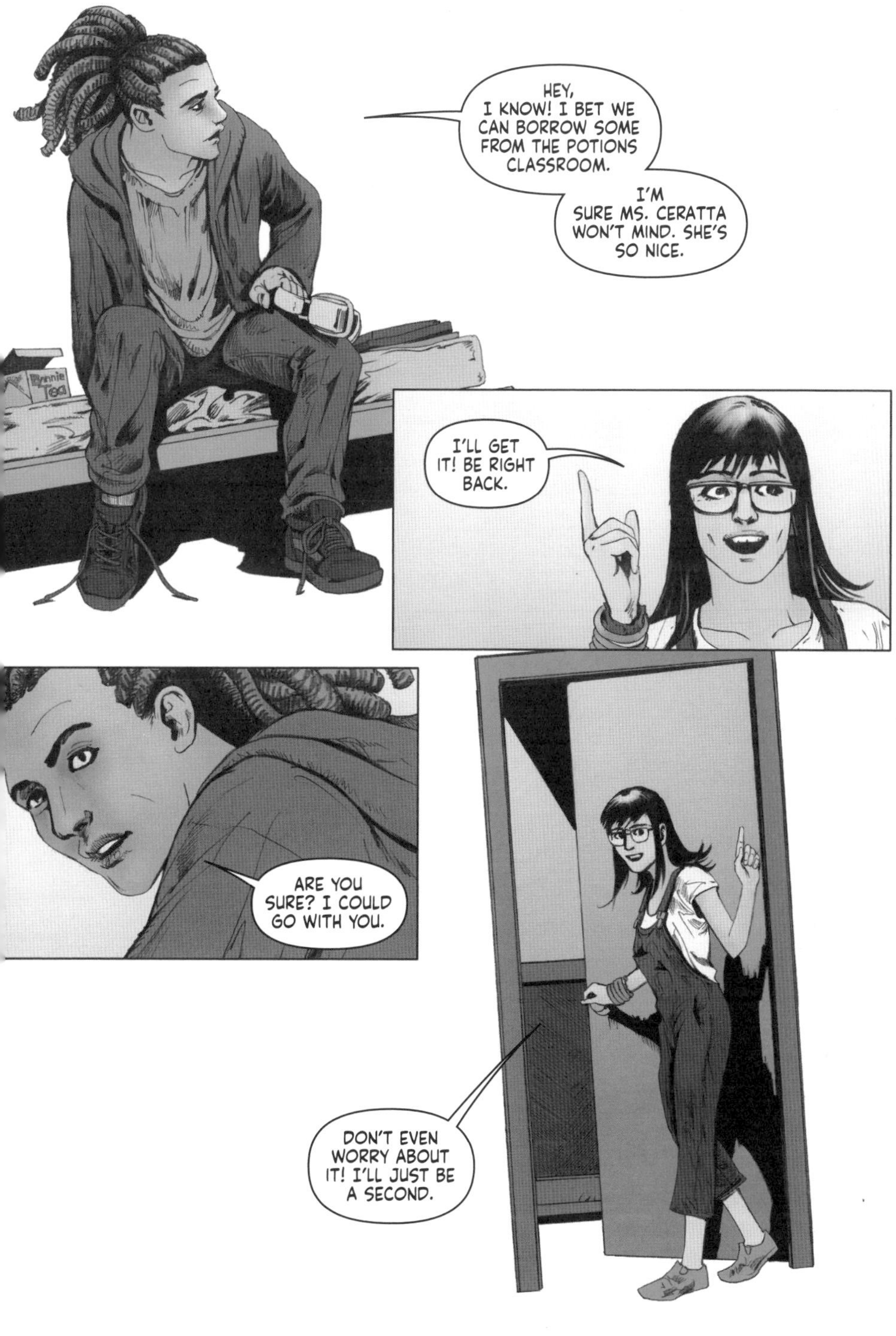
HEY, I KNOW! I BET WE CAN BORROW SOME FROM THE POTIONS CLASSROOM.
I'M SURE MS. CERATTA WON'T MIND. SHE'S SO NICE.
I'LL GET IT! BE RIGHT BACK.
ARE YOU SURE? I COULD GO WITH YOU.
DON'T EVEN WORRY ABOUT IT! I'LL JUST BE A SECOND.

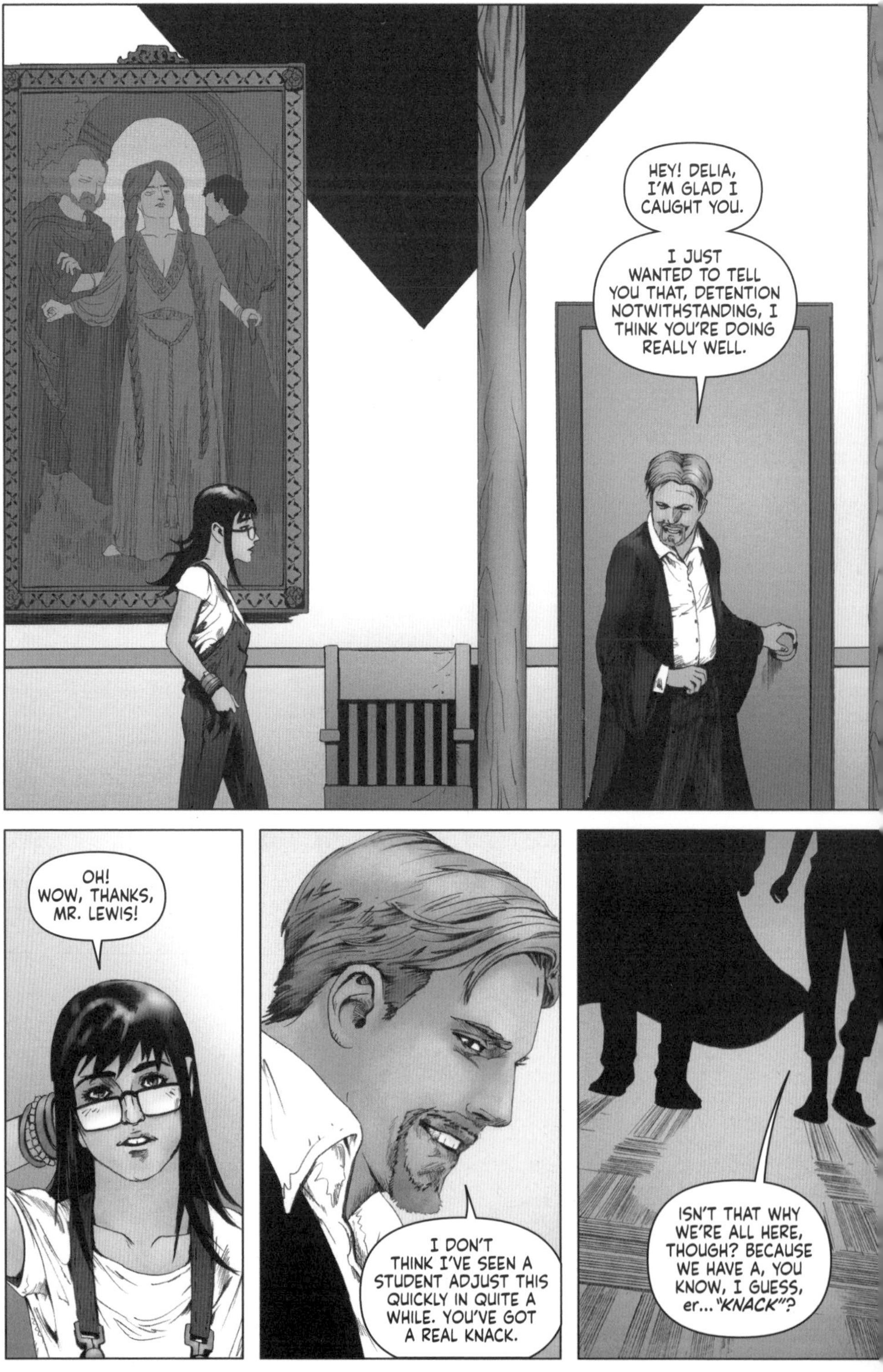
HEY! DELIA, I'M GLAD I CAUGHT YOU.
I JUST WANTED TO TELL YOU THAT, DETENTION NOTWITHSTANDING, I THINK YOU'RE DOING REALLY WELL.
OH! WOW, THANKS, MR. LEWIS!
I DON'T THINK I'VE SEEN A STUDENT ADJUST THIS QUICKLY IN QUITE A WHILE. YOU'VE GOT A REAL KNACK.
ISN'T THAT WHY WE'RE ALL HERE, THOUGH? BECAUSE WE HAVE A, YOU KNOW, I GUESS, er..."*KNACK*"?

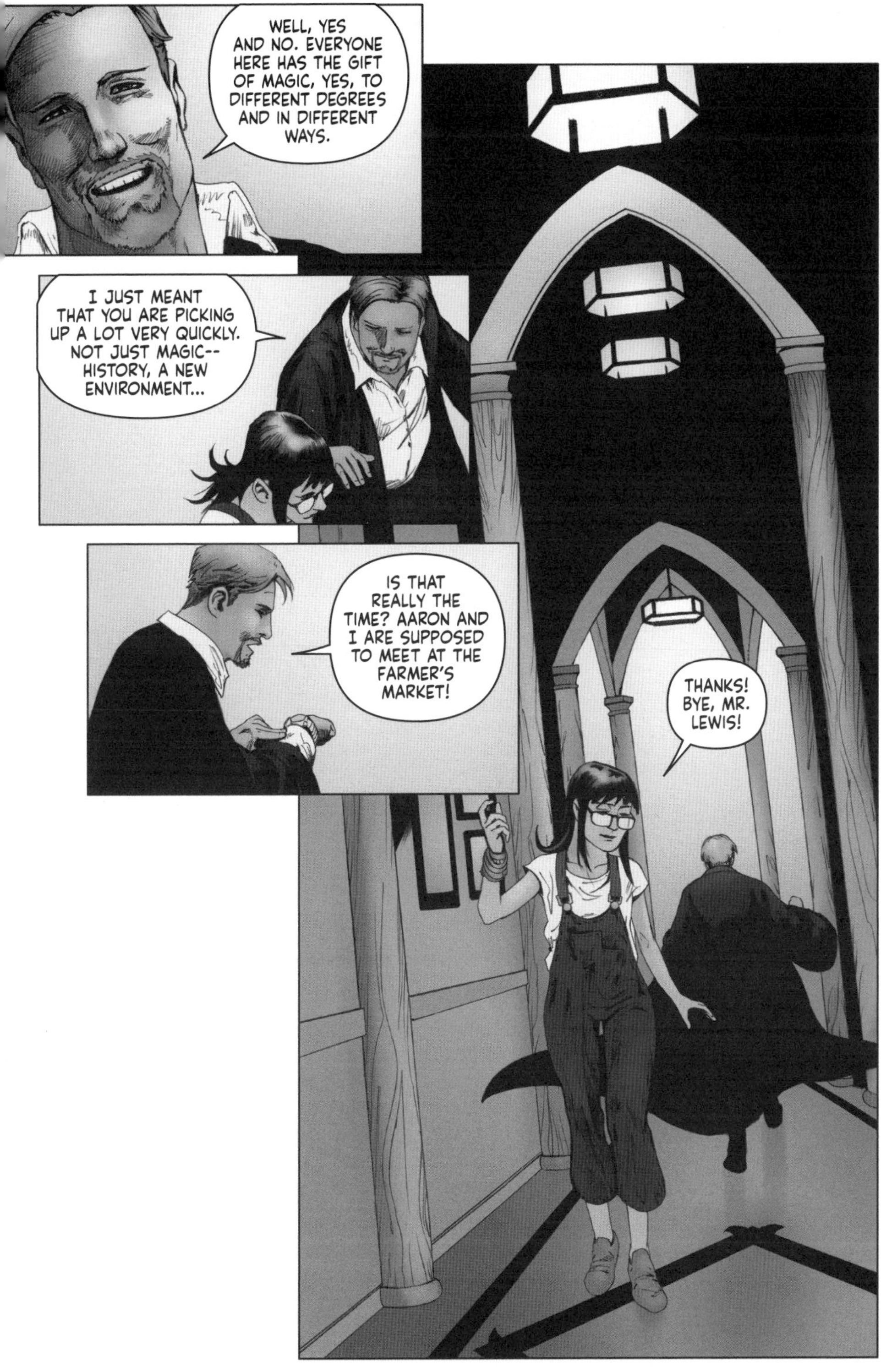
WELL, YES AND NO. EVERYONE HERE HAS THE GIFT OF MAGIC, YES, TO DIFFERENT DEGREES AND IN DIFFERENT WAYS.
I JUST MEANT THAT YOU ARE PICKING UP A LOT VERY QUICKLY. NOT JUST MAGIC-- HISTORY, A NEW ENVIRONMENT...
IS THAT REALLY THE TIME? AARON AND I ARE SUPPOSED TO MEET AT THE FARMER'S MARKET!
THANKS! BYE, MR. LEWIS!

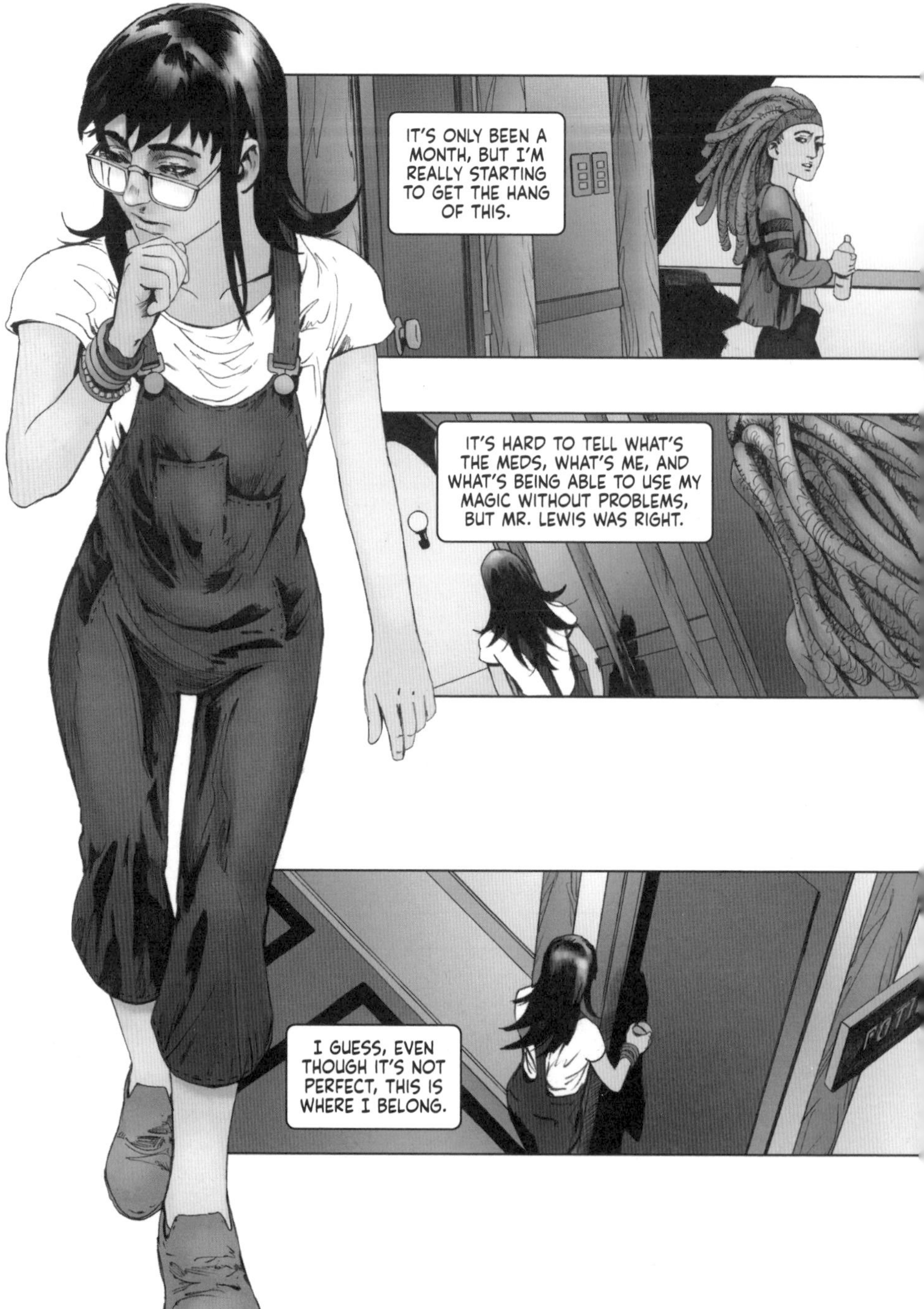
IT'S ONLY BEEN A MONTH, BUT I'M REALLY STARTING TO GET THE HANG OF THIS.
IT'S HARD TO TELL WHAT'S THE MEDS, WHAT'S ME, AND WHAT'S BEING ABLE TO USE MY MAGIC WITHOUT PROBLEMS, BUT MR. LEWIS WAS RIGHT.
I GUESS, EVEN THOUGH IT'S NOT PERFECT, THIS IS WHERE I BELONG.

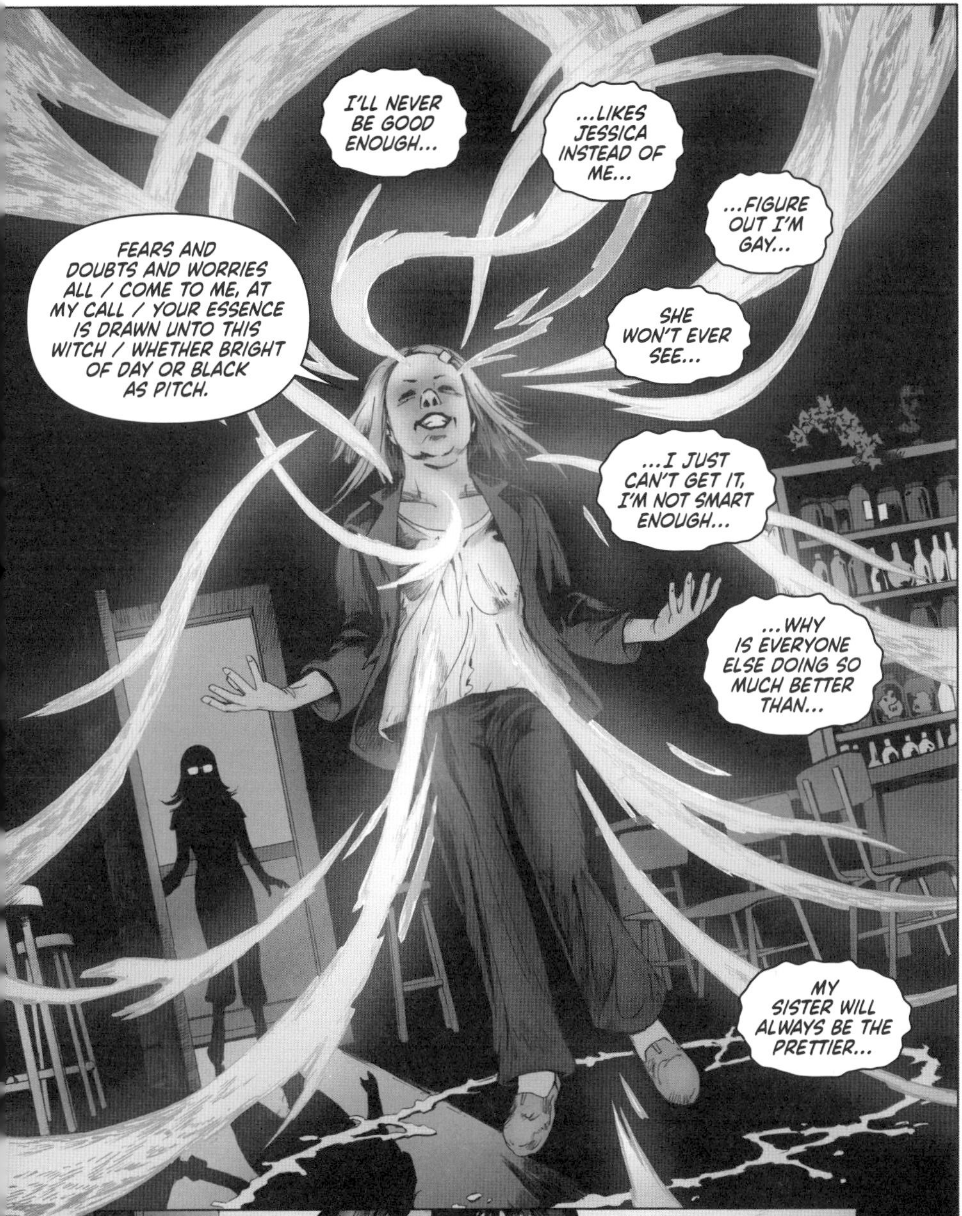
FEARS AND DOUBTS AND WORRIES ALL / COME TO ME, AT MY CALL / YOUR ESSENCE IS DRAWN UNTO THIS WITCH / WHETHER BRIGHT OF DAY OR BLACK AS PITCH.
I'LL NEVER BE GOOD ENOUGH...
...LIKES JESSICA INSTEAD OF ME...
...FIGURE OUT I'M GAY...
SHE WON'T EVER SEE...
...I JUST CAN'T GET IT, I'M NOT SMART ENOUGH...
...WHY IS EVERYONE ELSE DOING SO MUCH BETTER THAN...
MY SISTER WILL ALWAYS BE THE PRETTIER...
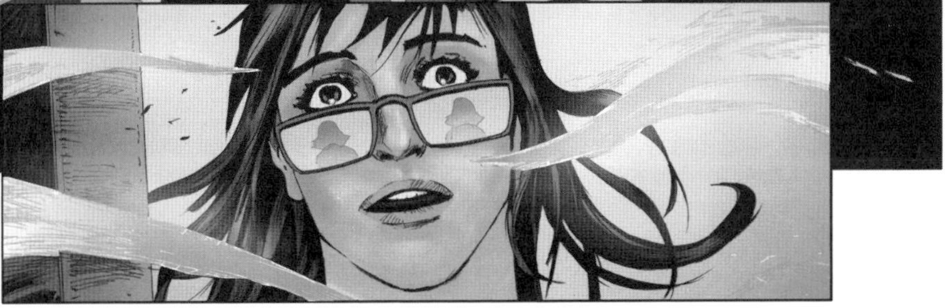

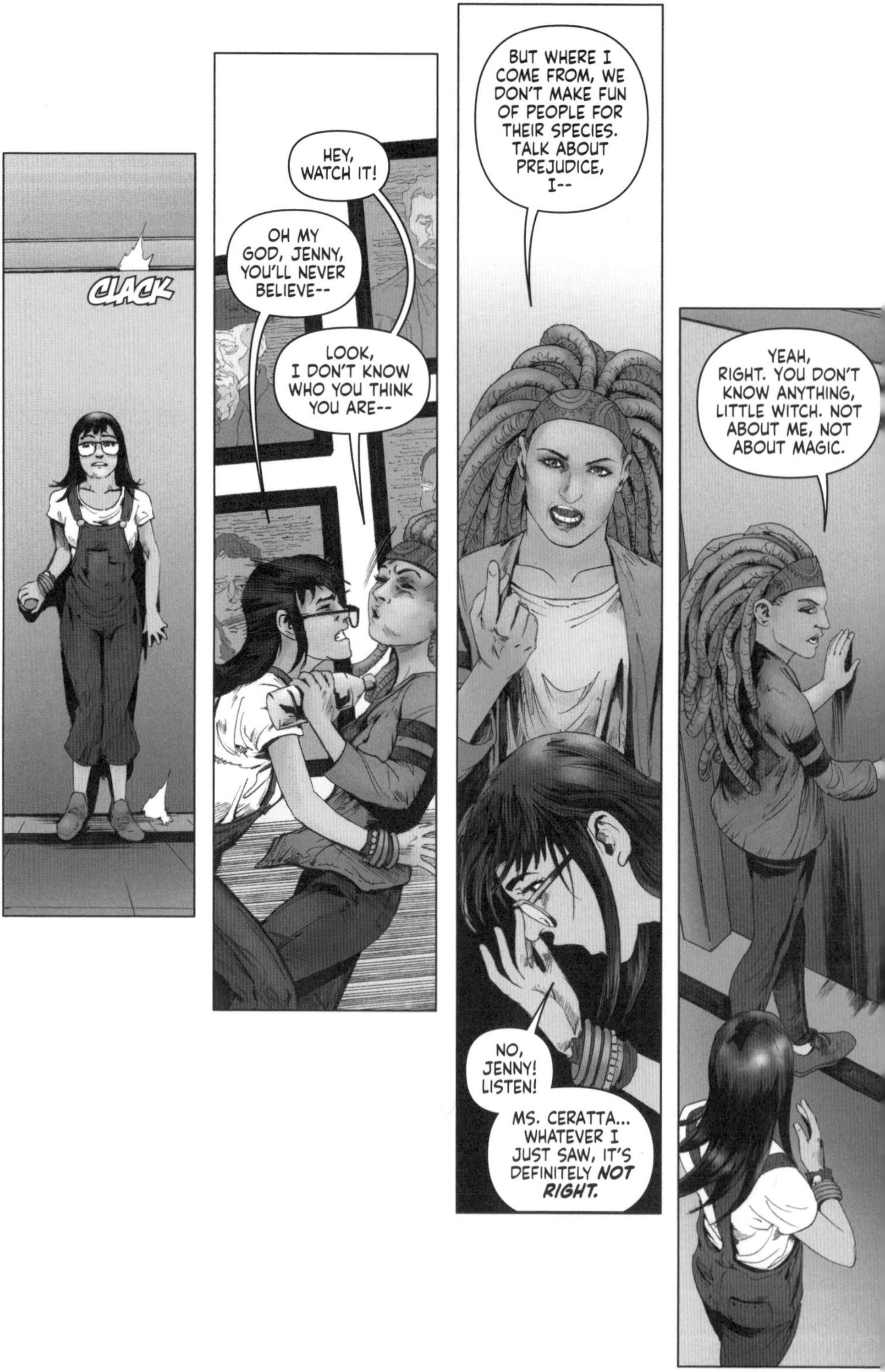
CLACK
HEY, WATCH IT!
OH MY GOD, JENNY, YOU'LL NEVER BELIEVE--
LOOK, I DON'T KNOW WHO YOU THINK YOU ARE--
BUT WHERE I COME FROM, WE DON'T MAKE FUN OF PEOPLE FOR THEIR SPECIES. TALK ABOUT PREJUDICE, I--
NO, JENNY! LISTEN!
MS. CERATTA... WHATEVER I JUST SAW, IT'S DEFINITELY **NOT RIGHT.**
YEAH, RIGHT. YOU DON'T KNOW ANYTHING, LITTLE WITCH. NOT ABOUT ME, NOT ABOUT MAGIC.

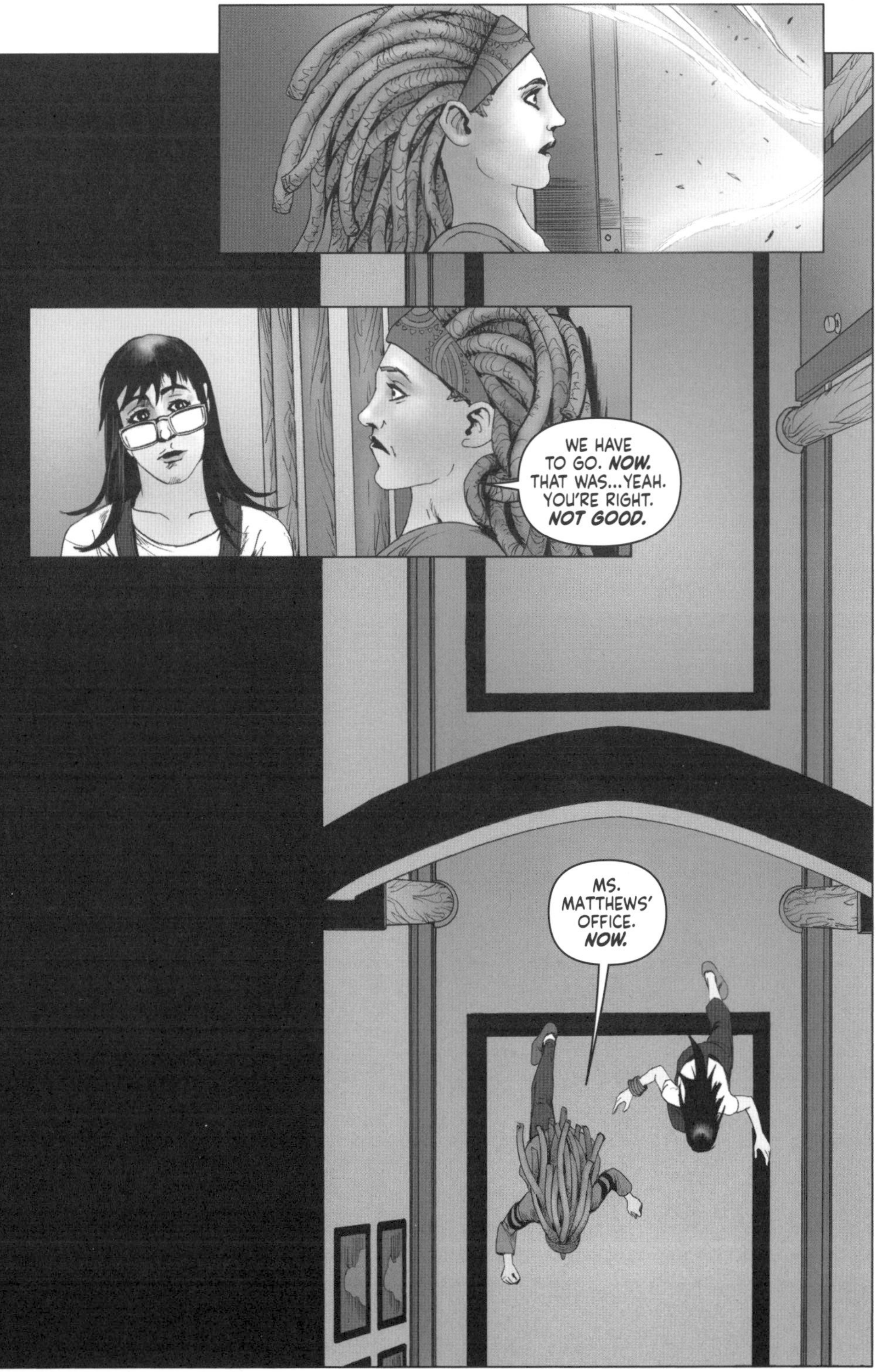
WE HAVE TO GO. NOW. THAT WAS...YEAH. YOU'RE RIGHT. NOT GOOD.
MS. MATTHEWS' OFFICE. NOW.

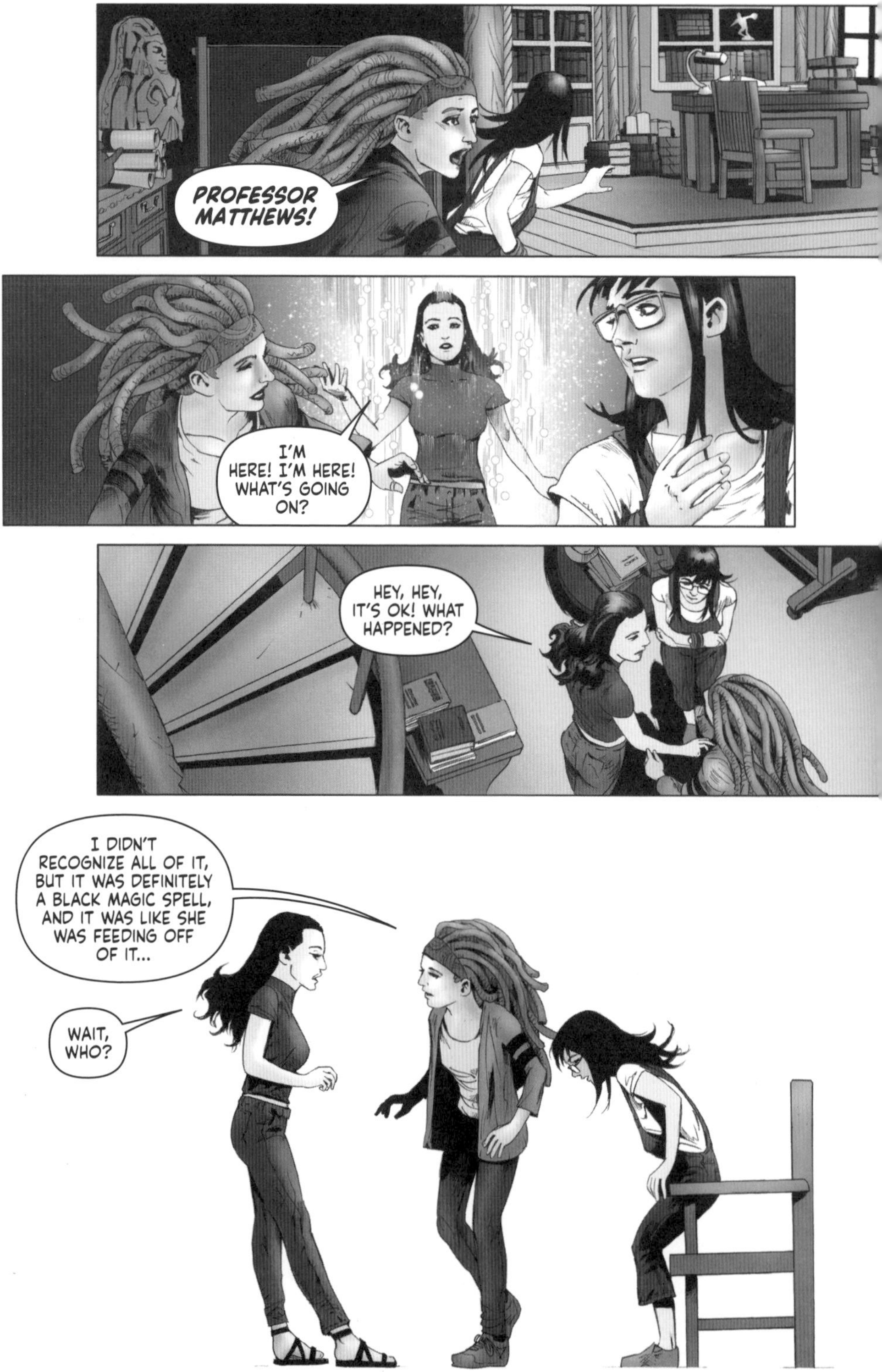
PROFESSOR MATTHEWS!
I'M HERE! I'M HERE! WHAT'S GOING ON?
HEY, HEY, IT'S OK! WHAT HAPPENED?
I DIDN'T RECOGNIZE ALL OF IT, BUT IT WAS DEFINITELY A BLACK MAGIC SPELL, AND IT WAS LIKE SHE WAS FEEDING OFF OF IT...
WAIT, WHO?

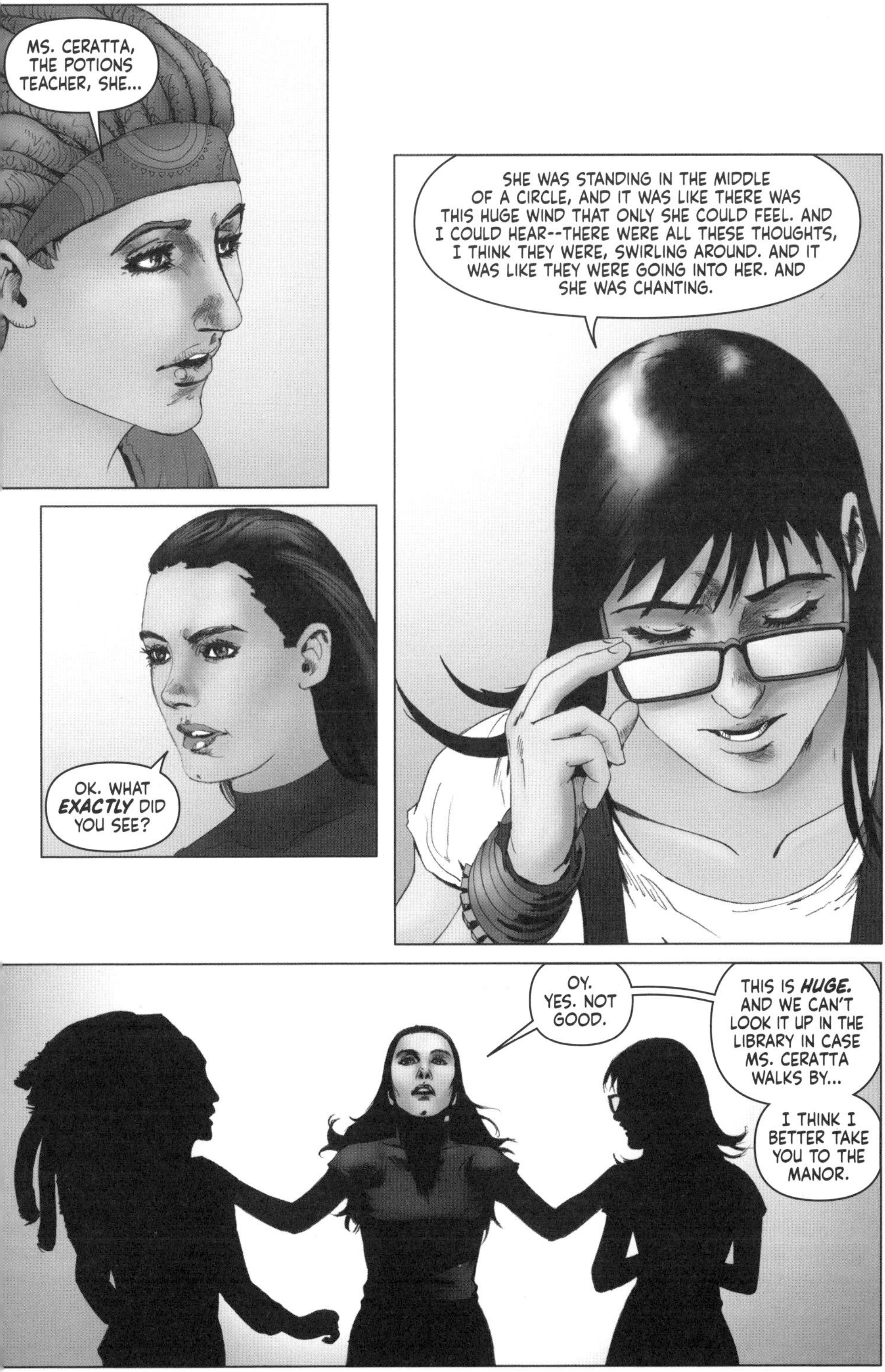
MS. CERATTA, THE POTIONS TEACHER, SHE...
OK. WHAT ***EXACTLY*** DID YOU SEE?
SHE WAS STANDING IN THE MIDDLE OF A CIRCLE, AND IT WAS LIKE THERE WAS THIS HUGE WIND THAT ONLY SHE COULD FEEL. AND I COULD HEAR--THERE WERE ALL THESE THOUGHTS, I THINK THEY WERE, SWIRLING AROUND. AND IT WAS LIKE THEY WERE GOING INTO HER. AND SHE WAS CHANTING.
OY. YES. NOT GOOD.
THIS IS ***HUGE.*** AND WE CAN'T LOOK IT UP IN THE LIBRARY IN CASE MS. CERATTA WALKS BY...
I THINK I BETTER TAKE YOU TO THE MANOR.

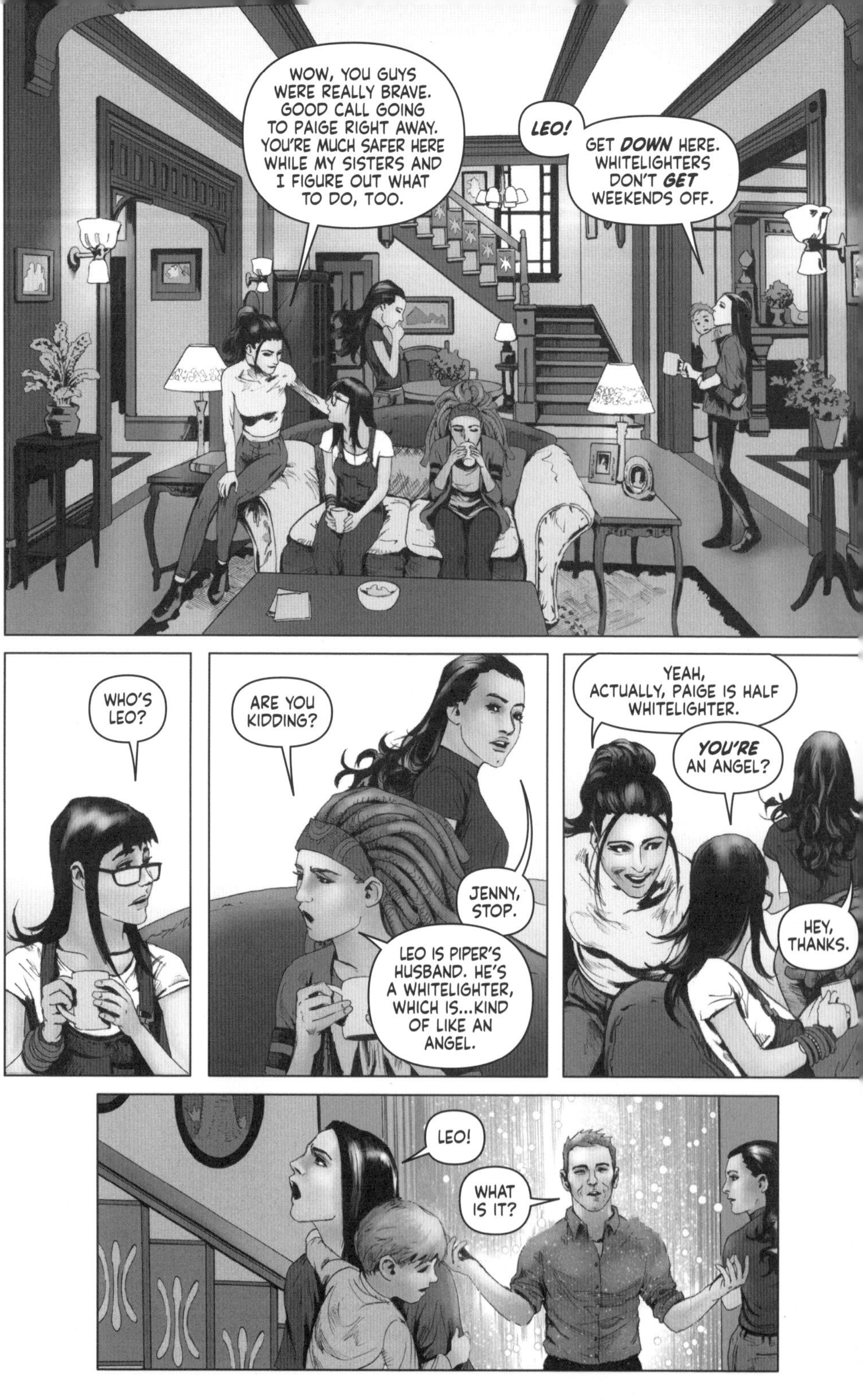
WOW, YOU GUYS WERE REALLY BRAVE. GOOD CALL GOING TO PAIGE RIGHT AWAY. YOU'RE MUCH SAFER HERE WHILE MY SISTERS AND I FIGURE OUT WHAT TO DO, TOO.
LEO!
GET **DOWN** HERE. WHITELIGHTERS DON'T **GET** WEEKENDS OFF.
WHO'S LEO?
ARE YOU KIDDING?
JENNY, STOP.
LEO IS PIPER'S HUSBAND. HE'S A WHITELIGHTER, WHICH IS...KIND OF LIKE AN ANGEL.
YEAH, ACTUALLY, PAIGE IS HALF WHITELIGHTER.
YOU'RE AN ANGEL?
HEY, THANKS.
LEO!
WHAT IS IT?

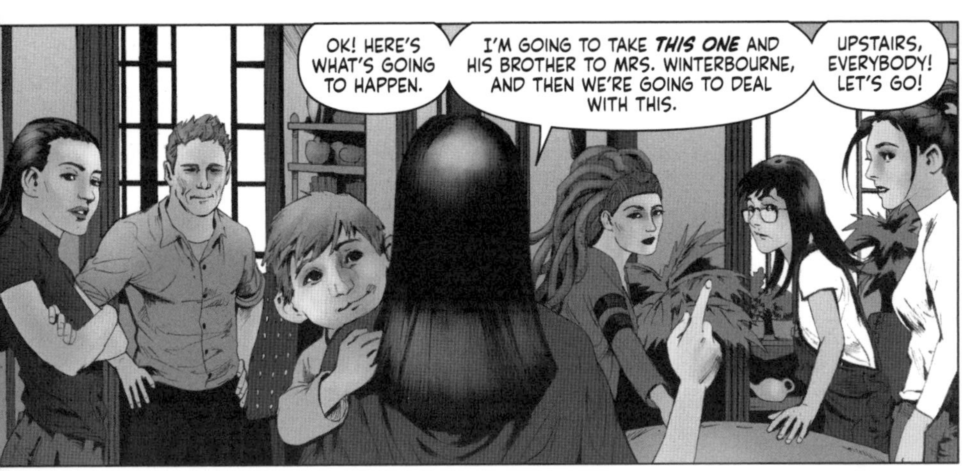
OK! HERE'S WHAT'S GOING TO HAPPEN.
I'M GOING TO TAKE **THIS ONE** AND HIS BROTHER TO MRS. WINTERBOURNE, AND THEN WE'RE GOING TO DEAL WITH THIS.
UPSTAIRS, EVERYBODY! LET'S GO!

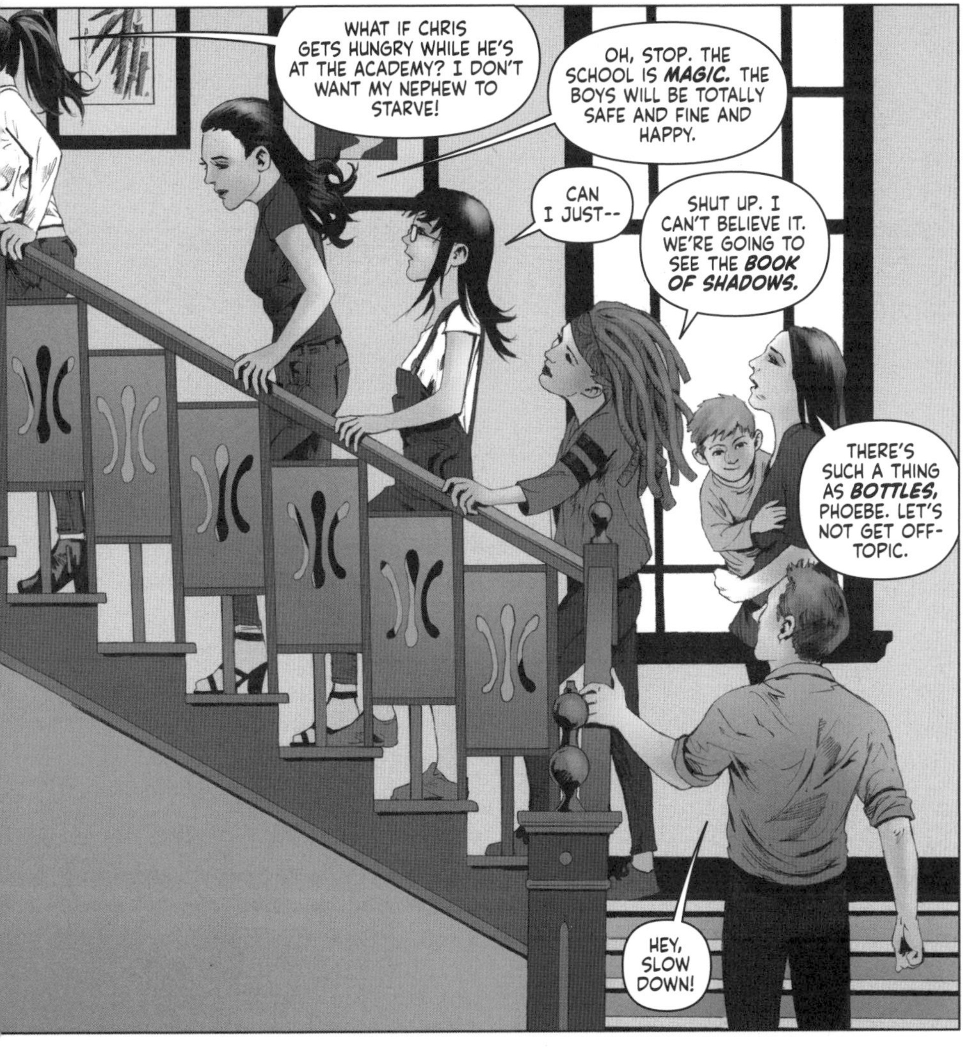
WHAT IF CHRIS GETS HUNGRY WHILE HE'S AT THE ACADEMY? I DON'T WANT MY NEPHEW TO STARVE!
OH, STOP. THE SCHOOL IS **MAGIC.** THE BOYS WILL BE TOTALLY SAFE AND FINE AND HAPPY.
CAN I JUST--
SHUT UP. I CAN'T BELIEVE IT. WE'RE GOING TO SEE THE **BOOK OF SHADOWS.**
THERE'S SUCH A THING AS **BOTTLES,** PHOEBE. LET'S NOT GET OFF-TOPIC.
HEY, SLOW DOWN!

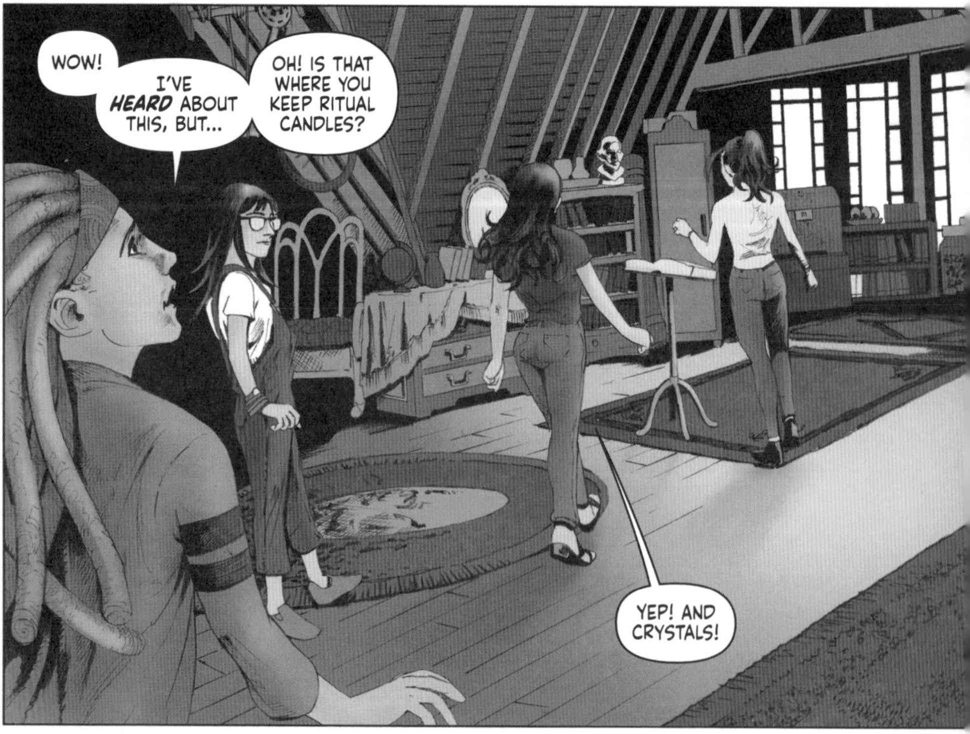
WOW!
I'VE **HEARD** ABOUT THIS, BUT...
OH! IS THAT WHERE YOU KEEP RITUAL CANDLES?
YEP! AND CRYSTALS!

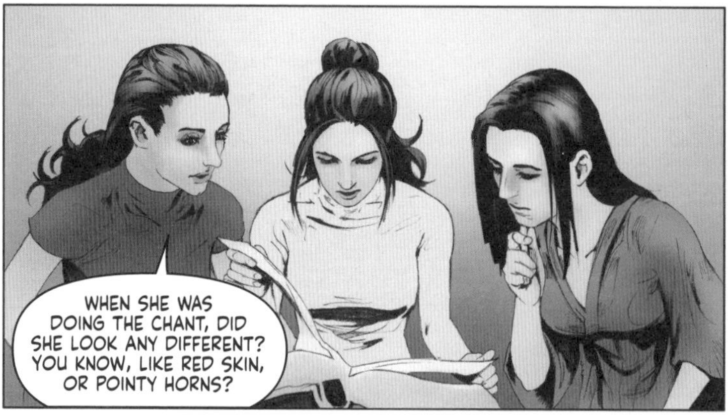
WHEN SHE WAS DOING THE CHANT, DID SHE LOOK ANY DIFFERENT? YOU KNOW, LIKE RED SKIN, OR POINTY HORNS?

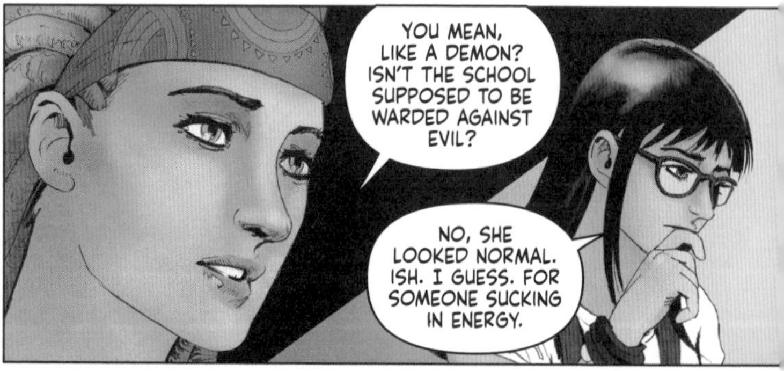
YOU MEAN, LIKE A DEMON? ISN'T THE SCHOOL SUPPOSED TO BE WARDED AGAINST EVIL?
NO, SHE LOOKED NORMAL. ISH. I GUESS. FOR SOMEONE SUCKING IN ENERGY.

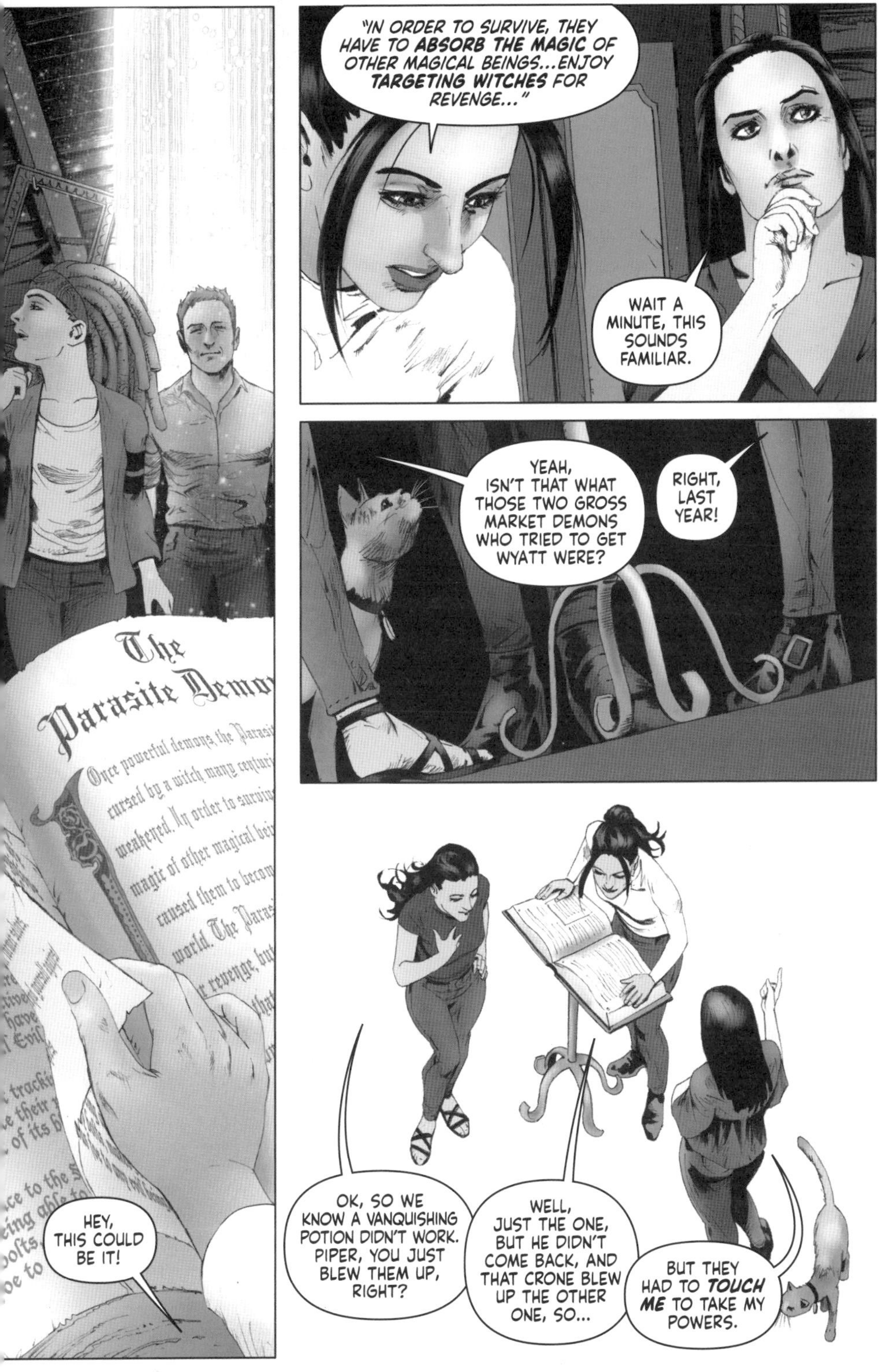
The
Parasite
Once powerful demons, the
cursed by a witch many
weakened. In order to
magic of other magical
caused them to become
world. The
HEY, THIS COULD BE IT!
"IN ORDER TO SURVIVE, THEY HAVE TO ABSORB THE MAGIC OF OTHER MAGICAL BEINGS...ENJOY TARGETING WITCHES FOR REVENGE..."
WAIT A MINUTE, THIS SOUNDS FAMILIAR.
YEAH, ISN'T THAT WHAT THOSE TWO GROSS MARKET DEMONS WHO TRIED TO GET WYATT WERE?
RIGHT, LAST YEAR!
OK, SO WE KNOW A VANQUISHING POTION DIDN'T WORK. PIPER, YOU JUST BLEW THEM UP, RIGHT?
WELL, JUST THE ONE, BUT HE DIDN'T COME BACK, AND THAT CRONE BLEW UP THE OTHER ONE, SO...
BUT THEY HAD TO TOUCH ME TO TAKE MY POWERS.

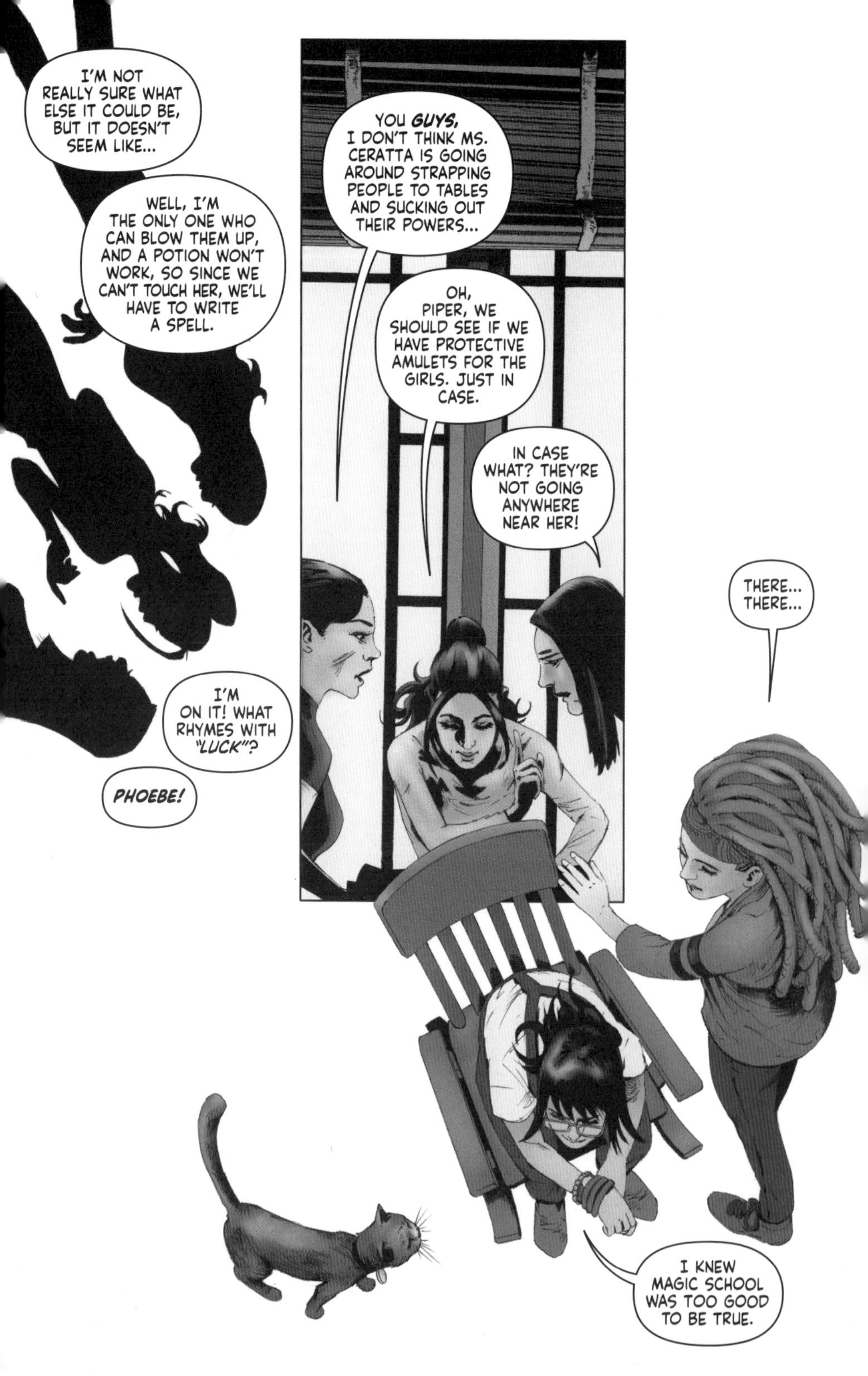
I'M NOT REALLY SURE WHAT ELSE IT COULD BE, BUT IT DOESN'T SEEM LIKE...
WELL, I'M THE ONLY ONE WHO CAN BLOW THEM UP, AND A POTION WON'T WORK, SO SINCE WE CAN'T TOUCH HER, WE'LL HAVE TO WRITE A SPELL.
I'M ON IT! WHAT RHYMES WITH *"LUCK"*?
PHOEBE!
YOU ***GUYS,*** I DON'T THINK MS. CERATTA IS GOING AROUND STRAPPING PEOPLE TO TABLES AND SUCKING OUT THEIR POWERS...
OH, PIPER, WE SHOULD SEE IF WE HAVE PROTECTIVE AMULETS FOR THE GIRLS. JUST IN CASE.
IN CASE WHAT? THEY'RE NOT GOING ANYWHERE NEAR HER!
THERE... THERE...
I KNEW MAGIC SCHOOL WAS TOO GOOD TO BE TRUE.

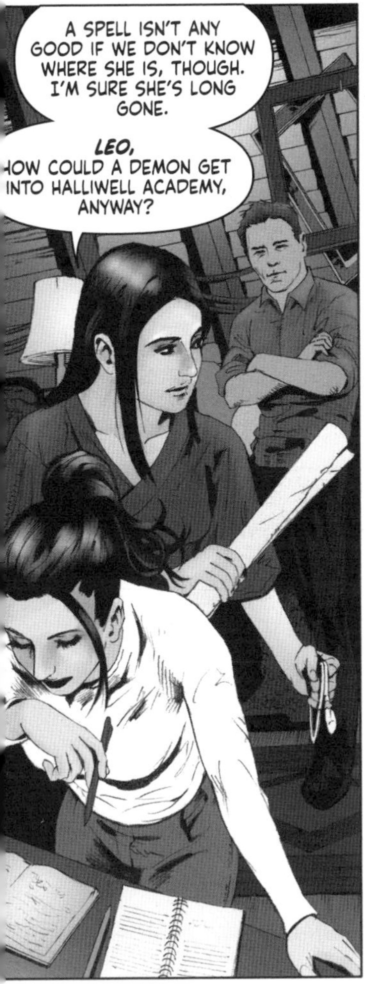
A SPELL ISN'T ANY GOOD IF WE DON'T KNOW WHERE SHE IS, THOUGH. I'M SURE SHE'S LONG GONE.
LEO,
HOW COULD A DEMON GET INTO HALLIWELL ACADEMY, ANYWAY?

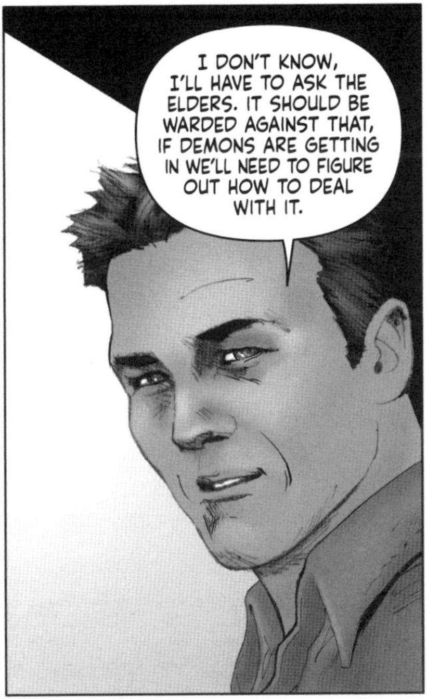
I DON'T KNOW, I'LL HAVE TO ASK THE ELDERS. IT SHOULD BE WARDED AGAINST THAT, IF DEMONS ARE GETTING IN WE'LL NEED TO FIGURE OUT HOW TO DEAL WITH IT.

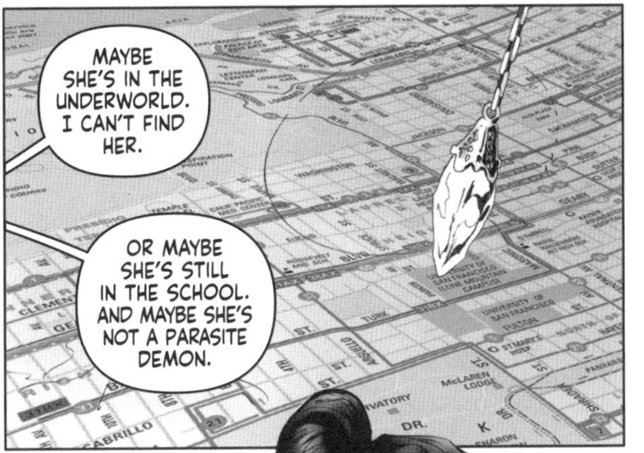
MAYBE SHE'S IN THE UNDERWORLD. I CAN'T FIND HER.
OR MAYBE SHE'S STILL IN THE SCHOOL. AND MAYBE SHE'S NOT A PARASITE DEMON.

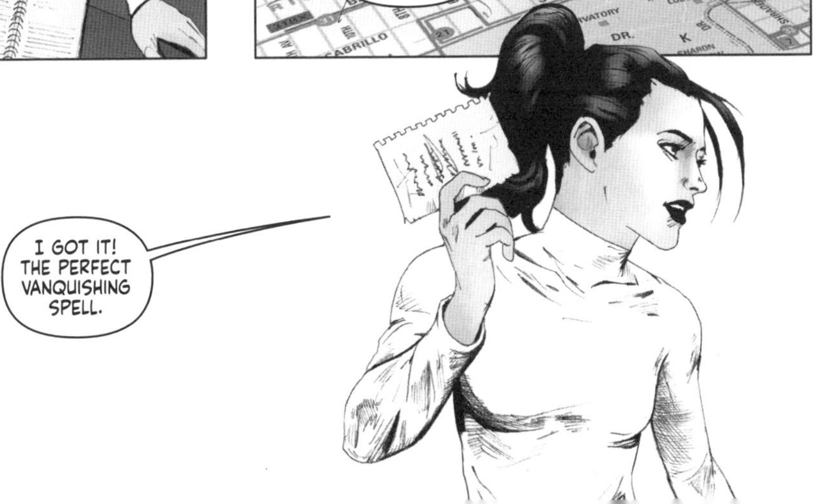
I GOT IT! THE PERFECT VANQUISHING SPELL.

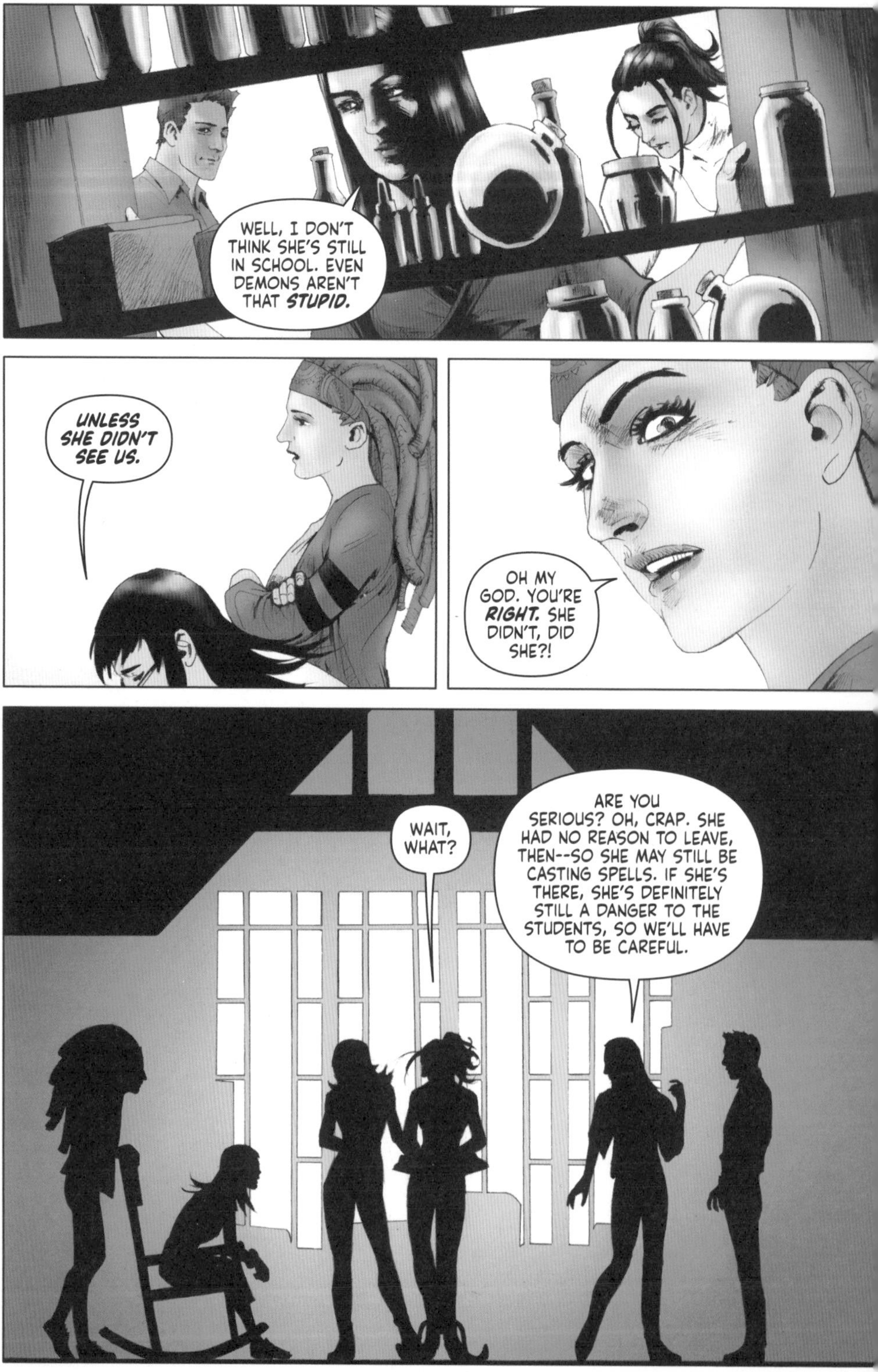
WELL, I DON'T THINK SHE'S STILL IN SCHOOL. EVEN DEMONS AREN'T THAT STUPID.
UNLESS SHE DIDN'T SEE US.
OH MY GOD. YOU'RE RIGHT. SHE DIDN'T, DID SHE?!
WAIT, WHAT?
ARE YOU SERIOUS? OH, CRAP. SHE HAD NO REASON TO LEAVE, THEN--SO SHE MAY STILL BE CASTING SPELLS. IF SHE'S THERE, SHE'S DEFINITELY STILL A DANGER TO THE STUDENTS, SO WE'LL HAVE TO BE CAREFUL.

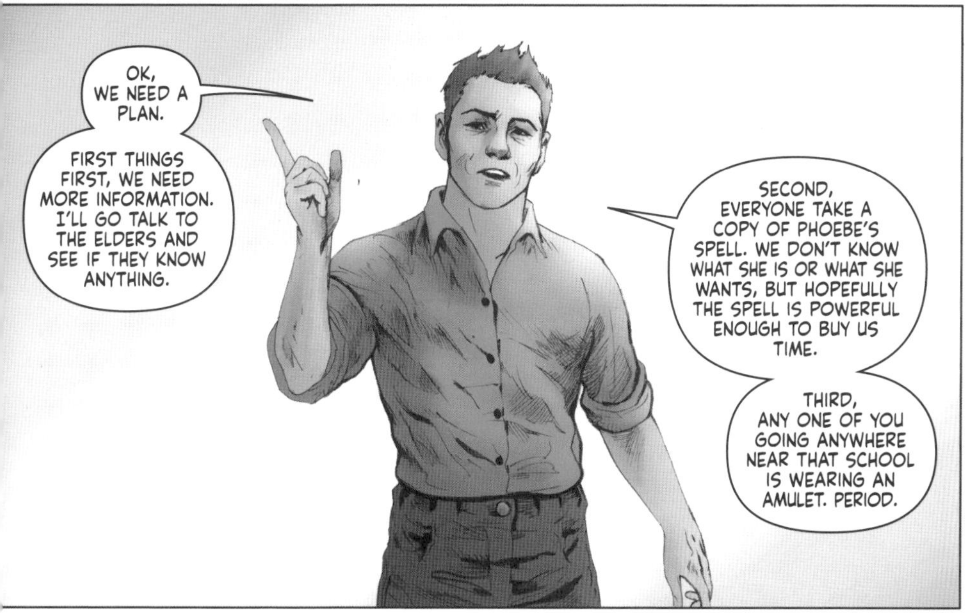
OK, WE NEED A PLAN.
FIRST THINGS FIRST, WE NEED MORE INFORMATION. I'LL GO TALK TO THE ELDERS AND SEE IF THEY KNOW ANYTHING.
SECOND, EVERYONE TAKE A COPY OF PHOEBE'S SPELL. WE DON'T KNOW WHAT SHE IS OR WHAT SHE WANTS, BUT HOPEFULLY THE SPELL IS POWERFUL ENOUGH TO BUY US TIME.
THIRD, ANY ONE OF YOU GOING ANYWHERE NEAR THAT SCHOOL IS WEARING AN AMULET. PERIOD.

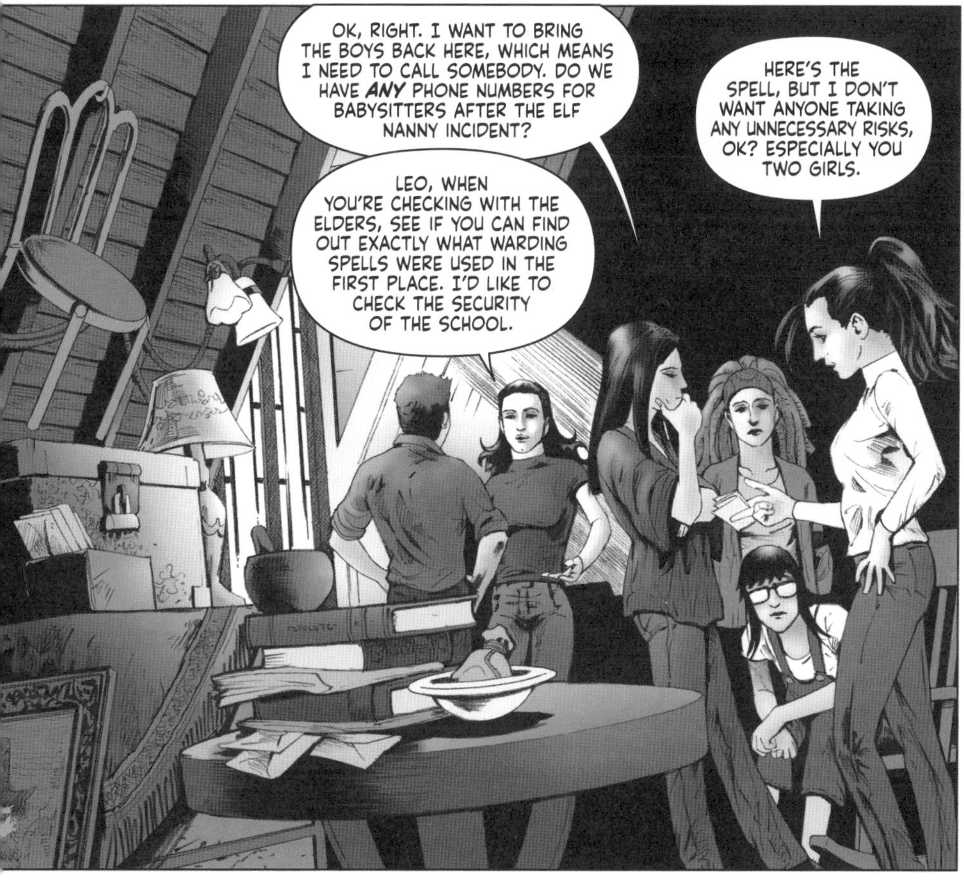
OK, RIGHT. I WANT TO BRING THE BOYS BACK HERE, WHICH MEANS I NEED TO CALL SOMEBODY. DO WE HAVE *ANY* PHONE NUMBERS FOR BABYSITTERS AFTER THE ELF NANNY INCIDENT?
LEO, WHEN YOU'RE CHECKING WITH THE ELDERS, SEE IF YOU CAN FIND OUT EXACTLY WHAT WARDING SPELLS WERE USED IN THE FIRST PLACE. I'D LIKE TO CHECK THE SECURITY OF THE SCHOOL.
HERE'S THE SPELL, BUT I DON'T WANT ANYONE TAKING ANY UNNECESSARY RISKS, OK? ESPECIALLY YOU TWO GIRLS.

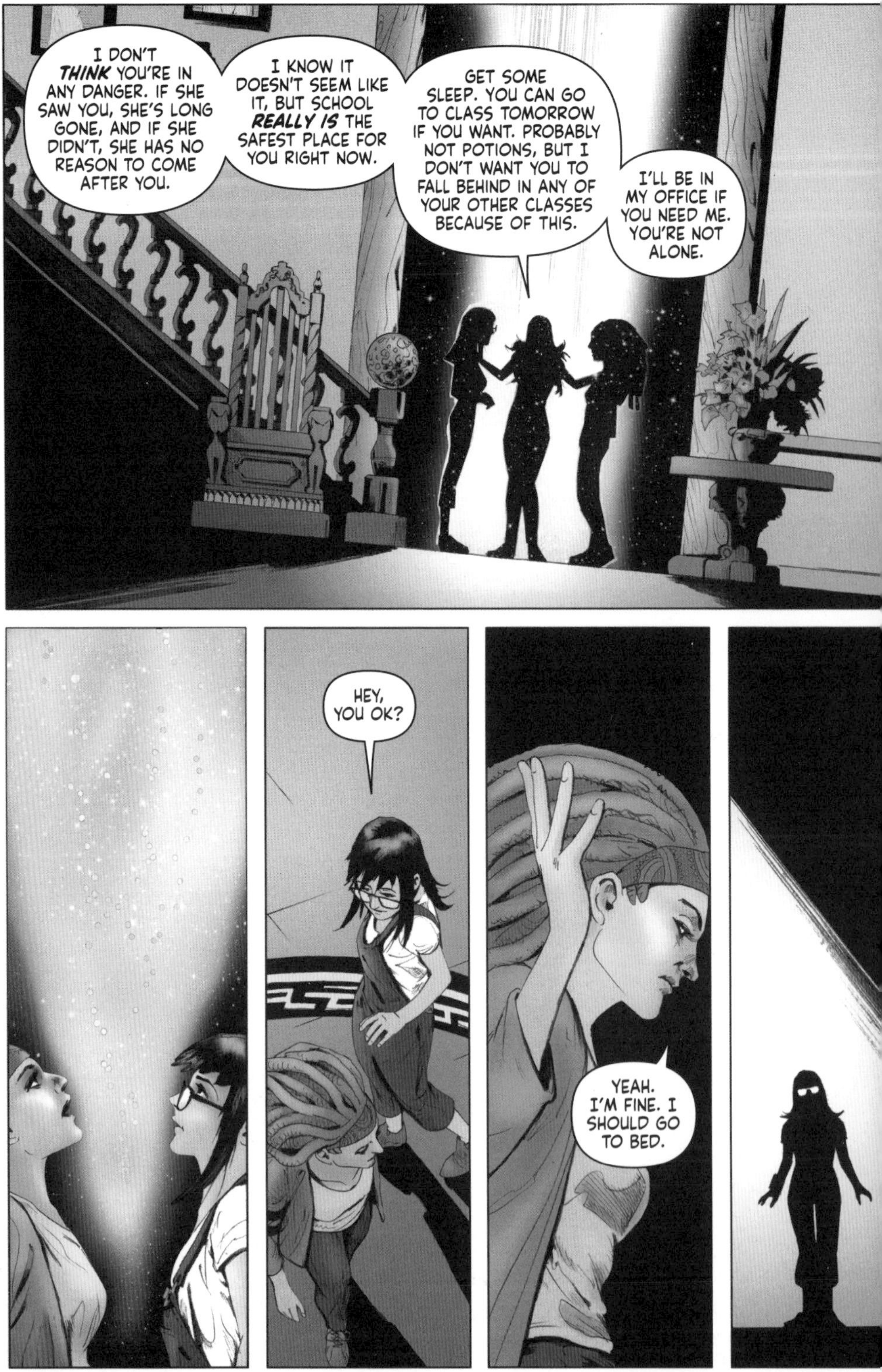
I DON'T **THINK** YOU'RE IN ANY DANGER. IF SHE SAW YOU, SHE'S LONG GONE, AND IF SHE DIDN'T, SHE HAS NO REASON TO COME AFTER YOU.
I KNOW IT DOESN'T SEEM LIKE IT, BUT SCHOOL ***REALLY IS*** THE SAFEST PLACE FOR YOU RIGHT NOW.
GET SOME SLEEP. YOU CAN GO TO CLASS TOMORROW IF YOU WANT. PROBABLY NOT POTIONS, BUT I DON'T WANT YOU TO FALL BEHIND IN ANY OF YOUR OTHER CLASSES BECAUSE OF THIS.
I'LL BE IN MY OFFICE IF YOU NEED ME. YOU'RE NOT ALONE.
HEY, YOU OK?
YEAH. I'M FINE. I SHOULD GO TO BED.

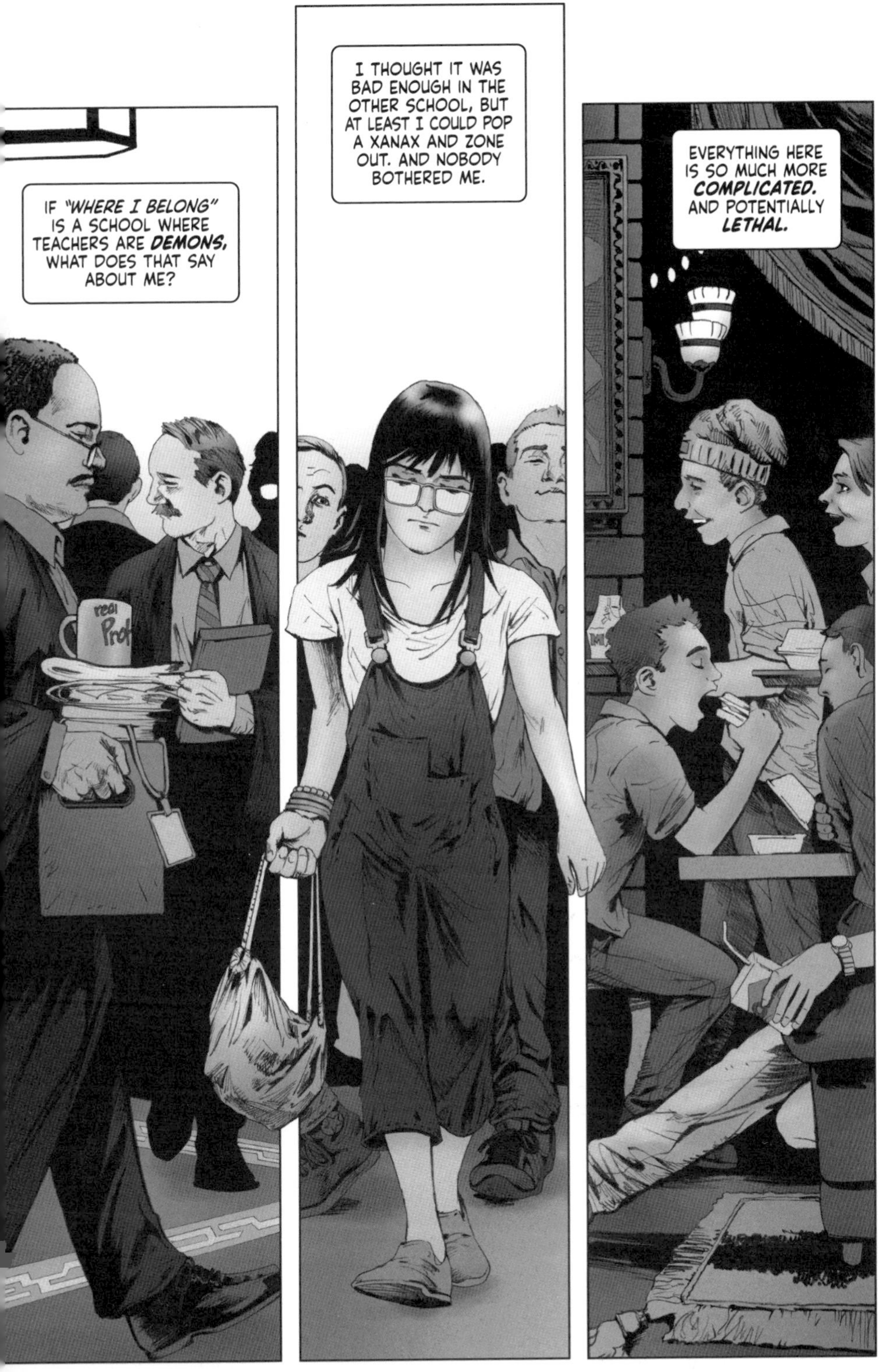
IF *"WHERE I BELONG"* IS A SCHOOL WHERE TEACHERS ARE ***DEMONS,*** WHAT DOES THAT SAY ABOUT ME?
I THOUGHT IT WAS BAD ENOUGH IN THE OTHER SCHOOL, BUT AT LEAST I COULD POP A XANAX AND ZONE OUT. AND NOBODY BOTHERED ME.
EVERYTHING HERE IS SO MUCH MORE ***COMPLICATED.*** AND POTENTIALLY ***LETHAL.***

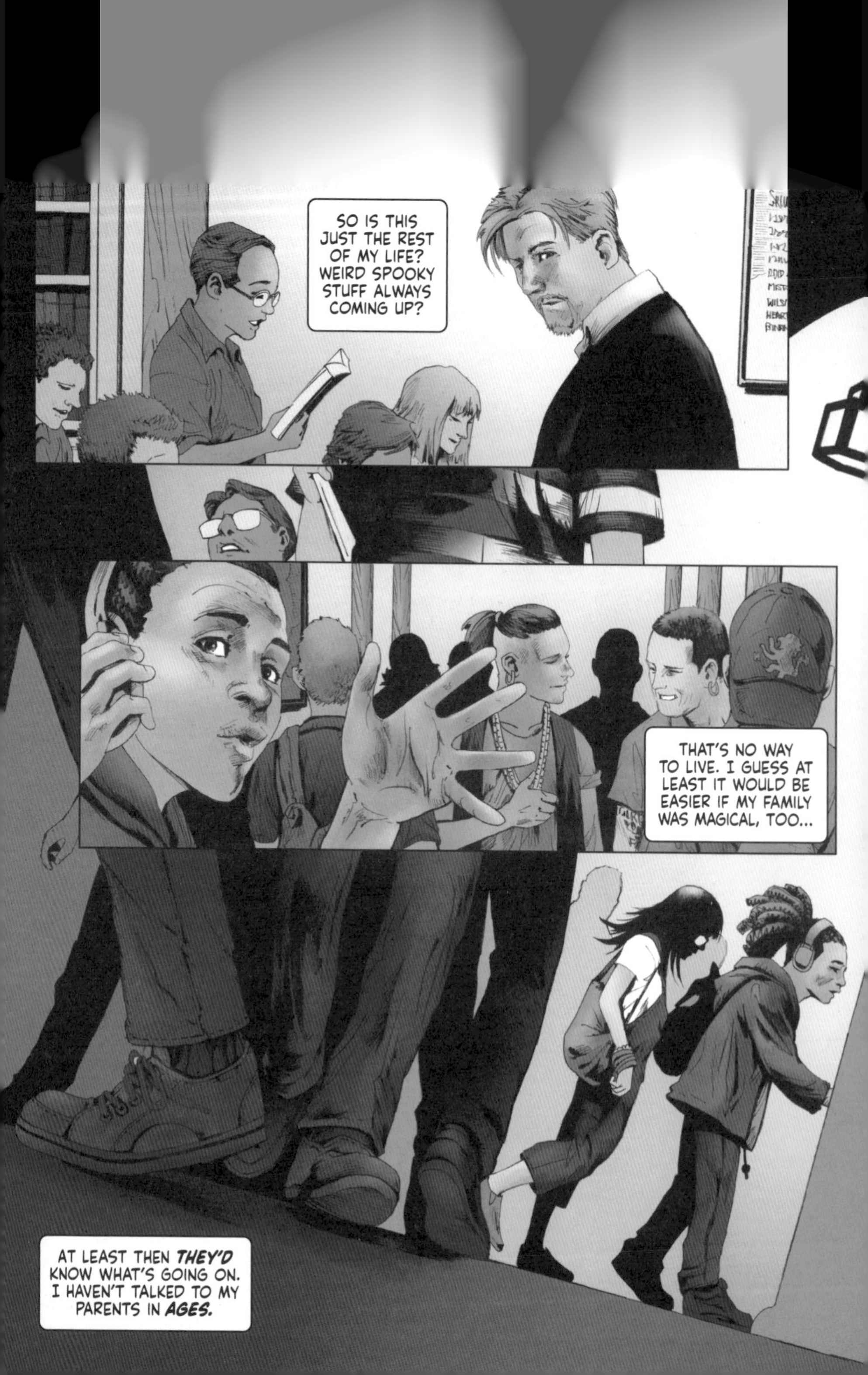
SO IS THIS JUST THE REST OF MY LIFE? WEIRD SPOOKY STUFF ALWAYS COMING UP?
THAT'S NO WAY TO LIVE. I GUESS AT LEAST IT WOULD BE EASIER IF MY FAMILY WAS MAGICAL, TOO...
AT LEAST THEN *THEY'D* KNOW WHAT'S GOING ON. I HAVEN'T TALKED TO MY PARENTS IN *AGES.*

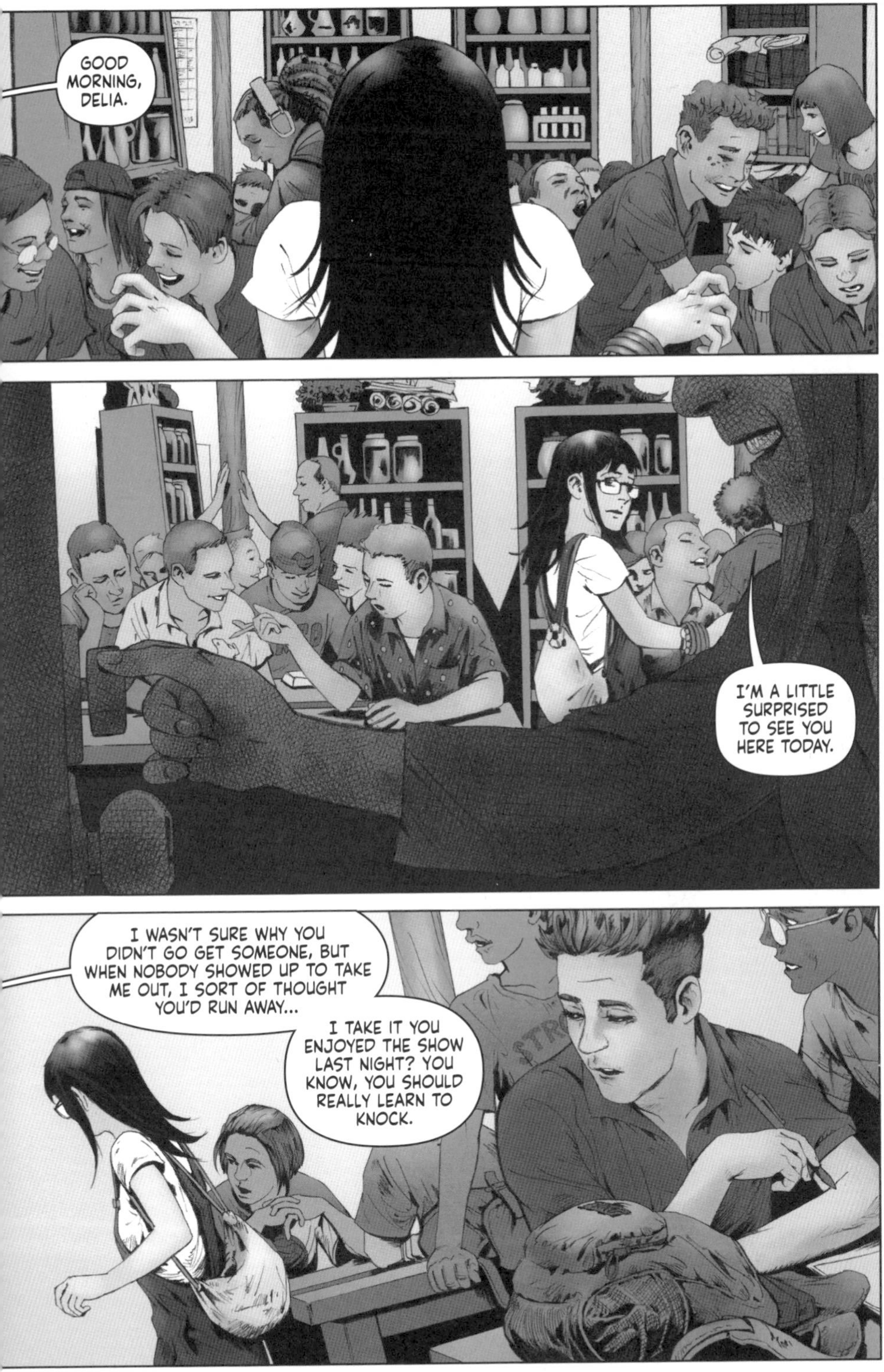
GOOD MORNING, DELIA.
I'M A LITTLE SURPRISED TO SEE YOU HERE TODAY.
I WASN'T SURE WHY YOU DIDN'T GO GET SOMEONE, BUT WHEN NOBODY SHOWED UP TO TAKE ME OUT, I SORT OF THOUGHT YOU'D RUN AWAY...
I TAKE IT YOU ENJOYED THE SHOW LAST NIGHT? YOU KNOW, YOU SHOULD REALLY LEARN TO KNOCK.

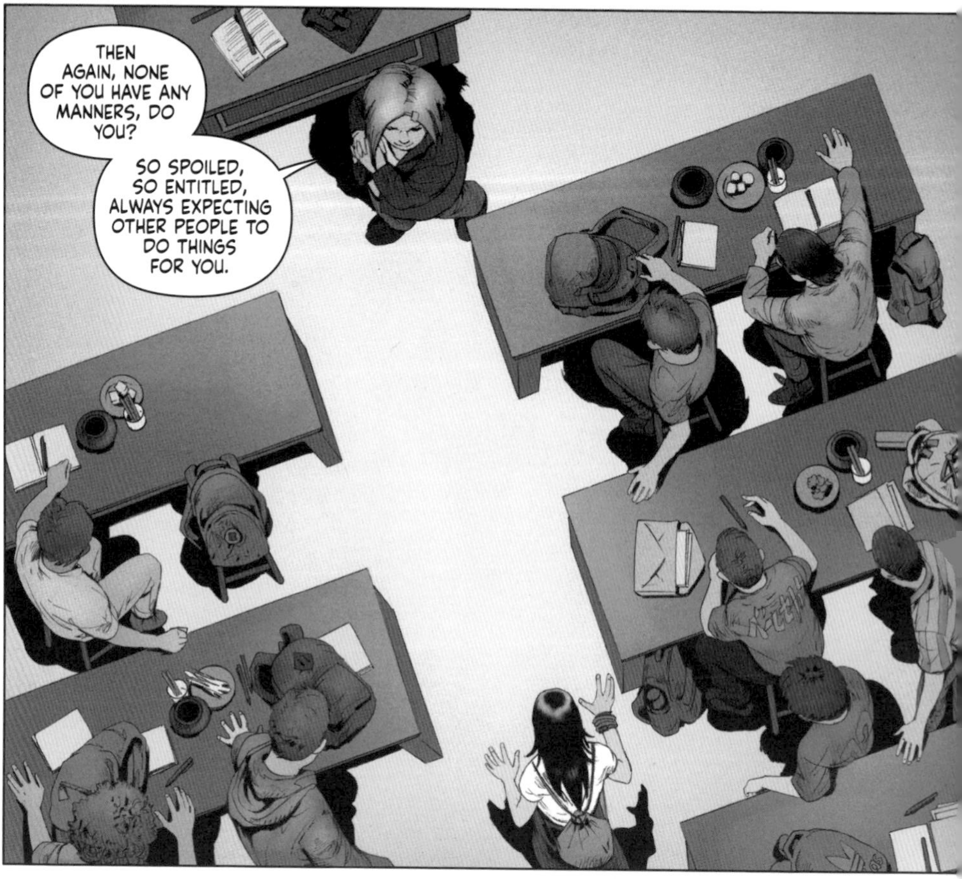
THEN AGAIN, NONE OF YOU HAVE ANY MANNERS, DO YOU?
SO SPOILED, SO ENTITLED, ALWAYS EXPECTING OTHER PEOPLE TO DO THINGS FOR YOU.

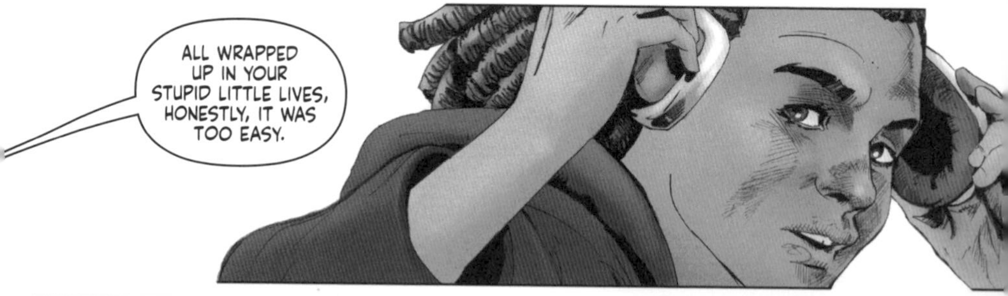
ALL WRAPPED UP IN YOUR STUPID LITTLE LIVES, HONESTLY, IT WAS TOO EASY.

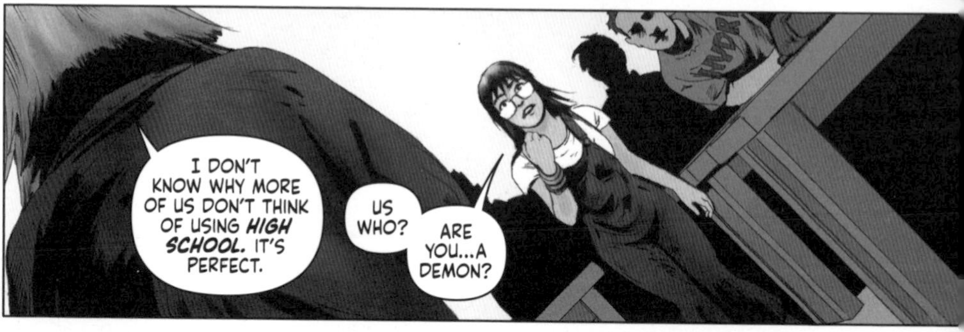
I DON'T KNOW WHY MORE OF US DON'T THINK OF USING ***HIGH SCHOOL.*** IT'S PERFECT.
US WHO?
ARE YOU...A DEMON?

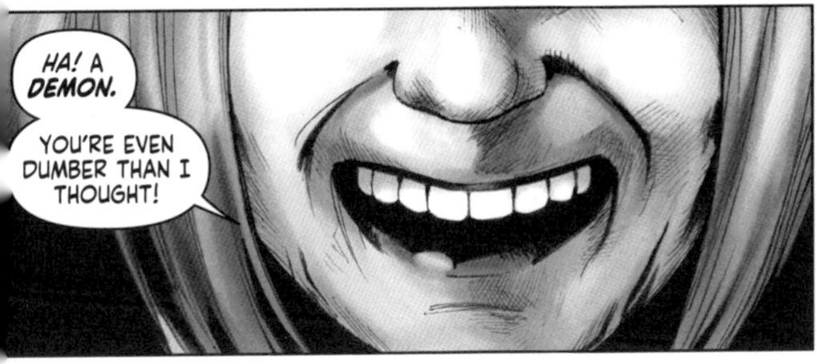
HA! A *DEMON.*
YOU'RE EVEN DUMBER THAN I THOUGHT!

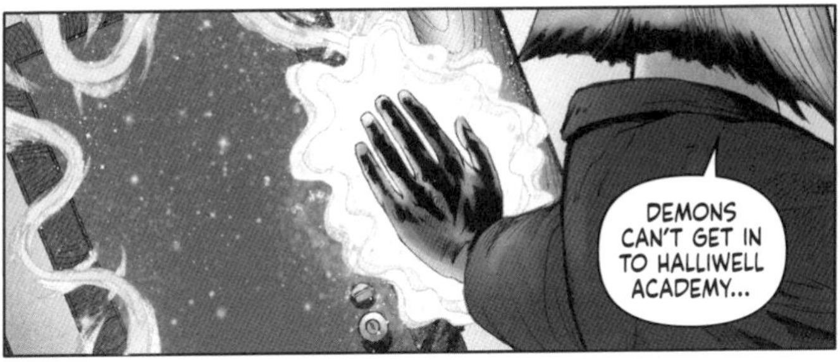
DEMONS CAN'T GET IN TO HALLIWELL ACADEMY...

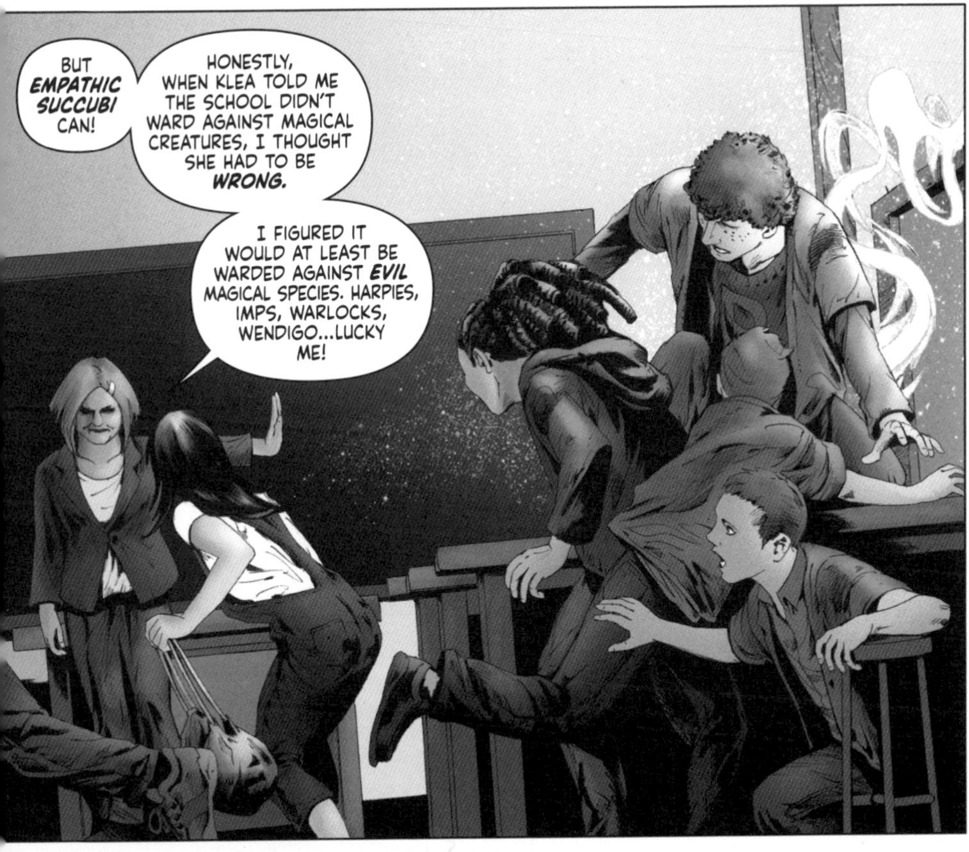
BUT *EMPATHIC SUCCUBI* CAN!
HONESTLY, WHEN KLEA TOLD ME THE SCHOOL DIDN'T WARD AGAINST MAGICAL CREATURES, I THOUGHT SHE HAD TO BE *WRONG.*
I FIGURED IT WOULD AT LEAST BE WARDED AGAINST *EVIL* MAGICAL SPECIES. HARPIES, IMPS, WARLOCKS, WENDIGO...LUCKY ME!

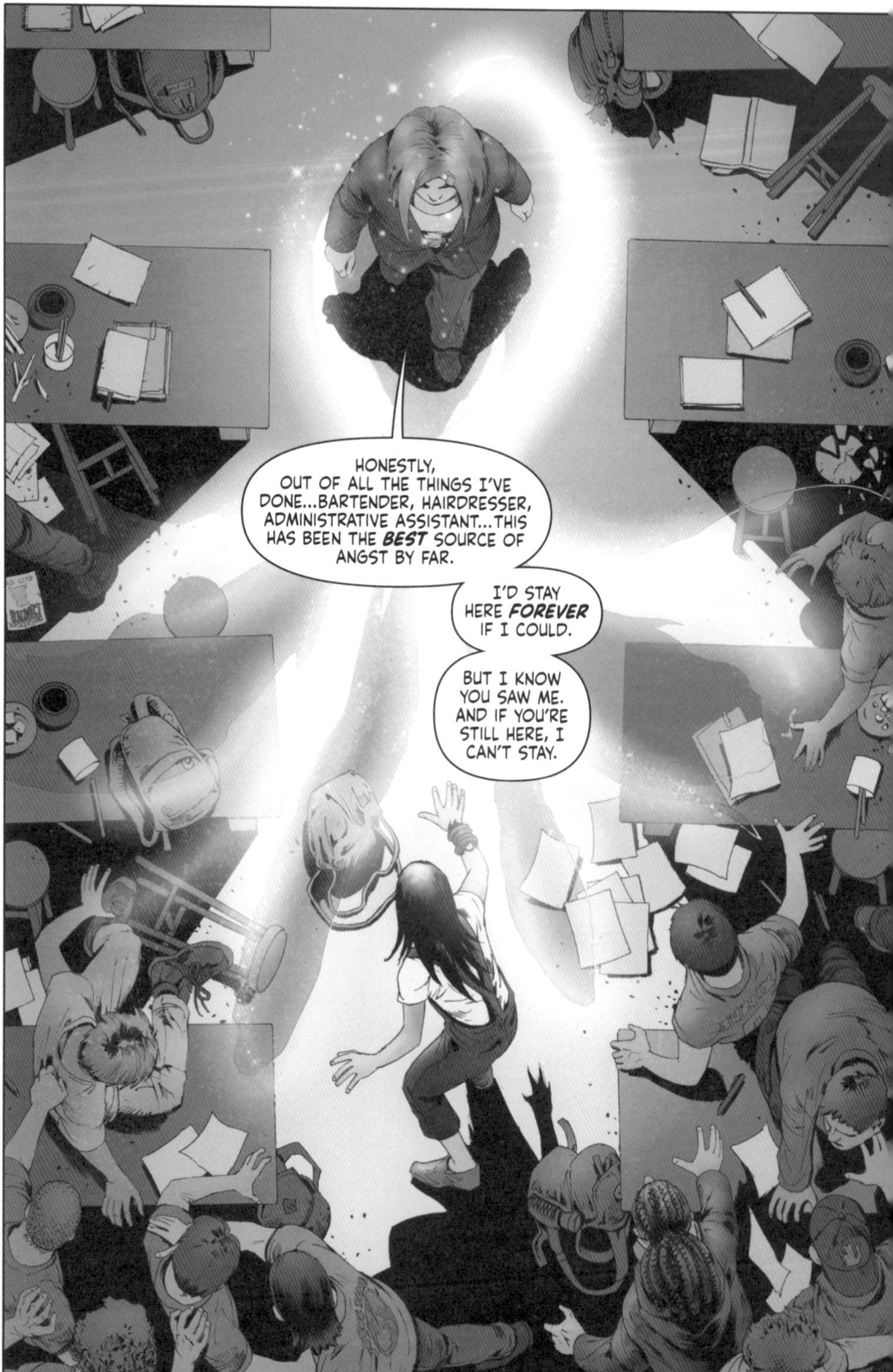
HONESTLY, OUT OF ALL THE THINGS I'VE DONE...BARTENDER, HAIRDRESSER, ADMINISTRATIVE ASSISTANT...THIS HAS BEEN THE ***BEST*** SOURCE OF ANGST BY FAR.
I'D STAY HERE ***FOREVER*** IF I COULD.
BUT I KNOW YOU SAW ME. AND IF YOU'RE STILL HERE, I CAN'T STAY.

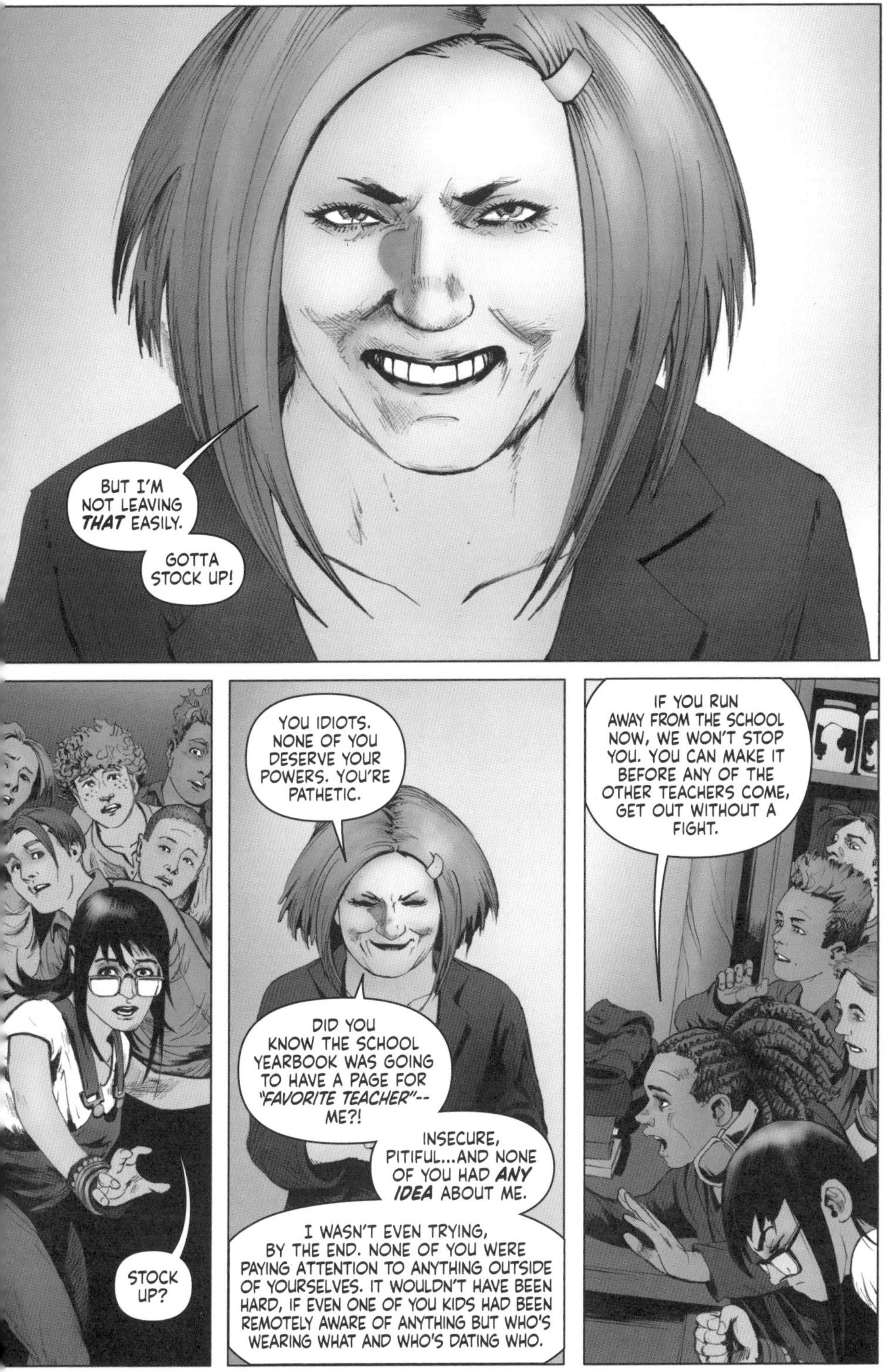
BUT I'M NOT LEAVING *THAT* EASILY.
GOTTA STOCK UP!
STOCK UP?
YOU IDIOTS. NONE OF YOU DESERVE YOUR POWERS. YOU'RE PATHETIC.
DID YOU KNOW THE SCHOOL YEARBOOK WAS GOING TO HAVE A PAGE FOR *"FAVORITE TEACHER"*-- ME?!
INSECURE, PITIFUL...AND NONE OF YOU HAD *ANY IDEA* ABOUT ME.
I WASN'T EVEN TRYING, BY THE END. NONE OF YOU WERE PAYING ATTENTION TO ANYTHING OUTSIDE OF YOURSELVES. IT WOULDN'T HAVE BEEN HARD, IF EVEN ONE OF YOU KIDS HAD BEEN REMOTELY AWARE OF ANYTHING BUT WHO'S WEARING WHAT AND WHO'S DATING WHO.
IF YOU RUN AWAY FROM THE SCHOOL NOW, WE WON'T STOP YOU. YOU CAN MAKE IT BEFORE ANY OF THE OTHER TEACHERS COME, GET OUT WITHOUT A FIGHT.

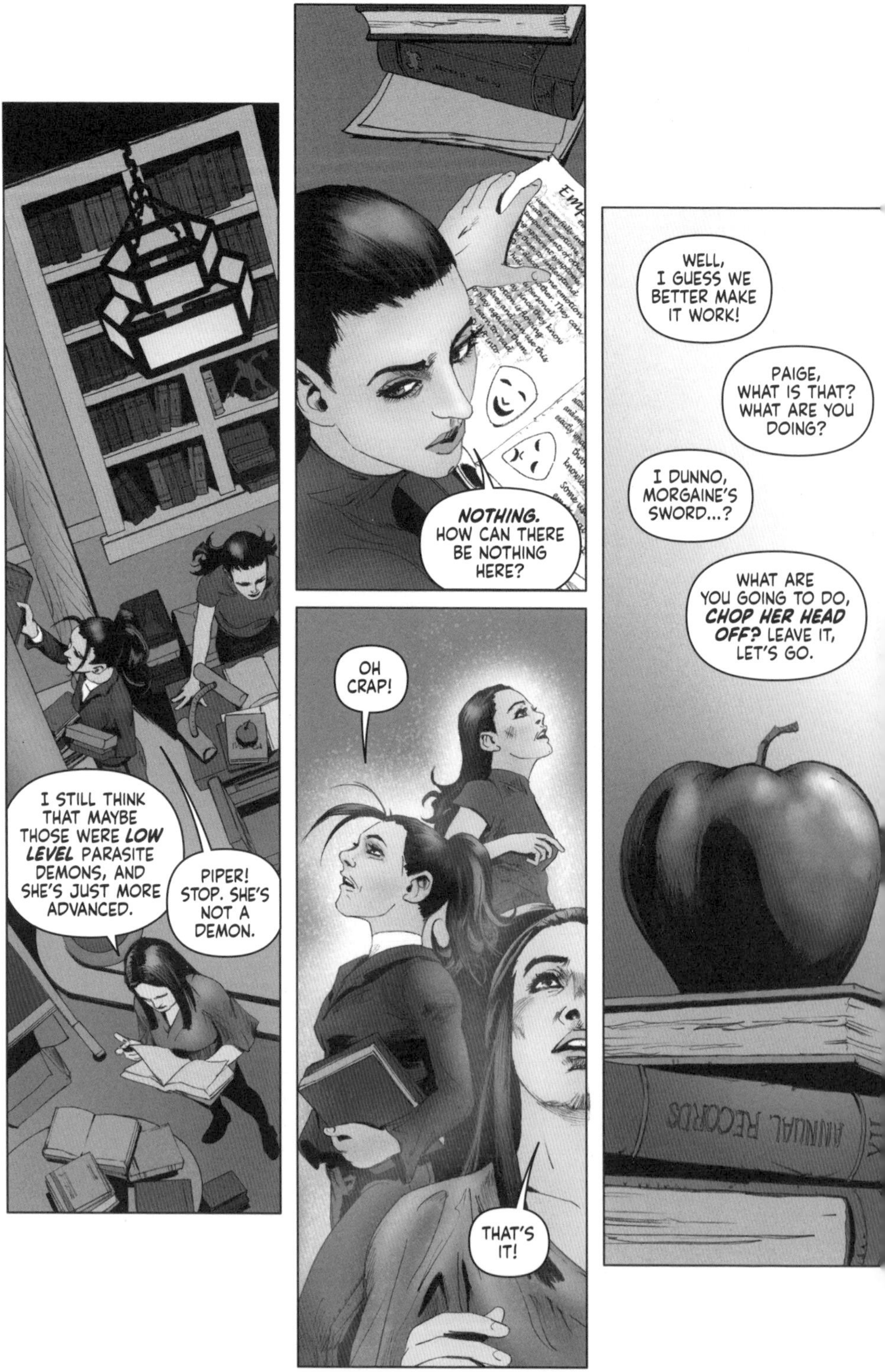
I STILL THINK THAT MAYBE THOSE WERE **LOW LEVEL** PARASITE DEMONS, AND SHE'S JUST MORE ADVANCED.
PIPER! STOP. SHE'S NOT A DEMON.
NOTHING. HOW CAN THERE BE NOTHING HERE?
OH CRAP!
THAT'S IT!
WELL, I GUESS WE BETTER MAKE IT WORK!
PAIGE, WHAT IS THAT? WHAT ARE YOU DOING?
I DUNNO, MORGAINE'S SWORD...?
WHAT ARE YOU GOING TO DO, **CHOP HER HEAD OFF?** LEAVE IT, LET'S GO.

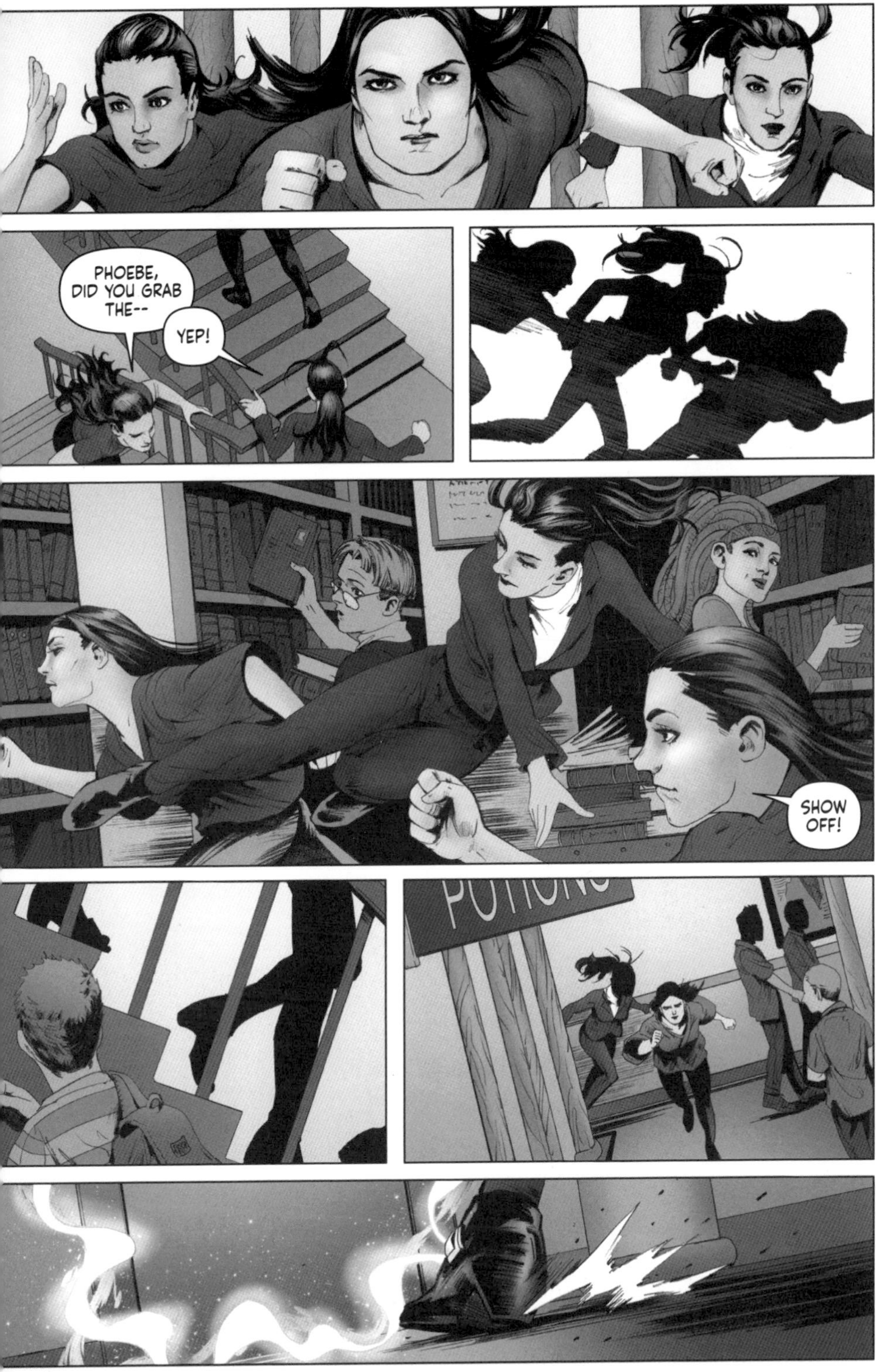
PHOEBE, DID YOU GRAB THE--
YEP!
SHOW OFF!

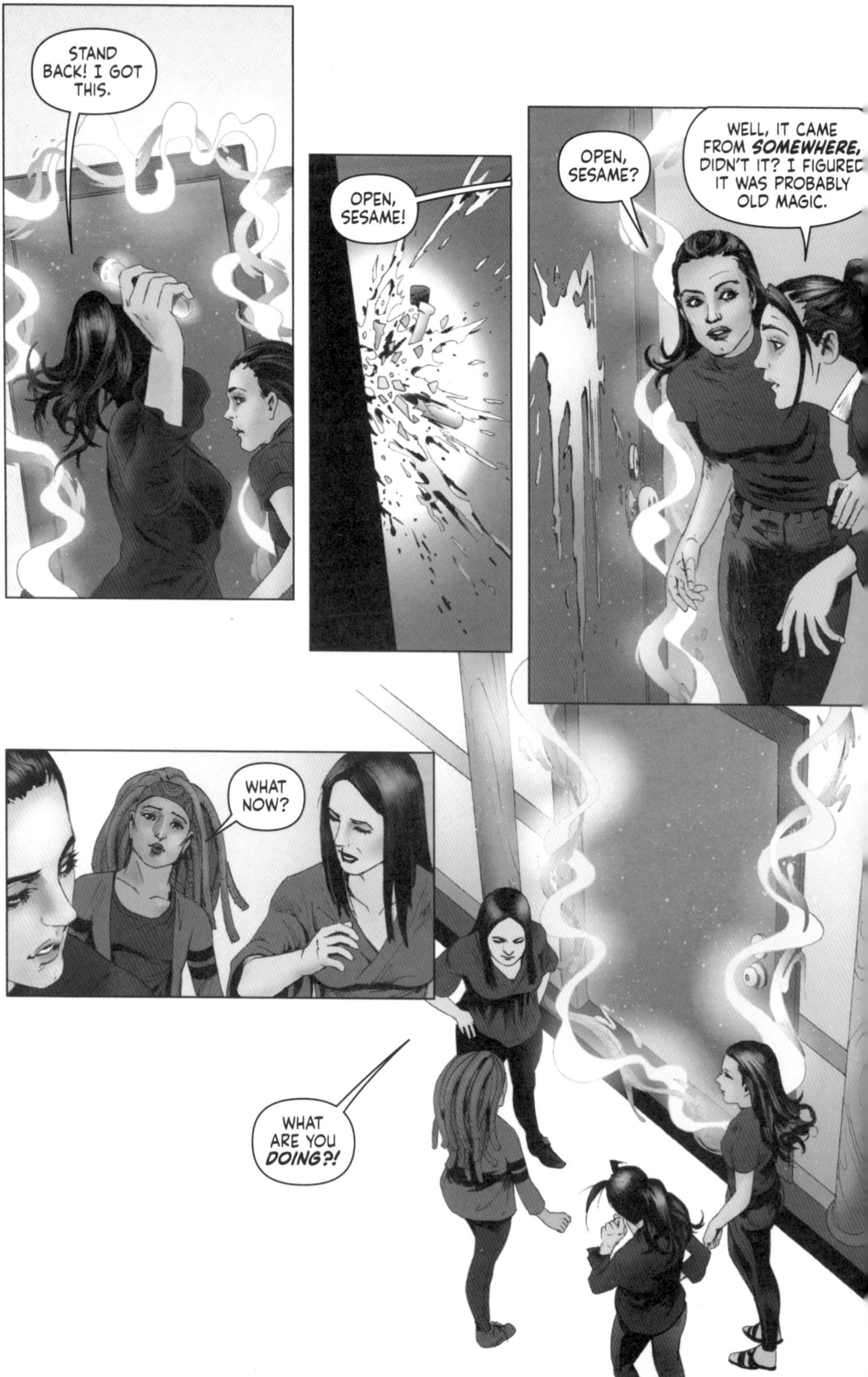
STAND BACK! I GOT THIS.
OPEN, SESAME!
OPEN, SESAME?
WELL, IT CAME FROM **SOMEWHERE,** DIDN'T IT? I FIGURED IT WAS PROBABLY OLD MAGIC.
WHAT NOW?
WHAT ARE YOU ***DOING?!***

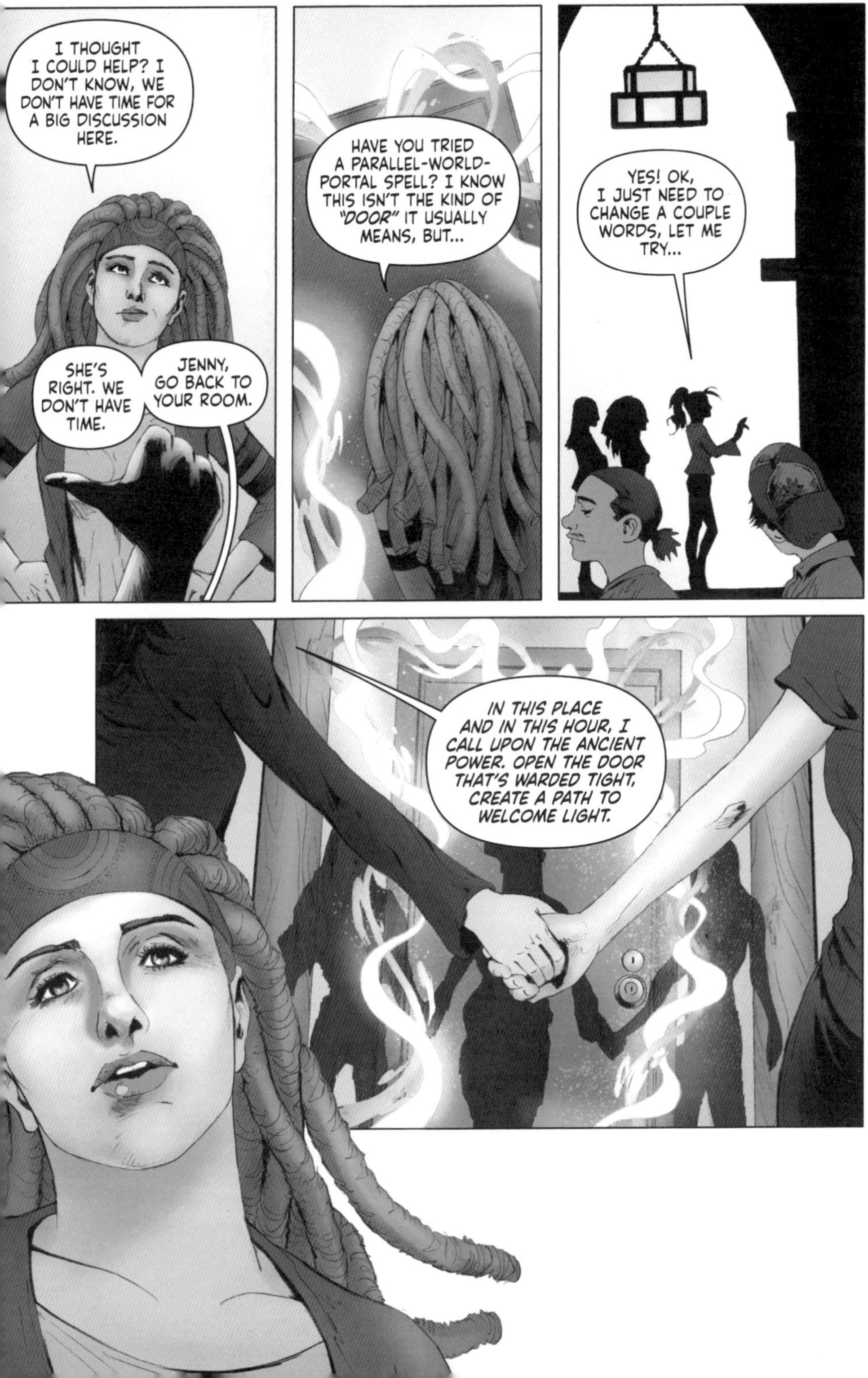
I THOUGHT I COULD HELP? I DON'T KNOW, WE DON'T HAVE TIME FOR A BIG DISCUSSION HERE.
SHE'S RIGHT. WE DON'T HAVE TIME.
JENNY, GO BACK TO YOUR ROOM.
HAVE YOU TRIED A PARALLEL-WORLD-PORTAL SPELL? I KNOW THIS ISN'T THE KIND OF "DOOR" IT USUALLY MEANS, BUT...
YES! OK, I JUST NEED TO CHANGE A COUPLE WORDS, LET ME TRY...
IN THIS PLACE AND IN THIS HOUR, I CALL UPON THE ANCIENT POWER. OPEN THE DOOR THAT'S WARDED TIGHT, CREATE A PATH TO WELCOME LIGHT.

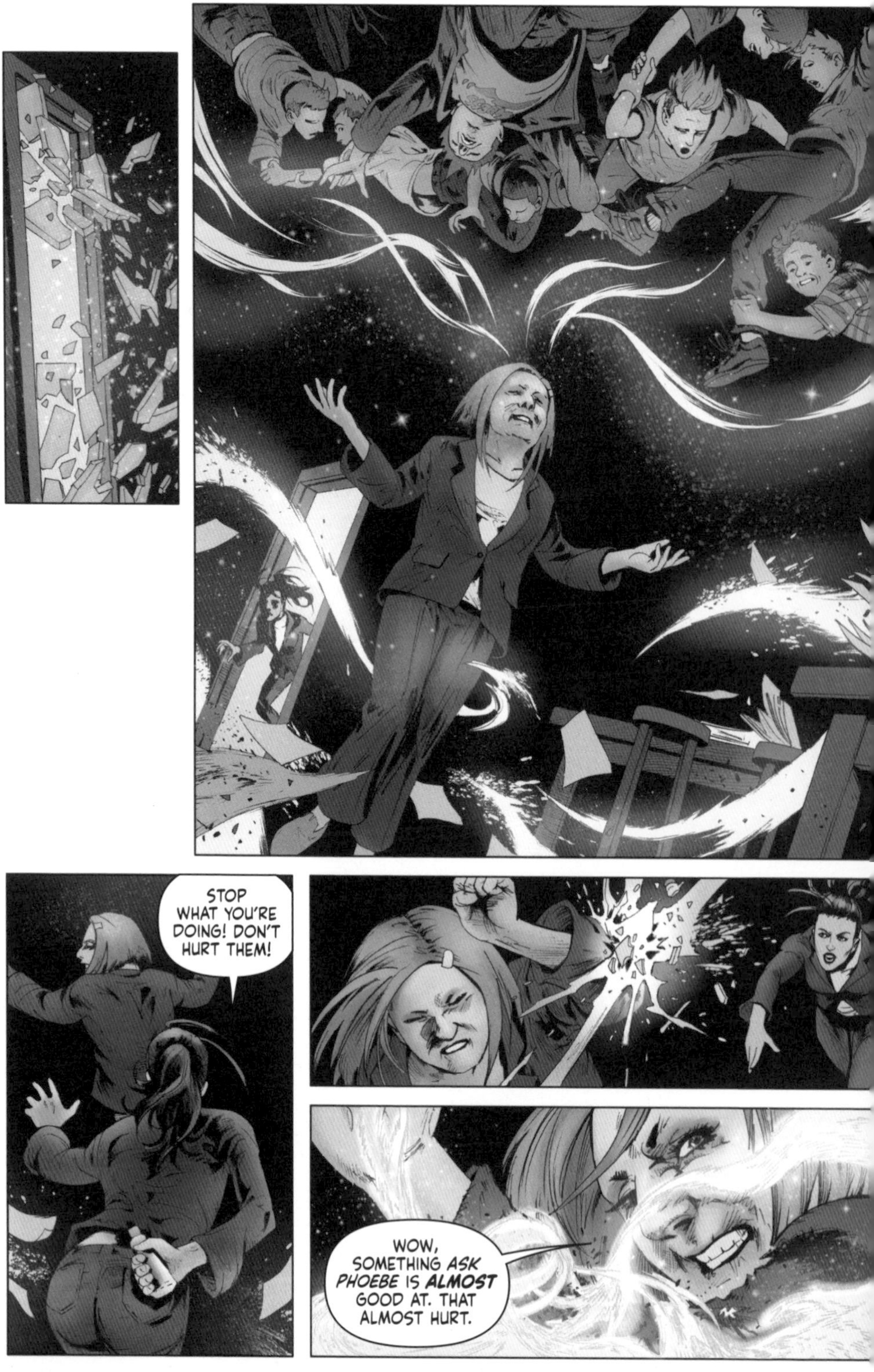
STOP WHAT YOU'RE DOING! DON'T HURT THEM!
WOW, SOMETHING *ASK PHOEBE* IS ***ALMOST*** GOOD AT. THAT ALMOST HURT.

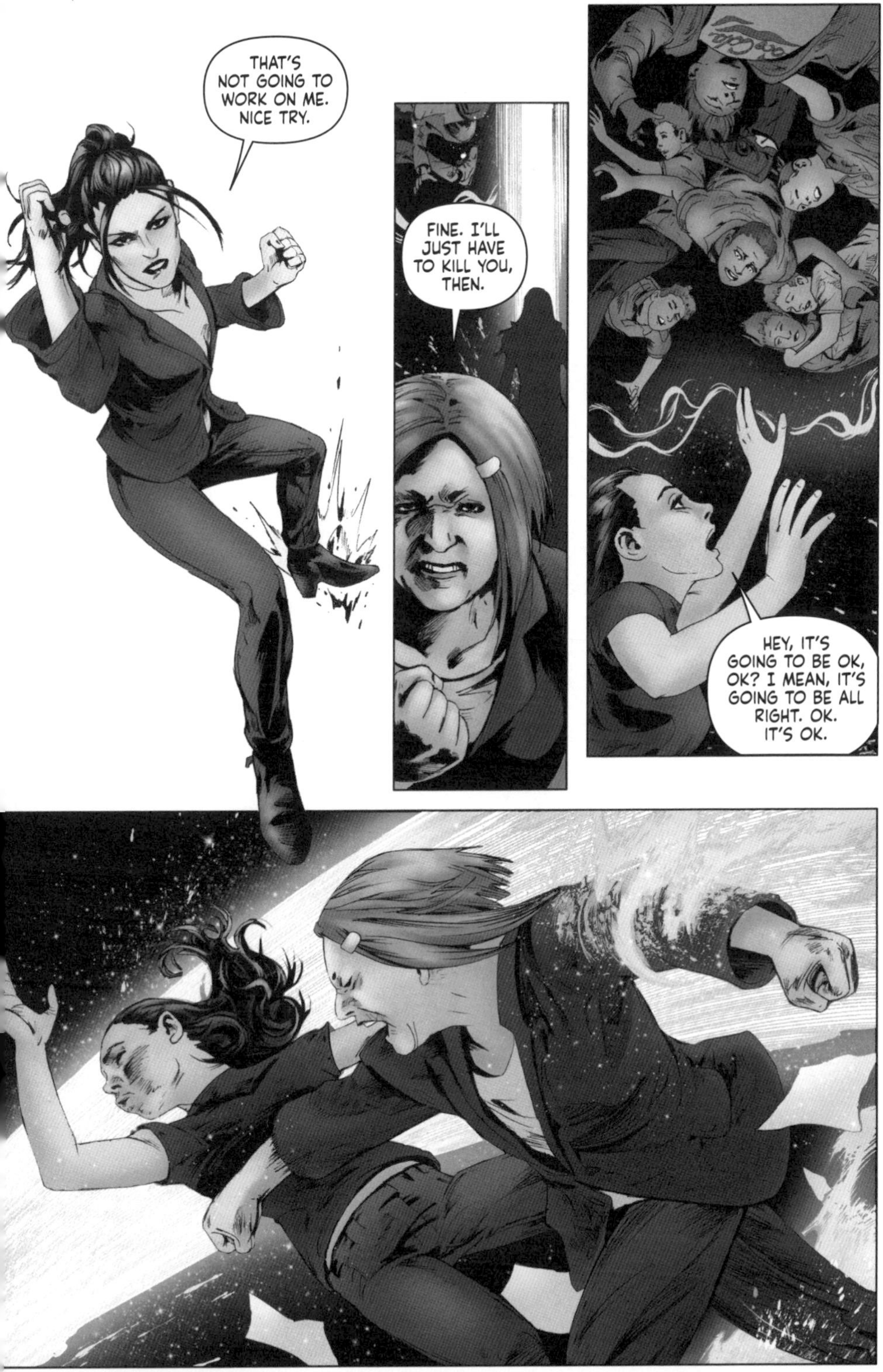
THAT'S NOT GOING TO WORK ON ME. NICE TRY.
FINE. I'LL JUST HAVE TO KILL YOU, THEN.
HEY, IT'S GOING TO BE OK, OK? I MEAN, IT'S GOING TO BE ALL RIGHT. OK. IT'S OK.

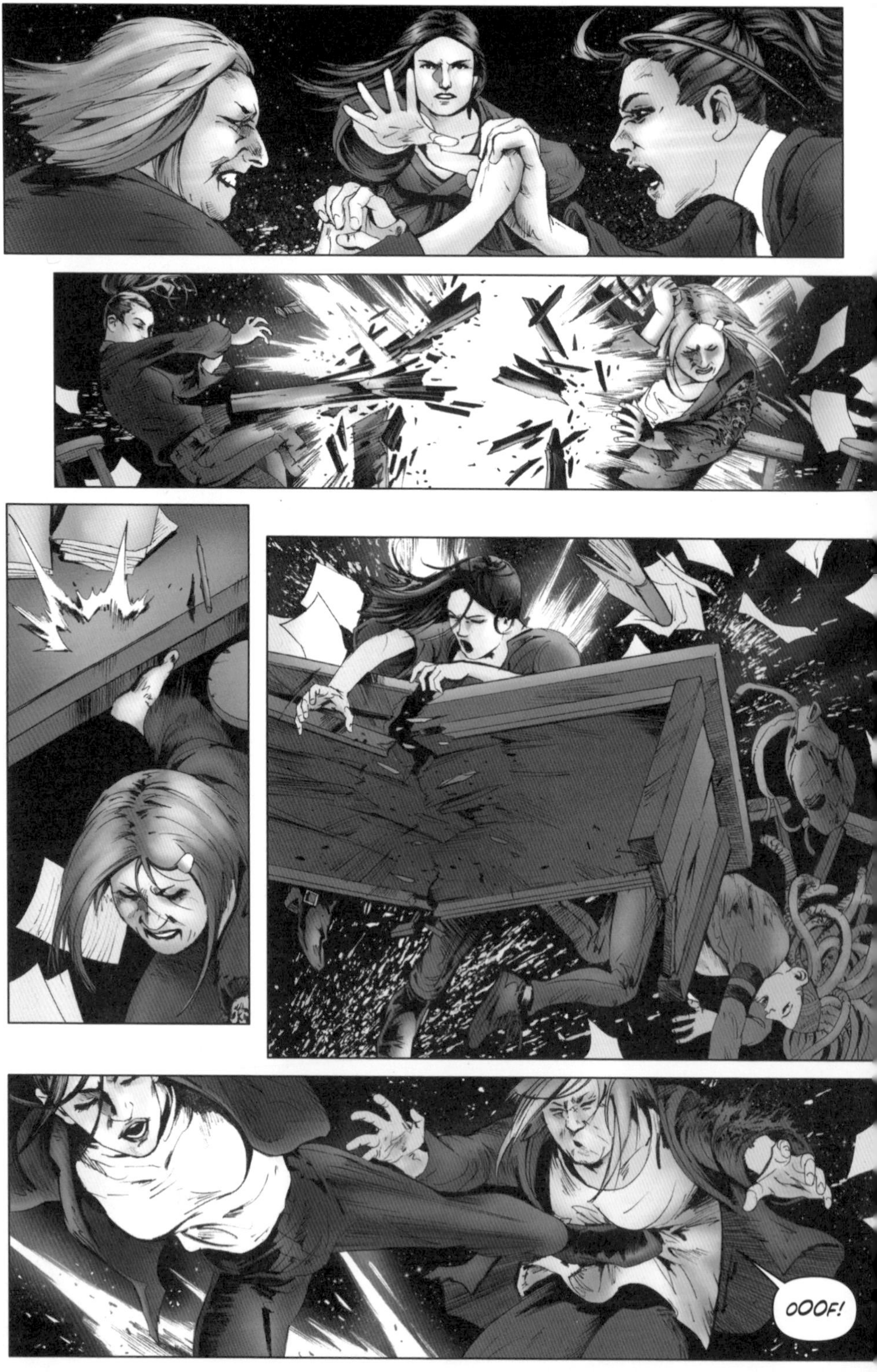
OOOF!

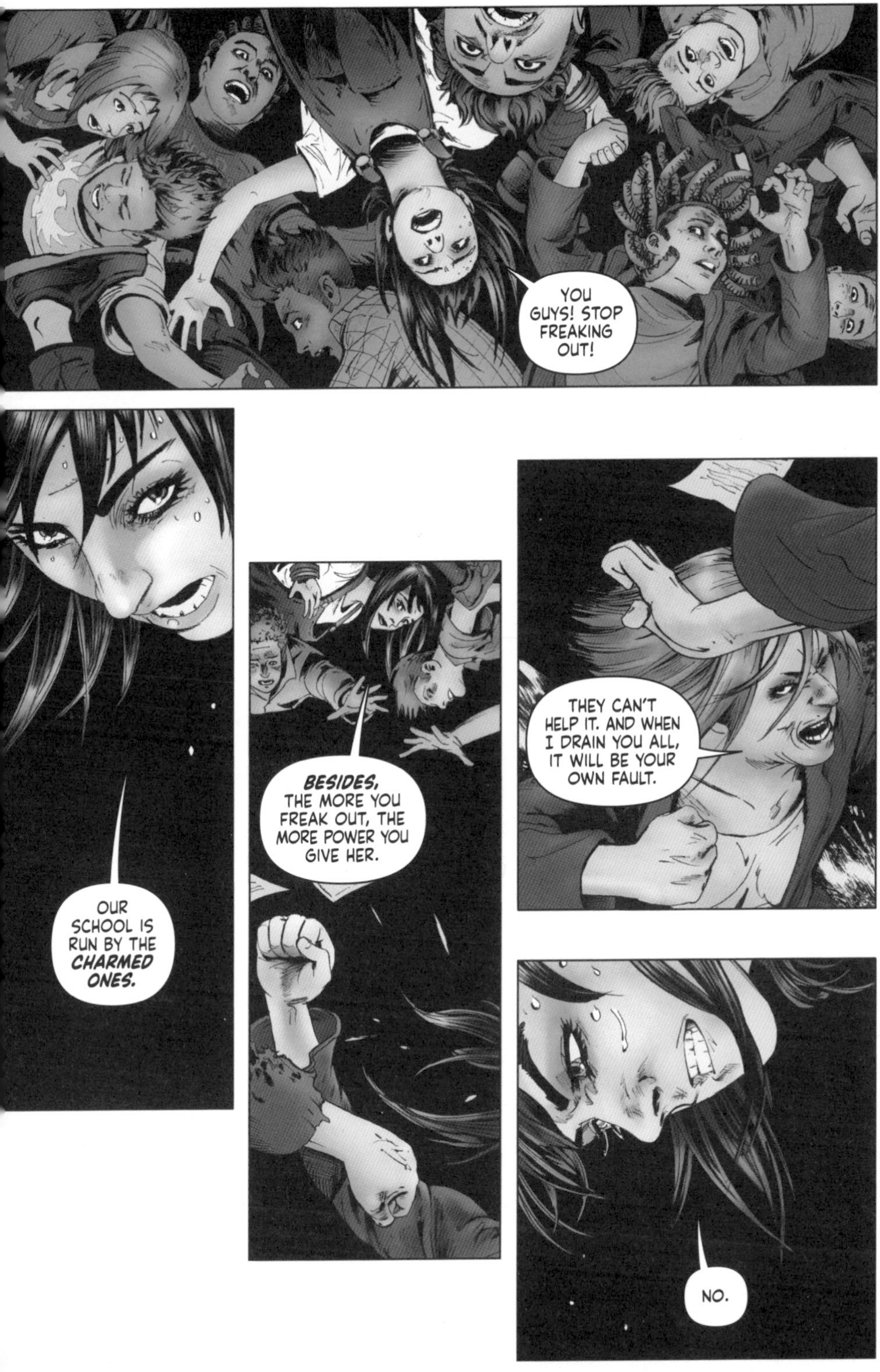
YOU GUYS! STOP FREAKING OUT!
OUR SCHOOL IS RUN BY THE ***CHARMED ONES.***
BESIDES, THE MORE YOU FREAK OUT, THE MORE POWER YOU GIVE HER.
THEY CAN'T HELP IT. AND WHEN I DRAIN YOU ALL, IT WILL BE YOUR OWN FAULT.
NO.

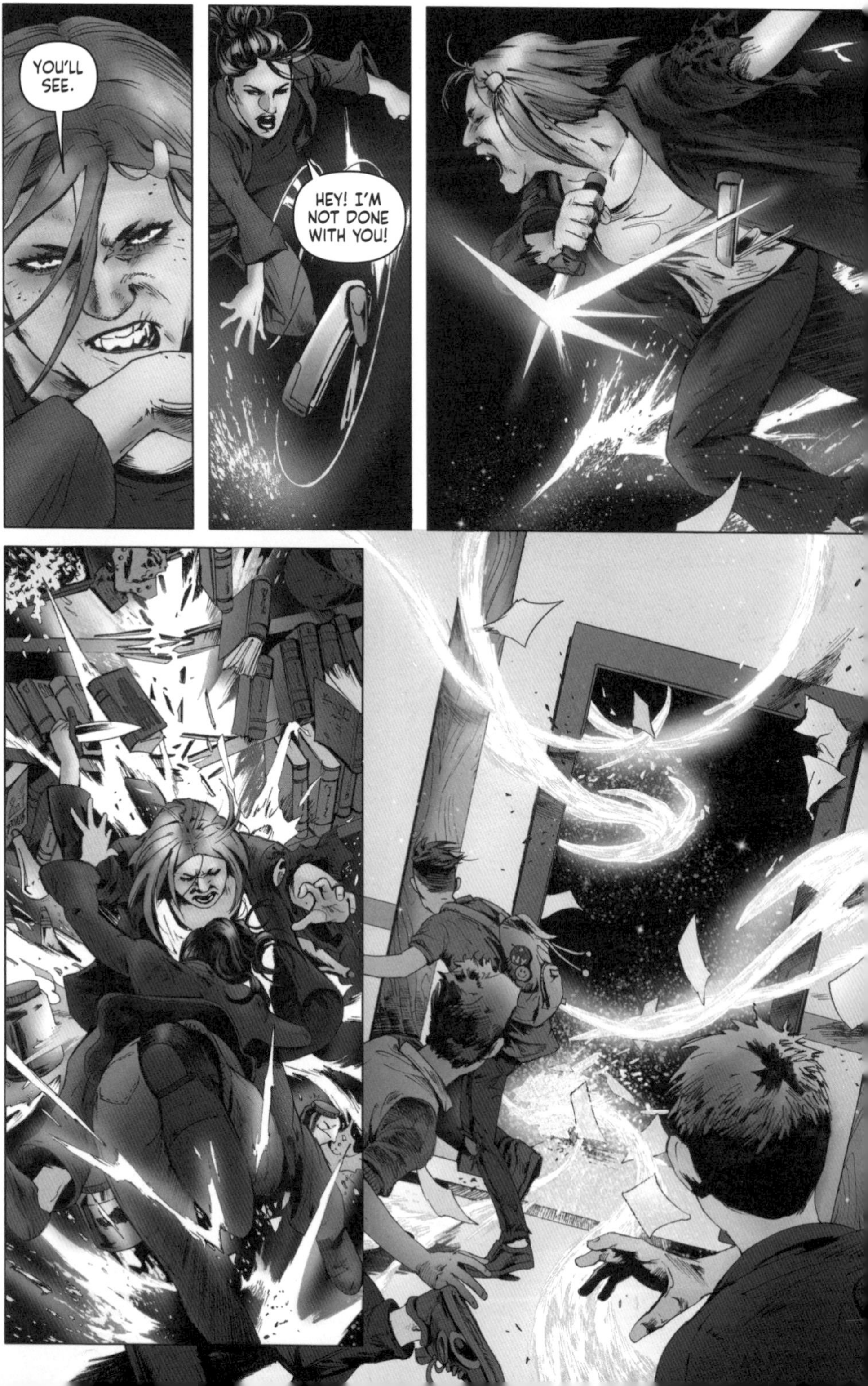
YOU'LL SEE.
HEY! I'M NOT DONE WITH YOU!

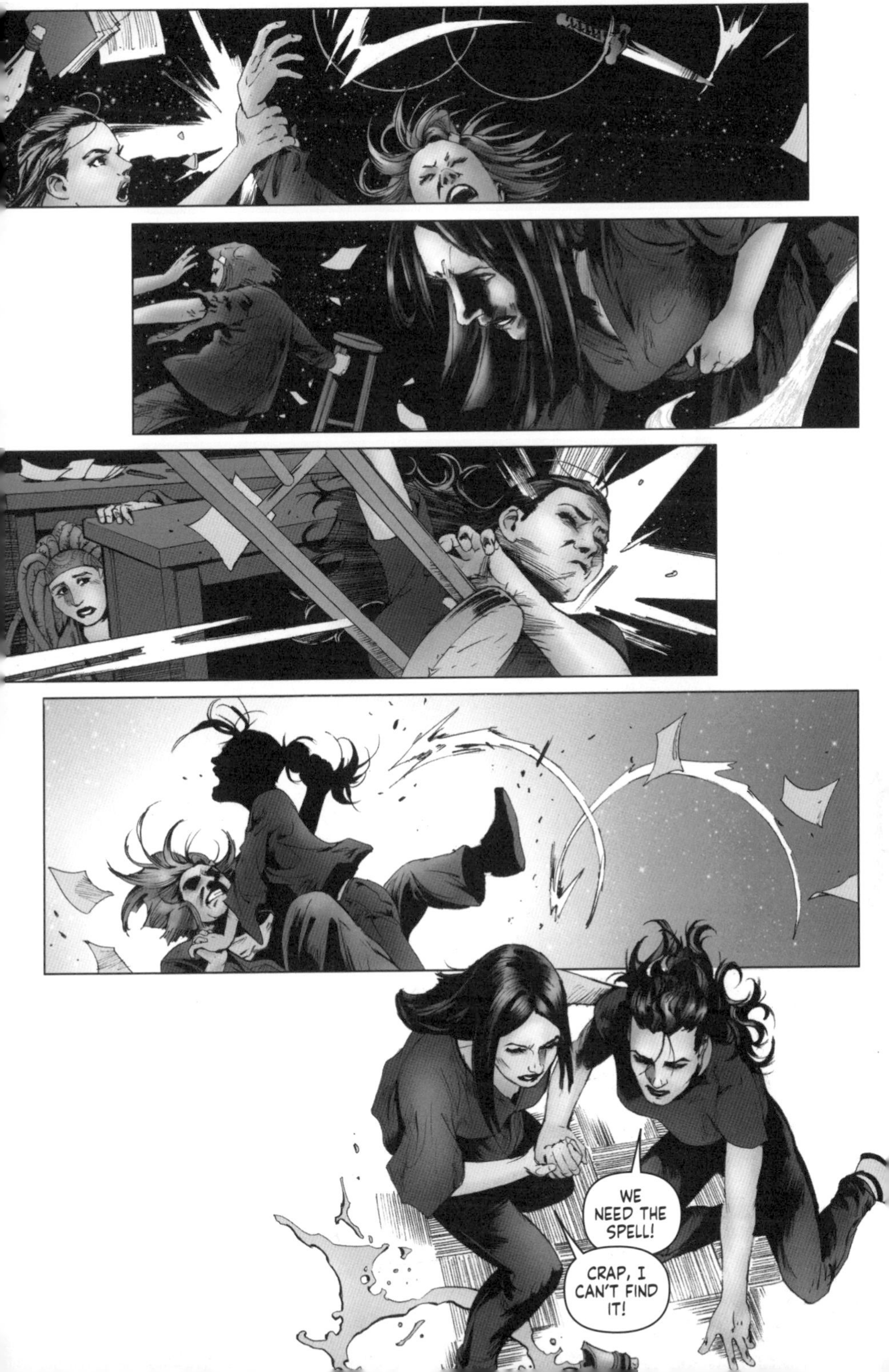
WE NEED THE SPELL!
CRAP, I CAN'T FIND IT!

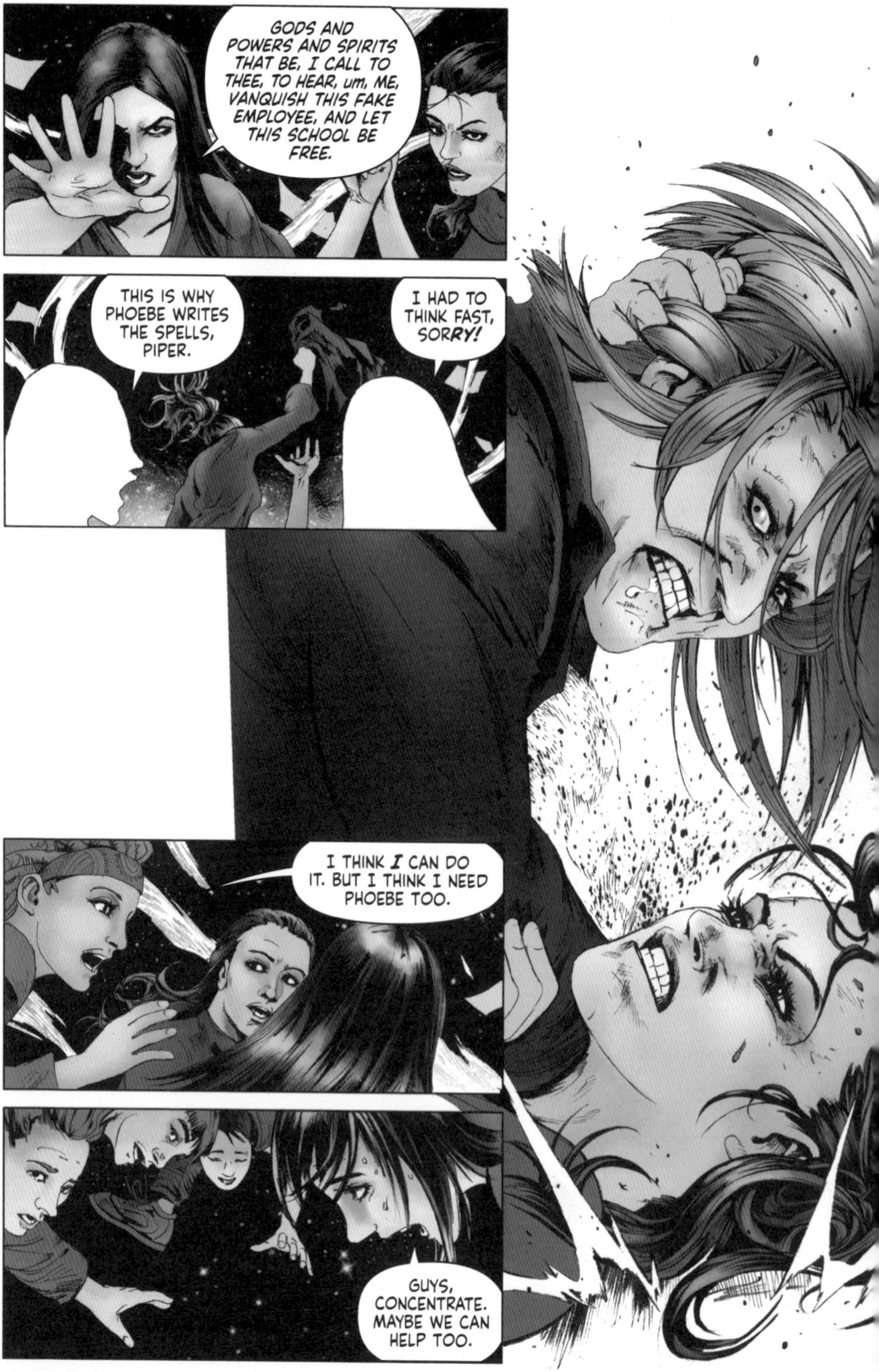
GODS AND POWERS AND SPIRITS THAT BE, I CALL TO THEE, TO HEAR, um, ME, VANQUISH THIS FAKE EMPLOYEE, AND LET THIS SCHOOL BE FREE.
THIS IS WHY PHOEBE WRITES THE SPELLS, PIPER.
I HAD TO THINK FAST, SORRY!
I THINK I CAN DO IT. BUT I THINK I NEED PHOEBE TOO.
GUYS, CONCENTRATE. MAYBE WE CAN HELP TOO.

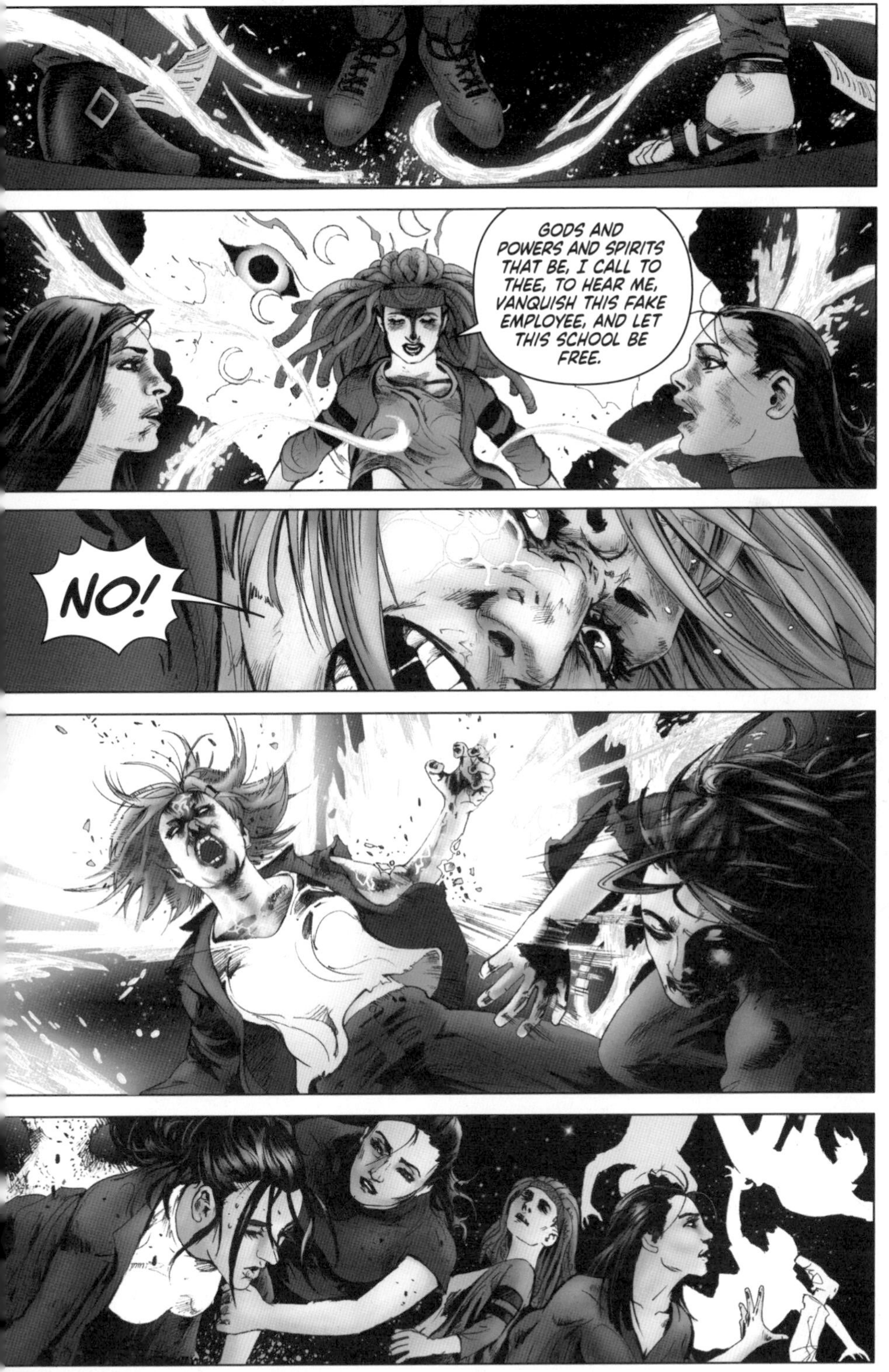
GODS AND POWERS AND SPIRITS THAT BE, I CALL TO THEE, TO HEAR ME, VANQUISH THIS FAKE EMPLOYEE, AND LET THIS SCHOOL BE FREE.
NO!

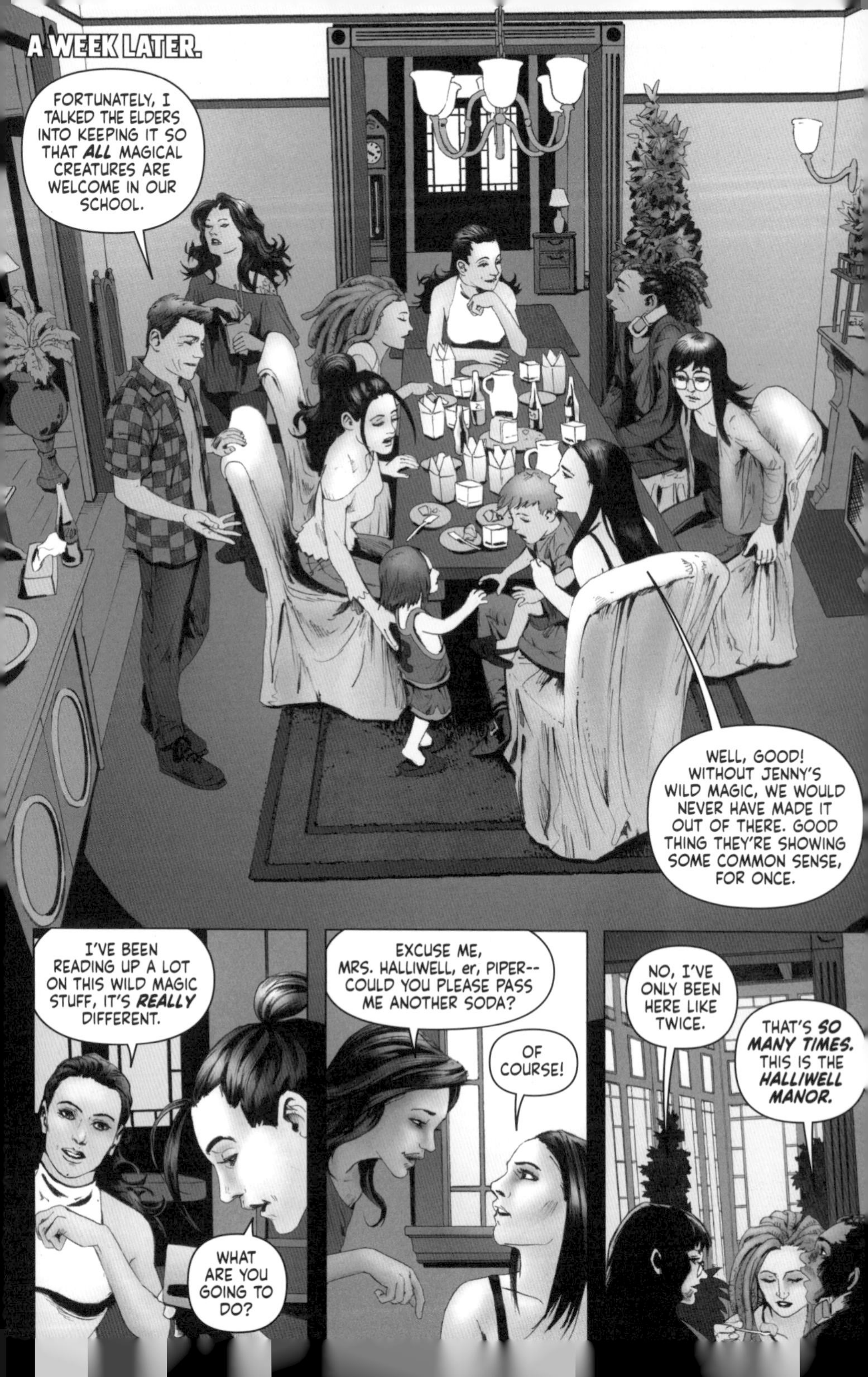
A WEEK LATER.
FORTUNATELY, I TALKED THE ELDERS INTO KEEPING IT SO THAT ALL MAGICAL CREATURES ARE WELCOME IN OUR SCHOOL.
WELL, GOOD! WITHOUT JENNY'S WILD MAGIC, WE WOULD NEVER HAVE MADE IT OUT OF THERE. GOOD THING THEY'RE SHOWING SOME COMMON SENSE, FOR ONCE.
I'VE BEEN READING UP A LOT ON THIS WILD MAGIC STUFF, IT'S REALLY DIFFERENT.
WHAT ARE YOU GOING TO DO?
EXCUSE ME, MRS. HALLIWELL, er, PIPER-- COULD YOU PLEASE PASS ME ANOTHER SODA?
OF COURSE!
NO, I'VE ONLY BEEN HERE LIKE TWICE.
THAT'S SO MANY TIMES. THIS IS THE HALLIWELL MANOR.

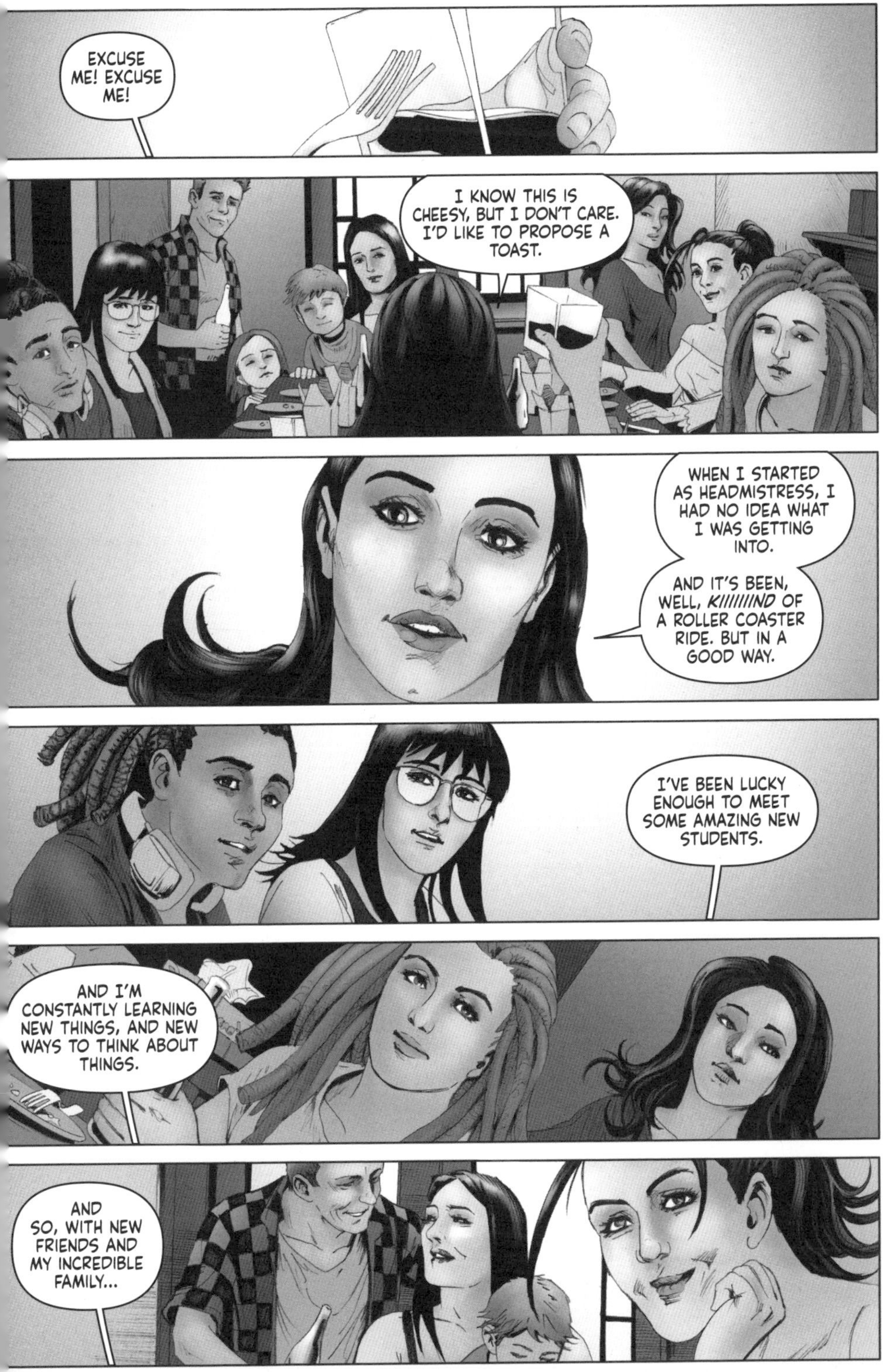
EXCUSE ME! EXCUSE ME!
I KNOW THIS IS CHEESY, BUT I DON'T CARE. I'D LIKE TO PROPOSE A TOAST.
WHEN I STARTED AS HEADMISTRESS, I HAD NO IDEA WHAT I WAS GETTING INTO.
AND IT'S BEEN, WELL, *KIIIIIIIND* OF A ROLLER COASTER RIDE. BUT IN A GOOD WAY.
I'VE BEEN LUCKY ENOUGH TO MEET SOME AMAZING NEW STUDENTS.
AND I'M CONSTANTLY LEARNING NEW THINGS, AND NEW WAYS TO THINK ABOUT THINGS.
AND SO, WITH NEW FRIENDS AND MY INCREDIBLE FAMILY...

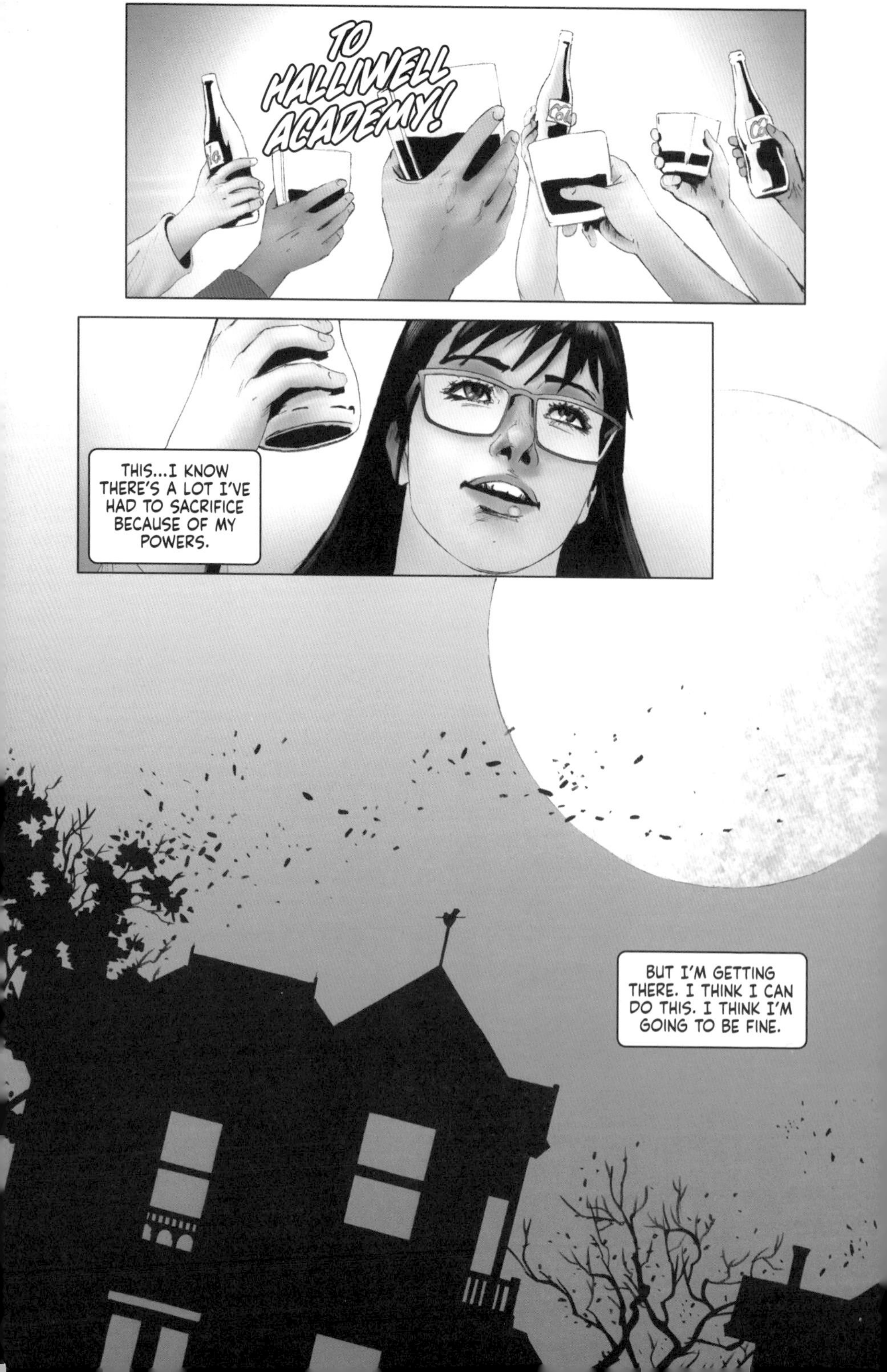
TO HALLIWELL ACADEMY!
THIS...I KNOW THERE'S A LOT I'VE HAD TO SACRIFICE BECAUSE OF MY POWERS.
BUT I'M GETTING THERE. I THINK I CAN DO THIS. I THINK I'M GOING TO BE FINE.

AN ORIGINAL STORY SET WITHIN THE FOURTH SEASON CONTINUITY OF THE HIT TELEVISION SERIES GRIMM!

What do Juliette, Adalind, Truble, and Rosalee have in common? They're the women in the life of Portland's own Grimm, Nick Burkhardt, and they're about to cross paths in a way they'd never expect!

Juliette's struggles to come to terms with becoming a Hexenbiest draw her into conflict with a new Wessen threat, and she finds she has nowhere to turn except her most hated enemy, Adalind (that's right, the woman who impersonated Juliette and slept with Nick)!

WRITTEN BY
CAITLIN KITTREDGE

ILLUSTRATED BY
MARIA SANAPO

ISBN13: 978-1-5241-0326-2
ON SALE NOW
AVAILABLE IN PRINT & DIGITALLY

Dynamite Entertainment is proud to continue the story of Phoebe, Piper, and Paige, television's fan-favorite witches, in all-new adventures set within the official continuity of *Charmed!*

The Halliwell (and Matthews) sisters may have defeated all manner of demons and monsters they've encountered so far, but now they're about to be challenged by a demon with a far grander plan. Having built a reputation as a wheeler and dealer in the Underworld, Djall is a demon with unmatched patience. He has concocted a scheme to take the sisters out of the picture for good, allowing every Tom, Dick & Demon to claim the souls of innocents. Throw in Paige's old flame from art school, a new charge to train, a demonic accountant, and a unicorn (yes, really), and you've got a new Charmed story you'll never forget!

WRITTEN BY
ERICA SCHULTZ

ILLUSTRATED BY
MARIA SANAPO

ISBN13: 978-1-5241-0413-9
ON SALE NOW
AVAILABLE IN PRINT & DIGITALLY

DYNAMITE. www.dynamite.com /dynamitecomics @dynamitecomics